A Marginal Majority

AMERICA'S BAPTISTS

Keith Harper, *Series Editor*

Mainstreaming Fundamentalism:
John R. Rice and Fundamentalism's Public Reemergence
Keith Bates

A Mere Kentucky of a Place:
The Elkhorn Association and the Commonwealth's First Baptists
Keith Harper

James Robinson Graves:
Staking the Boundaries of Baptist Identity, Second Edition
James A. Patterson

Doing the Word:
Southern Baptists' Carver School of Church Social Work
and Its Predecessors, 1907-1997
T. Laine Scales and Melody Maxwell

Apostle of the Lost Cause:
J. William Jones, Baptists, and the Development of Confederate Memory
Christopher C. Moore

Fundamentalism, Fundraising, and the Transformation
of the Southern Baptist Convention, 1919–1925
Andrew C. Smith

Edited by Elizabeth H. Flowers and Karen K. Seat

A Marginal Majority

Women, Gender, and a Reimagining of Southern Baptists

The University of Tennessee Press
Knoxville

First Edition.

Library of Congress Cataloging-in-Publication Data

Names: Flowers, Elizabeth Hill, editor. | Seat, Karen K., editor.
Title: A marginal majority : women, gender, and a reimagining of Southern Baptists / Elizabeth H. Flowers and Karen K. Seat.
Description: First edition. | Knoxville : The University of Tennessee Press, [2020] | Series: America's Baptists | Includes bibliographical references and index. | Summary: "This multiauthor volume represents a far-ranging effort to bring women into our understanding of recent Baptist history, thereby opening up the historiography of Baptist studies, which the editors argue has been too insular for far too long. This interdisciplinary approach extends the latest feminist scholarship to embrace racial issues within the denomination, the role that women had in the SBC takeover, Baptist women during the Progressive Era, a couple of essays on the Woman's Missionary Union, Baptist women in feminism (specifically the ERA), Beth Moore, and other topics"— Provided by publisher.
Identifiers: LCCN 2020028763 (print) | LCCN 2020028764 (ebook) | ISBN 9781621905998 (hardcover) | ISBN 9781621906001 (kindle edition) | ISBN 9781621906018 (pdf)
Subjects: LCSH: Southern Baptist Convention—History. | Baptist women—United States—History. | Feminism—United States—History.
Classification: LCC BX6462.3 .M37 2020 (print) | LCC BX6462.3 (ebook) | DDC 286/.132082—dc23
LC record available at https://lccn.loc.gov/2020028763
LC ebook record available at https://lccn.loc.gov/2020028764

Dedicated to
Robert and Carl Daoust
and
Darren and Jonathan Middleton

Contents

Foreword

In 1976 Laurel Thatcher Ulrich became a celebrity when she noted, "Well-behaved women seldom make history." In later interviews, Ulrich clarified her observation by adding "*but they should*." Southern Baptist women must have taken note. Within no time they found themselves at the center of a battle usually referred to as "The Controversy"; it was a battle that redefined the denomination.

Truth be told, women have always been at the heart of Southern Baptist life. Frequently, however, their contributions have either been shunted to the side or ignored altogether, and Elizabeth H. Flowers and Karen K. Seat want to change that. In *A Marginal Majority: Women, Gender, and a Reimagining of Southern Baptists*, Flowers, Seat, and the contributors to this outstanding collection of essays want to move women from the shadows of Baptist life to center stage.

A casual reading of the denomination's story reveals a lopsided tale best described as insular, male-centered, and triumphal. It is insular in that it tends to focus on intra-denominational life apart from broader national and international contexts. It is largely a male-centered narrative in that denominational good guys (literally guys) fought denominational bad guys (literally guys) in a tidy dialectic. It was triumphal in that the denomination advanced on all fronts, seemingly invincible. Or so the story goes.

Of course, it was never really that simple. The essays in *A Marginal Majority* demonstrate that women played a significant role in denominational development. As such, the Southern Baptist story is neither strictly male centered, nor a saga of triumph. It is a story that features women playing key roles both in shaping and paying for a denomination that grew into an international entity. It is a continuing story of Southern Baptist women who remain loyal to the denomination well into the twenty-first century, even though they remain shut out from the denomination's highest positions of power and influence. It is a complicated story that demands a reimagining, one that is nuanced and more broadly contextual. With Flowers and Seat as editors, it is a story that rests in very capable hands.

Readers may recognize elements of Ann Braude's "Women's History *Is* American Religious History" and Catherine Brekus's edited volume, *The*

Religious History of American Women: Reimagining the Past, in these essays, influences that Flowers and Seat gratefully acknowledge. They further grant that these essays do not arrive at a common agreement. But divergent viewpoints are strong evidence of a diverse legacy. As part of the reimagining process, the editors and contributors to this volume invite further inquiry.

Ulrich was right: well-behaved women really ought to make history. When it comes to American religious history, their stories form the fiber of denominational life. The University of Tennessee Press is excited to offer these essays, and we echo the editors' invitation to join in the reimagining project.

Acknowledgments

Numerous individuals supported us during the lengthy process of editing *A Marginal Majority*. We would like to take this opportunity to thank the anonymous peer reviewers with the University of Tennessee Press; the press's copyediting team, particularly Jon Boggs; the women of "GAs Gone Bad" (they know who they are), many of whom grew up feeling themselves the red-headed stepsisters of Southern Baptists; Susan Shaw and Eileen Campbell-Reed, who partnered with us and organized events where many contributors developed their initial ideas for this volume; and the many others who read parts of the manuscript, offered advice, or encouraged us in assembling this volume, including Allison Brown, Shannon Cate, Judy Dodd, Curtis Freeman, Theresa Gaul, Ann George, Charlotte Hogg, Lydia Hoyle, Mandy McMichael, Grant Wacker, Doug Weaver, and Jennifer Woodruff Tait.

We are grateful for the support of our academic institutions and the camaraderie of thoughtful colleagues. For Betsy, this includes both the Department of Religion at Texas Christian University and the Department of Religion at Baylor University; for Karen, the University of Arizona's Department of Religious Studies and Classics, School of International Languages, Literatures, and Cultures (SILLC), College of Humanities, and Confluencenter for Creative Inquiry. The Southern Baptist Historical Library and Archives provided us with a Lynn E. May Jr. Study Grant, and its director, Taffey Hall, generously devoted her time to answering our endless questions and guiding us to the appropriate historical resources.

We count ourselves fortunate to contribute one of the first books to appear in the America's Baptists series, published by the University of Tennessee Press. The enthusiasm of Keith Harper, series editor, kept us moving forward, and both his extensive knowledge of Baptist history and his editorial skill proved invaluable. As director of the University of Tennessee Press, Scot Danforth expressed his belief in the project from the beginning and demonstrated patience throughout the long process.

Finally, we are most appreciative of our families, especially Betsy's husband and son, Darren and Jonathan Middleton, and Karen's husband and son, Robert and Carl Daoust.

Elizabeth H. Flowers
Karen K. Seat
Fall 2019

Introduction

A MARGINAL MAJORITY

Women, Gender, and a Reimagining of Southern Baptists

Elizabeth H. Flowers
Karen K. Seat

For decades, the Southern Baptist Convention (SBC) has attracted national attention for its rightward trajectory regarding issues of women and gender. As the largest Protestant denomination in the United States, the SBC has long been a dominant religious force. It has served as a window into Southern culture and, as the politics of Dixie spread throughout the country as a result of migration and political clout, a window into the nation itself. The denomination's internal conflicts, which ultimately led to fissure in the 1980s and the triumph of the SBC's ultraconservatives by the end of the twentieth century, have been an indicator of the increasing polarization of American culture and politics. And the denomination's ability to successfully push back against feminist ideals of gender equality helps to explain broader, ongoing conflicts in American culture over women's roles and rights. The story of the SBC is a story of the nation's fraught history of gender and how this history is inexorably linked to those of race, class, and sexuality.

The complications and contradictions of American history itself may be better understood when examining this decentralized but widely influential denomination. The tensions and paradoxes within the SBC are manifest in numerous ways. Founded in 1845 when it cut ties with Baptists in the North because of Southern Baptists' support of slavery, the SBC has publicly declared its intention to pursue "racial reconciliation" since 1995 while simultaneously stoking anti-feminist theologies and politics. The denomination takes pride in its ancestral roots battling established religion while simultaneously expanding its religious influence in modern party politics; and it raises up the authority of the individual, with its embrace of the "priesthood of the believer," while simultaneously glorifying a gendered spiritual and social hierarchy.

Much of the historiography of the SBC does not present such a multidimensional story. In line with traditional church history of the past century, the prevailing annals of the denomination have been rather confessional in approach and triumphalist in character. They tell an androcentric tale of a people led by (male) clergy, in turn guided by (male) denominational officials, to achieve tremendous growth and successful institution building amidst occasional theological skirmishes and, later, a final battle from which ultraconservatives emerged victorious.[1] Writing in 1987, the church historian H. Leon McBeth, then a professor at Southwestern Baptist Theological Seminary, chided his Southern Baptist male peers: "If any of you men want to get away from women, here is one way you can do it: just get into the pages of Baptist history. Women will not bother you there."[2]

McBeth made this observation as a critique and a call for change just as the SBC was coming under the firm control of the denomination's most conservative forces. Thus, the institutions best able to support the work of Southern Baptist history became even further entrenched in their own academic subculture.[3] Most significant here, those at the helm of the denomination required a theology of women's submission, so the SBC's seminaries largely shunned the scholarship in the wider field attentive to women, gender, and sexuality, contributing to a delay in the study of Southern Baptist women precisely at the moment it seemed paramount.[4] Moreover, while a number of scholars from outside the denomination's official institutions produced works analyzing Southern Baptists as major players in American religious history, few focused specifically on women and gender.[5]

This has begun to change, however, and we count ourselves as part of a new generation of scholars who are grappling with the gendered history of the SBC, largely from within the field of American religious history.[6] We conceptualized *A Marginal Majority* as a means both to collectively "reimagine" Southern Baptist history from the perspective of women and issues of gender and to showcase the innovative work being accomplished by this new generation. Women have formed the majority in the Southern Baptist churches that crowded and eventually dominated the Southern landscape, and they have served as their congregations' most active members, tithers, Sunday school teachers, and mission leaders. Yet, as our title indicates, these Southern Baptists have been consigned to the margins of history, reflecting how they have also been excluded from their denomination's highest positions of power, including the roles of ordained minister and senior pastor. *A Marginal Majority* reimagines the story of the SBC from the vantage point of the Southern Baptist women who, despite their lack of visibility, have supported their denomination and enabled its prominent position in American Protestantism.

As many women's historians have maintained, starting with women is far more than adding female figures to the story's overall cast of characters. Switching the point of view changes our sense of the tale, in this case complicating and even reversing the logic of triumphalism that has driven Southern Baptist history. In contrast to the celebratory historiography of the past, *A Marginal Majority* shows how Southern Baptists often fell short in transcending the most oppressive contours of their culture. Not only in spite of but often because of the denomination's increasing growth and power, the SBC's male leadership could be hostile to women's expanding roles in American religion and culture, driving conservatives to move the denomination even further to the right. As many of our authors conclude, even as women promoted the growth and success of the SBC, the institutional politics and habits of culture also frustrated and restricted female agency. At the same time, while women within the denomination were often marginalized and constricted by patriarchal structures and norms, these predominantly white women themselves often served as agents in perpetuating a racial hierarchy that ensured them greater privilege and power. As an overwhelmingly white denomination, the SBC provides a case study of the construction of whiteness in relationship to gender and the ways in which individuals negotiate multiple identity markers within overlapping structures of power.

To be sure, as our contributors demonstrate, Southern Baptist women did not speak in any one voice; progressive impulses competed with conservative ones, and attempts at change were hindered by a desire to maintain the status quo. Taken as a whole, however, the volume's overarching narrative is ultimately one of loss and decline. The optimism apparent in several of the earlier chapters diminishes and is qualified by the stories of conflict and disillusionment in the later chapters. Reimagining the denomination by starting with women does uncover new plot twists, understandings of conflict, and novel genealogies of authority and power, but it also offers a window into the past through which it is not always easy to peer.

A Reimagining Project

At the end of the twentieth century, Ann Braude's seminal essay "Women's History *Is* American Religious History" made evident that one cannot fully understand American religious history without examining women as central figures and that one cannot understand American women's history without seriously engaging with religion.[7] Over twenty years later, Braude's message continues to resonate in the scholarship of American religious history as the work of women's and gender studies challenges scholars to reimagine old narratives. Those familiar with American religious history will inevitably hear in our title an echo of another seminal work, *The Religious History of American Women: Reimagining the Past* (2007), edited by Catherine Brekus and inspired, in part, by Braude. Because of the longstanding ghettoization of women's experience and agency in American religious history, Brekus and the contributors to her volume took Braude's call seriously to bring careful scholarly attention to women. So too do we. *A Marginal Majority* explores ways to bring Braude's insights to bear on Southern Baptist history and the history of women in the American South. While we draw on gender as a category of analysis, and certainly understand gender as it concerns men as well as women, constructions of masculinity as well as femininity, and issues of power around sex and sexual identity, in this volume we are most concerned with providing a corrective to the historiography of Southern Baptists by focusing on women in Southern Baptist life.

Yet in other ways *A Marginal Majority* does not fit neatly with the goals of these earlier works in American women's religious history, which, in the words of Brekus, sought to "demonstrate women's agency in creating historical change."[8] Unlike the chapters in the Brekus volume, for instance, those in our volume narrate the history of a single denomination, and one that has perpetuated and expanded its conservative, anti-feminist culture, moving since the 1980s even further to the right. While some women certainly were agents in this rightward turn, others, including conservative as well as progressive Southern Baptist women, encountered increasing limitations on their ability to effect change. Moreover, contributors to *A Marginal Majority* were writing over a decade after those essayists in *The Religious History of American Women*. Not only had the scholarship begun, once again, to question the extent of human agency within the parameters of institutional religion, it was the era of Trump and the #MeToo movement. The SBC loomed large here. The denomination struggled publicly over how to respond to the 2016 presidential election amid concerns over the president's attitude toward women; this was followed by its own sexual abuse scandals coming into the national spotlight in 2018 and 2019. Overall, then, our history concentrates on the strictures that did indeed "surround, determine, and occupy" our subjects, to quote the religion scholar Katheryn Lofton.[9] Brekus's volume heralded a new era in the field of American religion, as being more inclusive of women and issues of gender and sexuality. But in contrast to the welcomed optimism of many reimagining projects, *A Marginal Majority* demonstrates that not every "reimagining" will prove uplifting.

Because of its focus on the SBC, and the ways we apply the work of feminist scholars to a denomination, *A Marginal Majority* additionally builds on what Robert Bruce Mullin and Russell E. Richey called "reimagining denominationalism." Since the late twentieth century, a growing number of scholars have joined Mullin and Richey to explore the potential for new directions in American denominational history, which take it away from that old confessional model and open it to the variety of perspectives that have informed the field of American religious history, bringing the two together.[10] Gone are the days of "white, male intellectual history that drearily recounted which preacher served where" declares the denominational Baptist historian Keith Harper.[11]

While that conventional model does still linger in some ecclesial circles, the underlying premise of "reimagining denominationalism," which likewise informs our volume, is that denominations remain vital to understanding American religion and history. After all, millions of Americans have organized their social lives and networks according to the denominational identities that inform their local churches and congregations.[12] Historical investigations of denominations uncover complex institutional networks that shape individuals and societies. And this new scholarship is demonstrating how the study of denominations can teach us about any number of social and cultural issues, from gender, race, and sexuality to consumerism and media. In our view, connecting denominational history with critical cultural analyses is crucial for making it meaningful to a broad range of scholars, including those who do not necessarily have personal or confessional connections to a specific religious identity.

The historiography of Southern Baptists has been slow to catch up with these new directions in denominational studies. As noted earlier, the scholarship on Southern Baptists has been rather insular, traditionally written from within the denomination and its seminaries with theologians and church historians treating the SBC as *sui generis*. Somewhat paradoxically, as the SBC grew and flourished in the post-War World II period, becoming more established in the American religious landscape, it increasingly stood apart from mainline Protestantism, which was embracing an ecumenism that made its denominations more open to critical inquiry, especially when it came to issues of gender.[13] The SBC also refused to join the National Association of Evangelicals, which prompted some to question its evangelical identity.[14] But the bottom line for the SBC was that it did not need these alliances to flourish. It had the money and means to pursue its own historical endeavors, and inside scholars proudly saw their denomination's narrative and heritage as unique unto itself.

The internecine SBC battles of the latter twentieth century did, however, push many Southern Baptists moderates and progressives outward, especially when it came to the study of religion. Many of *A Marginal Majority*'s contributors, ourselves included, are a part of this history. While representing a variety of perspectives, most of this volume's contributors share a Southern Baptist heritage but have left the official SBC fold, ourselves again included here. Through their research, all the contributors to this volume now engage with the denomination through the academic study of religion, history, and/or gender. Together, then, as scholars shaped by a particular history and turn of events, we draw upon and hope to push other reimagining projects in new directions.[15]

We would certainly acknowledge here that there have been recent histories of Baptists in the field of American religious history that have modeled the cultural analysis so significant to new denominational studies.[16] But they are not close studies of the SBC per se. And while *A Marginal Majority* does not provide an exhaustive history of the SBC, we do uphold the value of probing Southern Baptists specifically, as a denomination and a people, to secure a deeper sense of their multilayered and complicated history, one that has profoundly shaped the American story.

Who Are Southern Baptists?

Throughout their history, Southern Baptists have defied simple categorization. Despite the dominant conservatism of Southern Baptists, they have demonstrated a surprising degree of theological and ecclesial diversity that can be tied to regional and class differences throughout the South. Because the SBC, unlike many other Christian denominations, was not formed with a doctrinal or organizational center, Southern culture and piety, along with a zeal for missions, filled this void for much of its history to provide unity and a shared sense of purpose. The following overview moves both thematically and chronologically through Southern Baptist history, highlighting the culture that brought Southern Baptists together and the differences that made their unity unstable.

THE "ORIGINAL SIN" OF RACISM

The SBC infamously began with its members on the "wrong side" of history. White Baptists in the South broke from their Northern counterparts in 1845 to found the SBC as a denomination that would support slavery.[17] The founding of the SBC on the defense of slavery, and Southern Baptists' later defense of Jim Crow policies, informed the relationship of religion and race in the South. And yet, most white Southern Baptists at the denomination's founding did not own slaves. In 1845, Southern Baptists ranged from the few elite and wealthy plantation owners who ran the newly formed convention to the overwhelming number of poor whites who occupied the pews and led local churches. Still, despite their demographic diversity, the vast majority of Southern Baptists were socially and culturally conservative, defining themselves over and against their Northern counterparts, Baptists and otherwise. This conservatism involved a shared commitment to race and gender hierarchies. Indeed, the democratic impulses evidenced in a low church ecclesiology existed within and alongside an agreed upon strict social hierarchy that was rooted in slavery and segregation, as well as a culture that placed white women on a pedestal without formal power.

For a very brief period, before slavery was abolished, Southern Baptist churches had black and white members. But not surprisingly, after the Civil War freedmen and freedwomen formed their own congregations and established their own black Baptist conventions, separate from the SBC. Well into the twentieth century, members of the SBC, including Southern Baptist women, worked to maintain a paternalistic relationship with African Americans in the South, including efforts to instruct them on how to conduct their religious affairs. As *A Marginal Majority* shows, too often Southern Baptist women either ignored or inadequately struggled with their complicity in white supremacy. The complicated story of race and gender in the denomination reflects the paradox of the South as a region that has simultaneously held hierarchical impulses together with populist sentiments.

LOCALISM AND DIVERSITY

For most of the SBC's first century, its churches, congregations, and members embodied considerable internal diversity, as they resisted centralized power structures and top-down directives, making any straightforward description of this religious world a challenge. Many ordinary Southern Baptists either paid little heed to denominational politics or resented any imposition from above. Local congregations could simply ignore any denominational pronouncements and did frequently interpret them as meddlesome. Some churches went so far as to shun their local Southern Baptist associations, which were regional or county-based, along with their state conventions. Indeed, they often charted their own course, usually with an untrained, part-time preacher. Powerful pulpiteers emerged, although they too were most often kept in check by a strong sense of lay and individual authority.

Even when it came to their theology, Southern Baptists were heterogeneous. In matters as basic to Protestantism as personal salvation, Southern Baptists counted among their numbers both hard-core Calvinists who held to "once saved always saved" as well as free-will Wesleyans worried about the dangers of "backsliding" and a loss of salvation. Southern Baptists prized the Bible. But some advocated the power of the written Word, clinging doggedly to a literalism that proclaimed the inerrant and infallible Word of God, while others prioritized the inner Word, which, under the auspices of the Holy Spirit, led individuals to discern their own message from God. Even "believer's baptism," the hallmark of Baptist identity, divided as much as it united with opposing opinions on the reliable age for conversion and the necessity of rebaptism leading to church splits. Still, Southern Baptists clung to those traditional Baptist ideals of soul competency (the accountability of each individual before God) and the priesthood of the believer (in which the individual mediates his or her own salvation), even if they did not always articulate them as such or understand these concepts in the same way.

Theological variety was reflected in contrasting approaches to ecclesial life, including worship. To be sure, Southern Baptists squabbled over a range of issues here: open versus closed communion, the use of confessions of faith, the role of deacons, and church governance. If some Southern Baptist churches adopted a set liturgy for their weekly services, usually under the guidance of seminary-trained clergy, most were without the means or inclination to support a full-time preacher and relied more on a spontaneous revivalism for worship than any formalized model.

The devastating aftermath of the Civil War contributed to the SBC's lack of any strong, centralized denominational structure. The war crippled the South economically for years, and Southern Baptists were profoundly affected with many struggling for survival as poor scratch farmers (although their prospects certainly were not as bleak as the black share-cropping population laboring under a violent reign of terror). Even after its attempt to reorganize in 1914, creating a denominational executive board, headquartered in Nashville, and a streamlined plan of member giving, the SBC could hardly accomplish anything more than an annual convention meeting and could barely fund its two seminaries and three agencies: the Southern Baptist Theological Seminary in Louisville (founded in 1859); Southwestern Baptist Theological Seminary in Fort Worth (founded in 1908); the Home Mission Board (1874; founded in 1845 as the Board of Domestic Missions); the Foreign Mission Board (1845); and the Sunday School Board (1891). As the Southern historian Wayne Flynt has noted, well into the twentieth century three-fourths of Southern Baptist churches lacked any programming for children and young people with the vast majority of their members failing to register for or attend Sunday school—something that would later come to define Southern Baptist life and identity.[18]

Missions, however, were something of an exception here. If poorly organized and underfunded, both the Home and Foreign Mission Boards survived the denomination's lean years and even managed to grow the number of missionaries they appointed. This was largely due to the efforts of Southern Baptist women and the Woman's Missionary Union (WMU), as shown in *A Marginal Majority*'s early chapters.

THE WOMAN'S MISSIONARY UNION (WMU)

WMU leaders were at the forefront of the "woman question," as Southern Baptists were apt to call the social and ecclesial debates over the "permissible" parameters of women's roles and behaviors. Organized in 1888 as an auxiliary to the SBC, the WMU lasted well past the heyday of American women's missions. Numerous Protestant women's missions organizations had been established in the nineteenth century as separate women's boards, which independently appointed and supported single women missionaries. During the first half of the twentieth century, these autonomous women's mission boards merged with their larger denominational mission agencies. But rather than such mergers resulting in equality with men, they actually led to a loss of many Protestant women's independence and positions of denominational authority.[19]

In one of the many ironies of Southern Baptist history, the WMU's auxiliary status served as a form of protection from being absorbed into its denominational boards and thus helped Southern Baptist women to maintain a level of autonomy and agency in the realm of missions. Originally, the SBC's male leaders had been nervous that a separate women's missions organization at the national level would drain the denomination's monetary resources. They were also worried it might lead to women's public speaking, which could, in turn, be interpreted as preaching. But Southern Baptist women long involved in local mission societies were persistent. So, even though women could not serve as messengers (the SBC's term for delegates) to the annual convention, the men at the 1888 meeting voted for the formation of a national women's missions organization on the condition that it be established as an auxiliary rather than a denominational agency or board. Auxiliary status meant that the women would not appoint their own missionaries but rather use their time, energy, and funds to promote and support those serving the two SBC mission boards, which were under the leadership of men. Fearful that they would have to fund the women's efforts, the men also insisted that the women involved in the WMU would be responsible for their own budget and finances, so long as their charge focused on supporting the SBC mission boards. The SBC's male leadership later came to regret this decision, as women found avenues for autonomy in this structure, especially in the years before World War II. For example, social progressivism, relative to context, most often found expression in the SBC through the national leadership of the WMU, which succeeded in raising and managing its own funds along with selecting its own officers and publishing its own literature.

TWENTIETH-CENTURY GROWTH

The South and Southern Baptists were radically transformed in the period after World War II. In something of a reversal to its nineteenth-century postwar misfortune, the South benefited disproportionally from the country's post-World War II economic boom with Southern Baptists soon becoming more urban, educated, and solidly middle class. The SBC took advantage of its members' newfound status and rapidly expanded as financial giving increased exponentially. It added four new seminaries and grew the work of its boards and commissions. Through its church plant program, the Home Mission Board established congregations across the country, following Southerners as they moved west as well as north. Southern Baptist churches also were more apt to hire trained seminarians as pastors with larger churches boasting full-time staffs of ministers for every age group and activity. To assist local congregations, the SBC and its agencies supplied resources and materials for a wide range of programs. An accompanying convention calendar filled the year with events and activities. The hope was that programmatic unity would, in turn, create greater denominational loyalty and support.

But efforts toward programmatic unity had mixed results, as it also meant that underlying differences and conflicts, once contained at the local level, began to reach the highest levels of denominational life. And as differences between the North and South diminished, the culture of Dixie that had once knit Southern Baptist together began to unravel. The countercultural movements of the 1960s added to a sense of anxiety over change with civil rights and feminism leading the way. If most Southern Baptists responded similarly to civil rights by initially opposing desegregation and then eventually accepting the dismantling of Jim Crow, gender played a more prominent role than race in the large-scale divisions among Southern Baptists in the final years of the twentieth century. In fact, the SBC's resolution on racial reconciliation in 1995 occurred in the context of its hardening stance opposing feminism.[20]

As several of the chapters in *A Marginal Majority* demonstrate, as women found increasing opportunities for education and professionalization in wider American society and culture, the WMU entered a period of decline and found itself without the financial support and backing of the SBC's male leadership. Experiencing a backlash against feminism's gains, Southern Baptist women were increasingly marginalized in a denomination that resisted their entrance into arenas of power and authority other than missions, particularly those that involved ordained ministerial status. The WMU was further alienated during the 1980s and 1990s for assisting Southern Baptist Women in Ministry, a network organized to support the ordination and professional ministries of women.

BAPTIST BATTLES AND FRAGMENTATION

In histories of the SBC, the period from 1979 to 2000 has been described as the years of "The Controversy," the "Baptist Battles," or even the "Baptist Holy War." Indeed, the denomination was riven by conflict in the final decades of the twentieth century, namely between self-described moderates who had controlled the denomination since the mid-twentieth century and outlier conservatives who felt the SBC had been moving in a liberal—and "sinful"—direction under the moderates' leadership. The labels, of course, were relative. To most outsiders, it seemed an internecine war between white "born again" Christians with only differing degrees of conservatism. Still, from 1979 forward, an ultraconservative faction aligned itself with religious right leaders from outside the denomination and steadily assumed positions of power within the SBC. In the end, conservatives triumphed over moderates with complete control of all SBC agencies and seminaries. Their victory led to seismic shifts, fragmentation, and newly drawn institutional boundaries. While moderates on the losing side refer to these years as the "fundamentalist takeover," those further to the right call this period the "conservative resurgence."

The triumph of the ultraconservative faction had profound implications for the history of women and gender in the denomination. Once in power, for instance, conservatives revised the Baptist Faith and Message, Southern Baptists' official confessional document, to include several passages on women's roles. Most controversially, the 1998 amendment involved adding an article on family, which declared: "A wife is to submit herself graciously to the servant leadership of her husband even as the church willingly submits to the headship of Christ." The finalized 2000 statement also included: "While both men and women are gifted for service in the church, the office of pastor is limited to men as qualified by Scripture." Conservatives then drew on the revised document to determine those who did not tow the party line, thereby purging the SBC's seminaries, agencies, and mission fields of dissenters who supported women's ordination and other forms of women's leadership.

The question of Southern Baptist identity becomes more complicated here. While the SBC has traditionally defined a Southern Baptist as any person who belongs to a church that contributes to its fundraising organ (the Cooperative Program) and sends messengers to its annual convention, our volume includes studies of those who left or were expelled from the denomination as a result of its conflicts. Those self-described moderates who in 1991 formed the Cooperative Baptists Fellowship as an alternative to the hard-conservative turn in the denomination, for instance, were key players in the SBC's politics. Because of moderates' positions of power and leadership in the SBC's seminaries, agencies, and boards before the triumph of more conservative forces, they had long been known as "denominationalists." If mostly men, a few denominationalists in the moderate fold were women from the WMU. Eventually, women seeking ordination and ministerial status joined the moderate camp, often by default and feeling themselves the red-headed stepsisters of the movement. And some pushed further, joining the more progressive and much smaller Southern Baptist Alliance, which eventually became the Alliance of Baptists.[21] Our volume includes studies of women who left the denomination because of its newly codified positions on gender and women's roles, as we see them as integral to the Southern Baptist story.

As this overview makes obvious, a history of Southern Baptists focusing on women and gender has much ground to cover. Thus, *A Marginal Majority* is a beginning; and it is not intended to be exhaustive. We also would note that its chapters focus on the histories and stories of white women within a predominantly white denomination. While several contributors consider Southern Baptist women's attempts at racial reconciliation, and our work is informed by scholarship on black Baptist women, we hope to see more research from the perspectives of women of color regarding the SBC as well as studies on women of color who have joined the denomination in more recent years.[22] In addition, the censoriousness around issues related to sexuality that has persisted in Southern Baptist life has created a deafening silence in the literature, our volume only touching upon the relevant issues here. And finally, while several recent monographs have considered the ways the Baptist battles affected progressive women, little attention has been paid to conservative women in the denomination.[23] We invite scholars to expand the work here and to further complicate the stories presented in *A Marginal Majority.*

Chapter Overviews

While *A Marginal Majority* presents an overall trajectory that is more somber than celebratory, we would emphasize here that the chapters are not necessarily uniform in their conclusions and the ways in which loss and decline are understood and delineated. Relatedly, our contributors did not always interpret our "reimagining" project in the same way. Some responded to it more historiographically, in that they, as scholars, were the ones doing the reimagining by questioning the narrative frameworks and storylines in denominational history and church lore. Others explored how certain women reimagined Southern Baptist life and culture and pushed for change. A few showed the ways in which women reimagined their own lives in light of the overarching patriarchal structures, even when that meant leaving the SBC. While these multiple interpretations of reimagining might push and pull at the reader, we came to appreciate that contributors understood reimagining in different ways and saw this as a means to expand the theme as well as provide nuance.

In *A Marginal Majority's* opening chapter, "'A Greater Influence Than You Imagine': Women Lead the Way to Southern Baptist Centralization," C. Delane Tew considers the gendered nature of the denomination's centralization. Here, Tew scrutinizes local church and associational records as well as minutes from the WMU and the SBC to explore how local laywomen organized the WMU as a modern para-denomination that promoted its members' knowledge and monetary support of the SBC's missions.

Because the SBC, namely its male leaders and ministers, dogmatically held to the principle of local church autonomy, it lagged well behind the WMU in bureaucratic efficiency and fundraising, so that turn-of-the-century and even depression-era women financed the bulk of Southern Baptists' missions endeavors. The WMU's auxiliary status was deceptive, as the SBC relied heavily on the women of the WMU to provide a template for a more a modern, streamlined funding model. The resulting Cooperative Program, the brainchild of the WMU, enabled the SBC's transformation from a loose network of local religious groups into a corporate denominational empire with missions at its core. Ironically, the success of the Cooperative Program also enabled the SBC's male leadership to marginalize WMU women and their accomplishments, ultimately forcing them to function much more as an actual auxiliary than in their earlier years.

In chapter two, "'I *Can't* Go In Alone': A Frontier Girl's Transformation into a Southern Baptist Missionary," T. Laine Scales, Chelsea Cichocki, and Kari Rood explore the dynamics at work leading women to pursue lives as Southern Baptist missionaries. Their chapter presents a focused case study of Jewell Legett's early life, following her path to become a Southern Baptist missionary to China from 1909 to 1914 and again from 1919 to 1926. Legett, like so many other Southern Baptists, was inspired by the legendary Lottie Moon, a missionary to China from 1873 to 1924, whose eponymous Christmas offering has raised millions of dollars for missions. Though never as well-known as Moon and scarcely studied, missionaries like Legett were central to the Southern Baptist story. Scales, Cichocki, and Rood reach back and explore how Legett, as an adolescent Southern Baptist girl growing up on the Texas frontier, imagined and achieved the life of a career missionary to China. Drawing on her girlhood diaries as well as written memoirs and oral interviews, the authors emphasize the gendered nature of Legett's trek and argue that a particular combination of frontier freedom, familial backing, and support from the WMU enabled her to follow the footsteps of the legendary Lottie Moon, whom she had admired since girlhood.

Joanna Lile, in chapter three, "'The Mammy Sues Are Scarce in the South Now': Southern Baptist Women, Domestic Workers, and Progressive Era Racial Uplift," draws upon literature popular among Southern Baptist women in the first decades of the twentieth century—including a 1910s novel series and WMU magazines—to examine how they viewed their own homes as mission fields when they employed black women as domestic workers. Southern Baptist novelist Isla Mae Mullins, an active WMU member and the wife of Southern Baptist Theological Seminary president E. Y. Mullins, published a series of books from 1913 through 1918 about a fictional Southern Baptist family who employed Mammy Sue, a stock black character reminiscent of white Southern depictions of the happy, faithful "house slave" of the "Old South," as well as Cahaba, a younger servant depicted as a degenerate. Mammy Sue is celebrated as a beloved member of the household who is fiercely loyal to her white church-going Southern Baptist superiors and contrasts sharply with Cahaba, who represents a new generation of morally suspicious black women in need of redemption. Read alongside the literature of the WMU from the same time period, the novels reveal how the WMU encouraged its women to adopt a missionary approach to their domestic servants as a form of lay piety and "racial uplift." As Lile argues, their "missionary work" also reaffirmed their notions of religious and moral superiority over black women. These Southern Baptist women took an ardent interest in "racial uplift," she claims, because it promised to reinstate some semblance of the hierarchical racial relationships they believed had created a form of racial "harmony" during slavery. Thus, white women imagined themselves to be agents of Christian piety while working to reinforce their own positions of dominance and privilege.

In chapter four, "Saving Souls and Society: The WMU and Social Reform in the Progressive Era," Carol Crawford Holcomb asks us to reconsider Southern progressivism. By centering women in her study of Southern Baptists in this period, Holcomb challenges the assumption that Southern Baptists had little to do with Progressive Era social reform, including the Social Gospel movement. Holcomb examines how WMU leaders institutionalized a social reform agenda in 1909 through creating a department called Personal Service. Examining the literature associated with Personal Service and the curriculum of the WMU's newly established Training School in Louisville, Holcomb argues that a form of Southern progressivism did indeed inform Southern Baptists in the work of these early twentieth-century women. While even the most progressive Southern Baptist women labored, for the most part, within the limitations of the social constructs placed upon them, especially when it came to race relations—and Southern Baptist women who adopted Progressive Era views likely were in the minority—nevertheless a group of influential WMU leaders in the first decades of the twentieth century was determined to provide a platform for progressive women's views and even a space within the SBC to consider new interpretations of missions and salvation.

T. Laine Scales also considers women's service activities in chapter five, "Making a Home in the New 'House Beautiful': The Woman's Missionary Union Training School Negotiates Change and Decline, 1942–1963." Established in 1909 to prepare Southern Baptist women for careers in missions and social service work, the Training School entered a period of steady and marked decline after World War II. Scales draws on oral histories with women students from these years to chronicle several developments: the conflict some women students felt between a "call" to denominational missions and societal pressures pushing them toward marriage and family; the short-lived racial integration of the Training School; and the pressures to follow coeducational trends and merge with the Southern Baptist Theological Seminary (Southern). In telling the story of the Training School, Scales challenges the assumption that the years 1942 to 1963 were ones of withdrawn quietism for Southern Baptist women, and she contrasts the empire-building of the SBC during this era with the struggles of WMU women over their beloved school. Forced to merge with Southern in 1963, the Training School was, on the one hand, following national trends, in which women began to enter Protestant seminaries in record numbers. On the other hand, the problem for Southern Baptist women, of course, was that both the denomination and the majority of its congregations limited their roles, forbidding them clergy positions. And the social reforming impulse that marked the Training School was of lesser value to the male leadership of Southern, who eventually closed the programming in social work entirely. Women's initiatives in the denomination, then, experienced a reversal of fortune during what most historians have seen as the SBC's heyday.

In chapter six, "'A Christian Attitude toward Other Races': Southern Baptist Women and Race Relations, 1945–1965," Melody Maxwell maintains that if Southern Baptists after World War II were overwhelmingly resistant to shifts that threatened their privileged racial position, some expressed more progressive views. WMU leaders, in particular, were the most consistent Southern Baptist advocates of racial equity during the civil rights era. Basing her research on WMU magazine publications and annual reports, Maxwell demonstrates that over this period thousands of Southern Baptist women repeatedly read articles challenging the racial status quo with some even embracing interracial social justice work. Although not formal leaders of their churches, and often falling short in their stance against racism, WMU members did influence their broader church communities through their efforts, at the very least preparing them for the dismantling of the Jim Crow South, with some even welcoming this new era.

The final four chapters in *A Marginal Majority* deal with the transformations brought about by rapid changes to women's roles and rights in the United States from the 1970s onward. These chapters do not consider the WMU, signaling that Southern Baptist women were now moving in other, multiple, directions when it came to their faith commitments, ecclesial work, and religious identities. Even if many conservative Southern Baptists joined the religious right that emerged during this period, in part to resist the feminist movement, they nevertheless benefitted from and even appropriated many of its tenets. To be sure, feminism forced Southern Baptists of all persuasions to deal more forthrightly with women's roles in home, church, and society.

In chapter seven, "'I'M FOR ERA': Faith, Feminism, and the 'Southern Strategy' of a Southern Baptist First Lady," Elizabeth H. Flowers examines First Lady Rosalynn Carter's support of the Equal Rights Amendment (ERA). Along with her husband, President Jimmy Carter, Rosalynn was a vocal and committed Southern Baptist. While many scholars have focused on the paradox of Jimmy Carter as both the first evangelical president and the one whose politics prompted Southern Baptists to abandon his platform for the Christian right, few have considered Rosalynn Carter's significance in Southern Baptist history. Yet the first lady has traditionally served as the most visible cultural symbol of American womanhood. And Rosalynn occupied that position at a pivotal moment, when women's roles were being reexamined as never before. Carter's activist approach to the first lady role, particularly her lobbying for the ERA, contradicted the model of womanhood and femininity upheld by the Christian right, which included those Southern Baptists who became her harshest critics. Creating what her staff called a "Southern strategy," Rosalynn attempted to downplay the more revolutionary elements of the feminist movement behind the ERA, insisting that the amendment was separate from the issues of abortion and homosexuality. While her efforts backfired, she helped give birth to an evangelical feminism that inspired progressive Southern Baptist women in the early 1980s and continued in more dissident Southern Baptist circles.

Feminist ideas found fertile ground for a brief period in some of the SBC's seminaries, particularly the Southern Baptist Theological Seminary (Southern) in Louisville, which is the focus of chapter eight, "Camelot Revisited: Women Doctoral Graduates of the Southern Baptist Theological Seminary, 1982–1992, Talk about the Seminary and Their Lives since SBTS . . . Again," by Susan M. Shaw, Kryn Freehling-Burton, O'Dessa Monnier, and Tisa Lewis. By the 1980s, Southern found an increasing number of Southern Baptist women entering its doors who intended to pursue ordained ministry, including the office of senior pastor. Women at Southern Seminary became prominent in founding Southern Baptist Women in Ministry in 1984, which supported and lobbied for the ordination of women. Not surprisingly, Southern stood at the center of the Southern Baptist battles, both because of its historical status as the denomination's flagship seminary and because of its reputation as a "liberal" institution. Its campus eventually came under the control of the denomination's conservatives commencing with the presidency of R. Albert Mohler Jr. in February 1993. Five years later, in 1998, Susan M. Shaw and Tisa Lewis published the article "'Once There Was a Camelot': Women Doctoral Graduates of the Southern Baptist Theological Seminary, 1982–1992, Talk about the Seminary, the Fundamentalist Takeover, and Their Lives since SBTS."[24] Based on oral interviews with twenty-nine women who had graduated with doctorates from Southern during the 1980s and early 1990s, the article generated widespread discussion and debate. After all, their subjects were both the first and last women to be doctoral students at Southern during a period when they were both institutionally supported and a focal point of the denomination's controversy. While these women were certainly critical of Mohler and those who took control of the seminary, they also called out the sexism of moderate Southern Baptists.

For this volume, Shaw and Lewis, joined by Freehling-Burton and Monnier, interviewed seventeen of the original participants of the 1998 article, revisiting the themes of their original "Camelot" piece. Their chapter is unique to our volume as it is not as much a reimagining of Southern Baptist history as a charting of the ways these women have reimagined their lives in the decades since their Southern years. Overall, it considers how the Southern Baptist controversy pushed these women to become more liberal in their values and identities, leading them to pursue paths of leadership outside of the SBC and even the Baptist fold altogether.

The final two chapters turn to the conservative side of the Southern Baptist story. In chapter nine, "From Molly Marshall to Sarah Palin: Southern Baptist Gender Battles and the Politics of Complementarianism," Karen K. Seat charts the genealogy of gender discourses in the SBC's increasingly political conservatism from the 1990s through the first decade of the twenty-first century to illustrate how Southern Baptist leaders came to delineate acceptable and unacceptable forms of leadership for women. Starting with Molly Marshall, whom conservatives ousted from Southern Seminary in 1994 largely due to her support of women's ordination, and ending with Sarah Palin, the 2008 Republican vice-presidential candidate whom conservatives enthusiastically endorsed, Seat examines the theological and rhetorical strategies of conservative Southern Baptists as they negotiated women's changing roles. The flashes of popularity that Palin and other conservative female politicians have had among Southern Baptists illuminate just how unique "complementarian" theology has become. According to Seat, complementarianism denotes a softer patriarchy that accepts the realities of universal suffrage and women's wage labor while demanding a loving gender hierarchy in the "private sphere." Seat argues that this form of patriarchy enabled denominational leaders to assert their relevance in the broader world of modern American conservatism.

In the book's final chapter, "'My Husband Wears the Cowboy Boots in Our Family': The Preacherly Paradox of Beth Moore," Courtney Pace evaluates one of the most popular, and increasingly controversial, proponents of complementarianism: Beth Moore. This folksy and famous Houstonian reportedly has been one of the highest-grossing authors for the SBC's publishing house, LifeWay Christian Resources, with her dynamic speaking tours attracting thousands of women. Probing Moore's writings, videos, speaking performances, and social media presence, Pace insists that Moore has been something of a Southern Baptist anomaly. On the one hand, from the early 1990s until 2016, her message endorsed conservative Southern Baptist views on the roles of women, particularly complementarianism. And yet, on the other hand, her vocation undermined complementarian understandings of womanhood. After all, she has been the primary breadwinner for her cowboy husband, held tremendous spiritual authority and power over men, and exposited scripture from behind the pulpit, leading many critics to accuse her of preaching, a charge she seems to have accepted in 2019. In addition, Moore's vocal advocacy of the #MeToo movement, as evidenced in her more recent tweets and blogs, can be seen as a new form of preaching. As Pace shows, the rise of #MeToo emboldened Moore, leading her to critique the SBC's male leadership not only in its handling of sexual harassment and abuse but in its overall treatment and dismissal of women. As Pace concludes, any thorough understanding of contemporary Southern Baptist culture demands an account of, or accounting for, the popularity and paradox of Moore.

Arranged chronologically, the chapters in *A Marginalized Majority* can be configured and read in a variety of ways. Each stands by itself as well as anticipates and connects to others. As seen in this overview, they touch on wide-ranging themes from missions, social reform, and race relations, to preaching and ordination, and then to politics and "family values." They are diverse in terms of methodology too. As historians, most contributors have spent countless hours in the libraries and archives of SBC life. But as typical in women's history, they follow creative archival twists and turns, uncovering those "diaries in the attic." Later chapters incorporate ethnographic studies and oral interviews. The biographical studies sidestep the usual suspects, and although they avoid traditional hagiography, Scales, Cichocki, and Rood address that sense of connectedness many (women) historians feel to their subject. Several chapters challenge the assumptions around a particular movement. By starting with women and switching the narratological perspective, Holcomb, for instance, complicates previous assumptions about Southern Baptists and the Social Gospel as Maxwell does with civil rights. There are also those chapters and contributors who consider how Southern Baptists responded, usually in mixed ways, to more secular issues of the day around gender such as coeducation (Scales), the ERA (Flowers), party politics (Seat), and the #MeToo movement (Pace).

As we have noted, the contributors to *A Marginal Majority* take reimagining in different directions and come to varied conclusions regarding women's agency and influence with race as a case in point (Liles, Holcomb, and Maxwell). Moreover, as we would emphasize again, the volume is not exhaustive, and in bringing together historians currently writing on Southern Baptist women, we also invite other scholars to consider historical absences and missing voices that might complicate or even challenge our narrative of loss and decline. We offer this volume, then, as a series of case studies that, when read together, tell a complicated and incomplete tale. Our reimagining is the beginning of a process crucial to the field of American religion and the historiography of Southern Baptists. And if sometimes bleak, perhaps that means we have successfully met the challenge of H. Leon McBeth: women will indeed bother you here.

Notes

1. See, for instance, William Wright Barnes, *The Southern Baptist Convention, 1845–1953* (Nashville, TN: Broadman Press, 1954); Robert A. Baker, *The Southern Baptist Convention and Its People: 1607–1972* (Nashville, TN: Broadman Press, 1974); and Jesse C. Fletcher, *The Southern Baptist Convention: A Sesquicentennial History* (Nashville, TN: Broadman and Holman Publishers, 1994). Each of these volumes addressed the work of women only briefly and mostly focused on the Woman's Missionary Union (WMU), leaving the impression that women's contributions to the denomination were marginal. See also note 15.
2. H. Leon McBeth, "Perspectives on Women in Baptist Life," *Baptist History and Heritage* 22, no. 3 (July 1987): 9. McBeth himself had written a brief but helpful overview of Baptist women nearly a decade earlier: *Women in Baptist Life* (Nashville, TN: Broadman Press, 1979), one of few such endeavors until the twenty-first century. The WMU also published its own in-house history: Catherine B. Allen's *A Century to Celebrate: History of Woman's Missionary Union* (Birmingham, AL:

Woman's Missionary Union, 1987). But beyond a scattering of articles, there was little scholarship on Southern Baptist women and no major scholarly monograph until the 2000s.

3. In 1987, those institutions would have included the SBC's six seminaries, the Sunday School Board, which housed Broadman Press, and the Historical Commission, which supported the work of the Southern Baptist Historical Society and oversaw the Southern Baptist Historical Library and Archives. Ten years later, in 1997, the SBC closed the Historical Commission placing operation of the Southern Baptist Historical Library and Archives under the Council of Seminary Presidents.
4. The scholarship of Keith Harper, professor of Baptist studies at Southeastern Baptist Theological Seminary since 1996, has proven an exception. See especially *The Quality of Mercy: Southern Baptists and Social Christianity, 1890–1920* (Tuscaloosa: Univ. of Alabama Press, 1996), which gave substantial consideration to Southern Baptist women; and his edited volume *Through a Glass Darkly: Contested Notions of Baptist Identity* (Tuscaloosa: Univ. of Alabama Press, 2012). Still, despite such exceptions, the 2018 sentiments of Thomas Nettles, emeritus professor of historical theology at Southern Baptist Theological Seminary, remain indicative. Against calls to reexamine the rhetoric of conservatives around women in light of the denomination's growing sexual abuse crisis, Nettles rejected any analysis of the SBC's rightward trajectory that examined gender as central to the story, doggedly declaring that for Paige Patterson, who was a target for his mishandling of sexual abuse cases, and other conservative leaders of the Baptist battles, "inerrancy was really the issue" (rather than culturally influenced opposition to changes in women's roles). See "Inerrancy Was Really the Issue," Founders Ministry website and blog, June 25, 2018, accessed August 17, 2019, https://founders.org/2018/06/25/inerrancy-was-really-the-issue/.
5. Two major works stood prominent and alone until the 1990s: Rufus Spain, *At East in Zion: A Social History of Southern Baptists, 1865–1900* (Nashville, TN: Vanderbilt Univ. Press, 1967); and John Lee Eighmy, *Churches in Cultural Captivity: A History of Social Attitudes of Southern Baptists* (Knoxville: Univ. of Tennessee Press, 1972). It was not until twenty years later that other works picked up where Spain and Eighmy had left off analyzing Southern Baptists in light of their social and cultural contexts. See Edmund L. Queen II, *In the South the Baptists Are the Center of Gravity: Southern Baptists and Social Change, 1930–1980* (Brooklyn, NY: Carlson Publishing, 1991); and Keith Harper, *The Quality of* Mercy (1996). Three studies of the late twentieth-century battles between conservatives and moderates, which moved the SBC further to the right, were likewise crucial here: Nancy Tatum Ammerman, *Baptist Battles: Social Change and Religious Conflict in the Southern Baptist Convention* (New Brunswick, NJ: Rutgers Univ. Press, 1990); Bill J. Leonard, *God's Last and Only Hope: The Fragmentation of the Southern Baptist Convention* (Grand Rapids, IL: William B. Erdman Press, 1990); and Barry Hankins, *Uneasy in Babylon: Southern Baptist Conservatives and American*

Culture (Tuscaloosa: Univ. of Alabama Press, 2002). Since 2000, there have been several noted studies of Southern Baptists and race relations as well: Luther E. Copeland, *The Southern Baptist Convention and the Judgement of History* (Lanham, MD: Univ. Press of America, 2002); Mark Newman, *Getting Right with God: Southern Baptists and Desegregation, 1945–1999* (Tuscaloosa: Univ. of Alabama Press, 2002); and Alan Scott Willis, *All According to God's Plan: Southern Baptist Missions and Race, 1945–1970* (Lexington: Univ. Press of Kentucky, 2005). Despite such progress, however, in the two decades after McBeth's chiding, from 1987 to 2007, only two scholarly monographs actually focused on women as key figures in the history, culture, and conflicts of the denomination, and the first did not appear until 2000. See T. Laine Scales, *All That Fits a Woman: Training Southern Baptist Women for Charity and Mission, 1907–1926* (Macon, GA: Mercer Univ. Press, 2000); and David T. Morgan, *Southern Baptist Sisters: In Search of Status* (Macon, GA: Mercer Univ. Press, 2003).

6. Susan M. Shaw's publication of *God Speaks to Us Too: Southern Baptist Women on Church, Home, and Society* (Lexington: Univ. Press of Kentucky, 2008) represented a turning point. Monographs that followed included: Elizabeth H. Flowers, *Into the Pulpit: Southern Baptist Women and Power Since World War II* (Chapel Hill: Univ. of North Carolina Press, 2012); Melody Maxwell, *The Woman I Am: Southern Baptist Women's Writings, 1906–2006* (Tuscaloosa: Univ. of Alabama Press, 2014); and Eileen Campbell-Reed, *Anatomy of a Schism: How Clergywomen's Narratives Reinterpret the Fracturing of the Southern Baptist Convention* (Knoxville: Univ. of Tennessee Press, 2016). It is worth noting that several chapters in *A Marginalized Majority* are by scholars currently working on monographs focused on Southern Baptist women.
7. Ann Braude, "Women's History *Is* American Religious History," in *Retelling U.S. Religious History*, ed. Thomas A. Tweed (Berkeley: Univ. of California Press, 1997), 87–107.
8. Catherine A. Brekus, "Introduction: Searching for Women in Narratives of American Religious History," in *The Religious History of American Women: Reimagining the Past*, ed. Catherine A. Brekus (Chapel Hill: Univ. of North Carolina Press, 2007), 33. As for earlier works emphasizing women's agency, particularly in more conservative spaces, see: R. Marie Griffith, *God's Daughters: Evangelical Women and the Power of Submission* (Berkeley: Univ. of California Press, 1997); Brenda E. Brasher, *Godly Women: Fundamentalism and Female Power* (New Brunswick, NJ: Rutgers Univ. Press, 1998); and Kristy Nabhan-Warren, *The Virgin of El Barrio: Marian Apparitions, Catholic Evangelizing, and Mexican American Activism* (New York: New York Univ. Press, 2005).
9. Kathryn Lofton, *Oprah: The Gospel of an Icon* (Berkeley: Univ. of California Press, 2011), 16.
10. Robert Bruce Mullin and Russell E. Richey, *Reimagining Denominationalism: Interpretive Essays* (New York, NY: Oxford Univ. Press, 1994). For an overall

historiography and analysis of denominational history, see Mullin and Richey, "Introduction," in *Reimagining Denominationalism,* 3–11; and Keith Harper, "Introduction," in *American Denominational History: Perspectives on the Past, Prospects for the Future,* ed. Keith Harper (Tuscaloosa: Univ. of Alabama Press, 2008), 1–6. For an ongoing discussion, see Lincoln A. Mullen, Margaret Bendroth, Thomas Kidd, Keith Harper, and Robert W. Prichard, "The Uses of Denominational History," *Fides et Historia* 49, no. 2 (Summer/Fall 2017): 57–66.

11. Harper, "Introduction," in *American Denominational History*, 4.
12. Harper, "Introduction," 4.
13. In 1951, the SBC agreed to support the Southern Baptist Historical Society under a newly formed Southern Baptist Historical Commission and began its own journal to promote the work of Southern Baptist history, *Southern Baptist History and Heritage*. The denomination's Broadman Press also commissioned several "in-house" histories of the denomination, including a six-volume encyclopedia and those by Baker and Fletcher. While other Protestant denominations had similar internal agencies, journals, and publishing houses, their "church historians" tended to support ecumenical and even secular scholarly organizations such as the American Society of Church Historians, the American Academy of Religion, and the American Historical Association. Such activities and involvements influenced how they understood and wrote their denominations' histories. Since the late 1990s, scholars such as Barry Hankins, Keith Harper, and Bill Leonard have been instrumental in bringing the scholarship on Southern Baptists into the field of American religious history.
14. The relationship between Southern Baptists and evangelicals has been a topic of several studies. See James Leo Garrett Jr., E. Glenn Hinson, and James E. Tull, *Are Southern Baptists "Evangelicals?"* (Macon, GA: Mercer Univ. Press, 1983); David S. Dockery, ed., *Southern Baptists and American Evangelicals: The Conversation Continues* (Nashville, TN: Broadman and Holman Publishers, 1993); and Collin Hansen and Justin Taylor, "From Babylon Baptist to Baptists in Babylon: The SBC and the Broader Evangelical Community," in *The SBC and the 21st Century: Reflections, Renewal and Recommitments*, ed. Jason Allen (Nashville, TN: Broadman and Holman Academic, 2016), 33–50. See also Thomas Kidd, "Are Southern Baptists 'Evangelicals'?" *The Gospel Coalition* (blog), June 16, 2016, https://www.thegospelcoalition.org/blogs/evangelical-history/are-southern-baptists-evangelicals/. As Kidd indicates, while moderates generally saw "evangelical" as a "Yankee word," thereby answering "no," for conservatives at the helm of the denomination in the twenty-first century, the answer would be a resounding "yes." Southern Baptists also figure largely in several recent studies of evangelicals, particularly those that chart the rise of the religious right. See, for example: Daniel K. Williams, *God's Own Party: The Making of the Christian Right* (New York, NY: Oxford Univ. Press, 2010); Darren Dochuck, *From Bible Belt to Sunbelt: Plain-folk Religion, Grassroots Politics, and the Rise of Evangelical Conservatism*

(New York, NY: W. W. Norton and Company, 2011); Molly Worthen, *Apostles of Reason: The Crisis of Authority in American Evangelicalism* (New York, NY: Oxford Univ. Press, 2013); Steven P. Miller, *The Age of Evangelicalism: America's Born Again Years* (New York, NY: Oxford Univ. Press, 2014); and Seth Dowland, *Family Values and the Rise of the Christian Right* (Philadelphia: Univ. of Pennsylvania Press, 2015).

15. Again, there are historians working within Southern Baptist seminaries and institutions who identify as conservative and are active in and engage the larger field of American religious history. Few, however, focus on women and issues of gender. And to our knowledge, all are male. Thus, as it exists within the denomination, the scholarship on Southern Baptist history and identity remains largely the realm of men. See, for example, Allen, ed., *The SBC in the 21st Century* as well as David S. Dockery, ed., *Southern Baptist Identity: An Evangelical Denomination Faces Its Future* (Wheaton, IL: Crossway Books, 2009).
16. For recent studies of Baptists in America that incorporate the complexities of race, class, and gender, as well as regional concerns, see especially Thomas S. Kidd and Barry G. Hankins, *Baptists in America: A History* (New York, NY: Oxford Univ. Press, 2015); as well as William H. Brackney, *Baptists in North America* (Oxford: Blackwell Publishing, 2006); and the overall work of Bill J. Leonard, particularly *The Baptists* (New York, NY: Columbia Univ. Press, 2005) and *Baptist Ways: A History* (Valley Forge, PA: Judson Press, 2003). For one that appeals to lay readers, see Pamela R. Durso and Keith E. Durso, *The Story of Baptists in the United States* (Brentwood, TN: The Baptist History and Heritage Society, 2006). For a general historiography of Baptists, see Harper, "From the Margins to the Middle to Somewhere in Between: An Overview of American Baptist Historiography," in American Denominationalism, 71–94. See too Harper's edited volume *Through a Glass Darkly* (2012).
17. For years, Southern Baptist historians and leaders followed the sentiments of the denomination's founders and insisted that the origin of the denomination was not racism or even slavery but the right of Baptists in the South to appoint and send missionaries, regardless of their support of slavery and slaveholding status. At its founding meeting, the SBC organized its mission boards and assumed responsibility for those Baptist missionaries from the South. Nevertheless, even if the SBC's founding was technically driven by the belief that they had the right to appoint as missionaries whomever they chose, even slaveholders, the break made clear that the denomination would not take a stand against slavery but would instead support the "rights" of slaveholders.
18. See J. Wayne Flynt, "Southern Baptist: Rural to Urban Transition," *Baptist History and Heritage* 16 (January 1981): 24–34.
19. For an overview of Protestant women's missions, see Dana L. Robert, *American Women in Mission: A Social History of Their Thought and Practice* (Macon, GA: Mercer Univ. Press, 1994).

20. See Flowers, *Into the Pulpit*, 140–48.
21. Southern Baptist Women in Ministry was founded in the mid-1980s by Southern Baptist women who had attended or were enrolled in seminary and seeking ordination. In its early years, it was largely supported by the WMU as well as other progressives, many of whom were connected to Southern Baptist Theological Seminary or Southeastern Baptist Theological Seminary. These progressives had long felt marginalized in the denomination, even when under moderate control. In 1987, they formed the Southern Baptist Alliance. For a history of the Alliance of Baptists, see Andrew Gardner, *Reimagining Zion: A History of the Alliance of Baptists* (Macon, GA: Nurturing Faith, 2015).
22. Important studies examining black Baptist women that have informed our own work include: Evelyn Brooks Higginbotham, *Righteous Discontent: The Women's Movement in the Black Baptist Church, 1880–1920* (Cambridge, MA: Harvard Univ. Press, 1993, revised 1994); and Marla Faye Frederick, *Between Sundays: Black Women and Everyday Struggles of Faith* (Berkeley: Univ. of California Press, 2003).
23. As for progressive women, see Flowers, *Into the Pulpit*; and Campbell-Reed, *Anatomy of a Schism*. Both Flowers and Campbell-Reed consider Southern Baptist Women in Ministry. Because it is represented in these more recent books, Southern Baptist Women in Ministry (now Baptist Women in Ministry) is not the subject of any chapter here. And while Flowers looks carefully at conservative women in her study, their perspectives remain understudied.
24. Susan M. Shaw and Tisa Lewis, "'Once There Was a Camelot': Women Doctoral Graduates of the Southern Baptist Theological Seminary, 1982–1992, Talk about the Seminary, the Fundamentalist Takeover, and Their Lives since SBTS," *Review and Expositor* 95 (1998): 397–423.

A Marginal Majority

One

"A GREATER INFLUENCE THAN YOU IMAGINE"

Women Lead the Way to Southern Baptist Centralization

C. Delane Tew

The Siloam Baptist Church in Marion, Alabama, faced a dilemma in 1902. There was not enough money in the church budget to pay for fire insurance on the parsonage. Female members, organized as the Ladies Aid Society, decided to raise the money themselves by conducting "A Measuring Party." The women chose the church basement as a suitable location for the party, set the date for one month hence, and sent out five hundred invitations. Each member pledged to make twenty "little silk bags" that were sent out with the invitations.[1] To explain the event to the community the women placed an invitation in the local newspaper giving instructions about the party.

A MEASURING PARTY

A measuring party is given to you,
'Tis something novel as well as new;
With the invitation is a sack
For use in bringing or sending back
Three cents for every foot you are tall –
Measure yourself on door or wall –
An extra cent for each inch give,
And thereby show how high you live.
With recitation, song, and pleasure
We will meet you at our party of measure.[2]

The party was a success, and the treasurer reported raising a total of $62.50, sufficient to cover the insurance costs.[3]

Women across the South endeavored throughout the postbellum years to rebuild their churches, spiritually and physically. As the nineteenth century began to wane, national organizations such as the Woman's Christian Temperance Union began to urge these women to look beyond their local communities to national issues. Southern Baptist women took up nation-wide organizing through the creation of the Woman's Missionary Union (WMU). Built on preexisting grassroots groups such as local Ladies Aid and Women's Missionary societies, the national WMU grew to become a centralized entity directing the work of these small gatherings to support the Southern Baptist mission effort. The industry demonstrated by women such as those of the Ladies Aid Society of Siloam Baptist Church became a denomination-wide force that aided an expanding foreign mission program and, as I argue here, shaped the Southern Baptist Convention (SBC) into the megalith it became in the twentieth century. Ironically, the denomination's rising stature, built upon women's grassroots organizing, ultimately came at a cost to women's agency, as it led to a decline of the WMU's power.

Organizing the Southern Baptist Convention

Southern Baptists today take pride that the SBC is the largest Protestant denomination in the United States. Those nurtured by its programs and supportive of its missions will speak of the large number of yearly baptisms and announce the chart-topping number of international missionaries the convention maintains. Church members read pronouncements made by Southern Baptist seminary presidents and boast that these presidents are quoted in secular media. Those interested in SBC history will read of mighty men who led the denomination to lofty heights.

Male Baptist leaders in the South created the SBC in 1845, pulling away from the Triennial Convention when it refused to appoint a slave-owning minister as a missionary. A fundamental tenet of the SBC was the autonomy of the local church, causing the founders to reject the idea of a centralized organization with power to control the churches. To carry out various ministries for the churches, the leaders created two mission boards in 1845 with the founding of the SBC itself: the Foreign Mission Board (FMB) and the Home Mission Board (HMB), located in separate cities, each responsible for its own fundraising. The SBC continued to add new agencies and institutions in the 1800s, such as the Southern Baptist Theological Seminary (1859) and the Sunday School Board (1891), all of which needed funding. Despite the creation of the convention and its boards and agencies, from its earliest days, the male-led SBC worked on the assumption that its authority derived from local churches and their male pastors.[4] The functions of the SBC relied on messengers from local churches coming together once a year for the SBC annual meeting.

This local autonomy hampered the growth of a unified, centralized organizational structure, a structure needed to support expensive programs such as a growing missionary force. However, it was not until the 1910s and 1920s that the convention began searching for a way to develop into a more modern, centralized organization. In 1917, the SBC established the Executive Committee whose purpose was to act for the convention between annual meetings and to advise the boards. This was a first tenuous step toward centralization, but the committee did not take the step to have a professional, full-time executive secretary-treasurer until 1927.[5]

An important move toward centralization was to develop a monetary plan to undergird a growing convention. Historians point to the Seventy-Five Million Campaign (1919–24), the first attempt at joint funding across the convention, and the succeeding Cooperative Program (CP) launched in 1925, which is still in place today, as key turnstiles on the path to centralization.[6] In these histories, readers have found names of the men leading this effort, but few, if any, female names.[7] These historical narratives ignore the role of women's organizing at the heart of Southern Baptist history. The WMU, founded in 1888, was the first centralized organization in the SBC, reaching from the national office to the local church societies. Southern Baptist leaders pulled from WMU's experience and relied on its network to launch the Seventy-Five Million Campaign and the Cooperative Program.

The efforts of women from the local level to the national female leadership created one of the most successful denominational organizations in Southern Baptist history. And it proved crucial for the development of the SBC in the early twentieth century. While the SBC had churches carpeting the Southeast, without the centralizing structure forged by WMU women, the convention would have remained a body of loosely connected houses of worship rather than the hegemonic denomination it became.

Southern Baptist Women and Collective Fundraising

The Civil War left the South in disarray, and its churches suffered greatly. Southern ministers had died by serving as both soldiers and chaplains. Many structures, including church buildings and sanctuaries, had been burned and leveled. Emancipation freed nearly four million slaves, who had to meld into an economy devastated by war. Families found it difficult to support themselves, much less to contribute financially to community institutions. And yet Southern Baptists, like others, still struggled to support and rebuild their institutions.

In the process, Southern Baptists revived and continued patriarchal gender roles and expectations. When it came to their local churches, men pursued recognized leadership roles, such as pastor, preacher, or deacon, while women organized themselves into societies focused on benevolence and missions. Women provided aid to families in need and supported their congregation's infrastructure. It was women's lack of individual authority and financial autonomy that led them to collective organizing, which later became the blueprint for the denomination's infrastructure.

These women's groups performed a wide variety of services to their congregations and the larger communities, and the WMU ultimately harnessed this activity into coordinated, disciplined support of the entire denomination. Early on, women proved to be resourceful in their efforts to support all aspects of church life. The women of the Benevolent Society of Pendleton Street Baptist Church in Greenville, South Carolina, for instance, raised funds to provide new carpet, pulpit furniture, and chandeliers for their sanctuary.[8] The Woman's Missionary Society (WMS) of First Baptist Church in Eden, North Carolina, contributed to their pastor's salary in 1891 at the request of the male leadership. Three years later the payments had become a regular monthly item in the WMS budget.[9]

In their efforts to aid the local church, both men and women sought to increase available funds. Pastors encouraged men to pay a regular portion of their income to the church. Women's organizations also sought contributions of regular dues from their members based on the means ordinary churchwomen had available to them. In 1889, the Ladies' Missionary and Aid Society of the Greensboro Baptist Church in North Carolina, for example, decided that each member was to contribute one dollar a year to the society "or its equivalent in sewing."[10] Societies could sell sewn items for cash or send the items as donations to missionaries or the needy. Women regularly developed group activities for generating funds, providing an early prototype for the cooperative pooling of resources. A ladies aid society in Alabama prepared an oyster supper, raising money to purchase new carpet for the sanctuary in 1890.[11] The Ladies Aid and Missionary Society of Terrell, Texas, held teas, a dinner, and one bazaar within a year's span, as well as conducted a "market" one Saturday a month to help raise funds.[12]

The records of women's societies include reports of various "entertainments" offered to the community, proving women could be creative in their essential role of fundraising. Most of the meanings behind these written records are lost to time and can only be surmised. For example, in Parsons, Tennessee, the women spearheaded a "poverty social" (with no explanation recorded for the modern historian); the Pendleton Street women organized a "tin plate" entertainment and a "mystery party"; and in Huntsville, Alabama, the women in the Ladies Aid and Missionary Society raised funds with a "candy stir."[13] Many of these activities were advertised to the community as a whole, thus demonstrating women's vital role in creating a needed sense of social cohesion in the wake of war. At the same time women were supporting a fundraising effort for their church, they were providing a needed social service for the wider community beyond the church. After all, residents of small towns in the late nineteenth and early twentieth centuries lacked opportunities for gathered entertainment that urbanites experienced. These newfound socials offered a chance to engage distant neighbors, creating a rare time of fellowship. Turn-of-the-century rural Southerners, as yet unaccustomed to the concept of a "weekend" of rest, cherished times when they could leave their work behind, gather for an evening of entertainment, and support a worthy cause. The society women provided this opportunity for the community.

Alongside raising funds for local needs, Southern Baptist women also began supporting the burgeoning mission movement in the denomination, focusing on the needs of missionaries, which soon became an impetus for a national organization. Donating monetary funds was challenging for women, forcing them to look to other options. One of the most common was to fill a "missionary box" as their contribution. Groups packed these boxes with items members gathered from their households such as used shoes or articles of clothing women could sew, the same items women provided for their own families. These boxes furnished needed goods to missionaries living on limited salaries in the Americas and overseas. Often missionaries received merchandise and provisions unavailable in their areas of service. Such ventures drove local women toward a more centralized organization.

The strikingly similar methods of fundraising demonstrated across women's groups in the South, with no national organization through which information could be shared, suggested a gendered approach to generating income. Southern women excelled at conducting fundraising activities that brought communities together while supporting a worthwhile goal. Whereas men responded to financial needs by asking individuals to make contributions, women, building on a preexisting women's culture and network, produced events that not only benefited the church financially but also strengthened the community.

The Gendered Nature of Centralization and Mission Work

The two Southern Baptist mission boards, the FMB and the HMB, experienced financial hardships in the last half of the nineteenth century. The male leadership of SBC churches resisted a centralized funding program, fearing that a national denominational structure would cause a loss of local control. Nineteenth-century Baptist men such as the Landmark leader J. R. Graves were fiercely opposed to centralization and accused elite, eastern Southern Baptist leaders of power grabbing through convention structures to the detriment of local church leaders.[14]

Due to deep gender divisions in the nineteenth-century South, Southern Baptist women were more likely than their male counterparts to accept organizational centralization and top-down directives. Women perceived the need for a more efficient method of mission support early on due to their lack of power in church and home. Initially, the process for raising money for SBC missions required that their local women's groups first give the funds to their local churches, whose male leaders would then forward the women's offerings to the mission boards. Yet women could never be certain that the full amount would be sent, as deacons—a male-only governing body—had the power to divert any funds if they perceived a greater congregational need. A national women's organization would serve as a secure channel for women's fundraising attempts and guarantee that their money would land in their intended destinations. Therefore, the desire for a centralized structure came from the marginalization women experienced in the local church. Pastors and deacons, who controlled finances in their congregations, felt little or no compunction to seek a central authority.

Moreover, supporting or participating in missions was one of the few respectable non-domestic activities open to Southern Baptist and other Protestant women of the era, and thus access to the denomination's work in missions was a top priority for many Southern Baptist women. As a result, women across the South agreed to participate in the national WMU's standard programing and activities. By contrast, men were regularly involved in the governance of the local church and so did not feel as much of a need for outside empowerment. If centralization gave women a sense of greater denominational authority and significance, centralization provided the opposite experience for local men, who in turn protested mightily.

WMU women were a part of a growing, nation-wide movement of female organizations to support mission efforts. The first such organization began in 1861 in New York. Disappointed at male-led mission boards' reluctance to appoint women, Sarah Doremus worked to create the interdenominational Woman's Union Missionary Society to send single women missionaries. Other women determined to remain more closely tied to their male-led denomination as an auxiliary such as the Woman's Board of Missions, auxiliary to the Congregationalist mission board, established in 1868.[15]

These organizations based their work on the concept of gently expanding the "women's sphere," which was gaining credence among women of the nineteenth century. American gender ideologies limited woman's sphere to her home and her family (despite the fact that this was not a universal reality, given society's race and class structures). The genius of women in postbellum America was to nudge the acceptable boundaries of their sphere ever broader. Female mission groups began to explain that if women were responsible for the creation of "Christian homes," then it was their responsibility to teach less privileged women (often described in their literature as "heathen") how to do the same. Leaders of women's mission groups discussed the fact that in many countries male missionaries were forbidden to speak directly to the native women, which meant that the spread of Christianity could not be fully achieved without female missionaries. As missionary wives were often preoccupied with the care of their own children, mission societies began to advocate for appointing unmarried women as missionaries, who could then focus all their energies on reaching "heathen" women. Thus, the theme of women's mission to women carried females far beyond the limited sphere where society had placed them. Ordinary church women passionately embraced the message that they could reach women in foreign nations with the message of Christ by supporting female missionaries.[16]

Overcoming Resistance to the WMU

The formation of the WMU met with significant resistance from men in the denomination. However, women's fundraising skills were so important to the SBC mission boards that they did find support for their activities among the convention's national leadership. H. A. Tupper, the FMB's executive secretary, was instrumental in supporting women to organize at the state level. Tupper proposed that each state form a WMU committee made up of elected women from across the state who would guide the societies. These elected women would oversee sending local women's mission groups literature, promoting contributions, and forwarding funds to the two national mission boards. These committees were the first organization of Southern Baptist women on the state level. Tupper was able to form central committees in a few states through his own efforts, though the male leadership in others rejected the idea. His greater success came during the 1878 SBC annual meeting when messengers approved a resolution declaring that states should form central committees that would function as women's auxiliaries to the state conventions "or to the SBC." The status of auxiliary meant that the women's organization would neither receive money from the SBC nor be controlled by its male leadership. The phrase "or to the SBC" allowed women to establish committees in states where the male leadership rejected the idea.[17] Tupper envisioned a network of local women raising funds for missions and sending those monies through the female-led state central committees to the FMB and HMB.

Southern Baptist women made several attempts to organize at the national level before they were finally successful. Mission-minded women first gathered with the intention of forming a national organization in Waco, Texas, during the 1883 SBC annual meeting. While the men filled the Baptist church, women congregated at the nearby Methodist church. Although the 1883 effort to create a national WMU was not successful, women organized themselves to continue to meet every year concurrently with the SBC annual meeting, with the wives of male SBC church delegates (referred to as messengers) often serving as leaders. At their gathering in 1884 in Baltimore, many women hoped again to form a national organization as reports from twelve states proved mission societies were continuing to grow, and delegates repeated the need for a guiding body—yet their efforts were defeated once again.

Fissures began to develop within the male-led convention as women continued to meet and call for a centralized body from 1885 to 1887. Men in the SBC split over the propriety of a women's entity. Several convention leaders recognized women were gaining strength and feared they would create separate mission boards as had a number of northern women's groups. Finally, during the 1888 SBC meeting in Richmond, Virginia, women officially organized themselves as the Woman's Missionary Union, Auxiliary to the Southern Baptist Convention. Ironically, even though this historic event took place in Virginia, the women of the Virginia Central Committee were relegated to the role of hostess, as the male leadership of the Virginia state convention refused to allow the women to participate as official representatives.[18] The Virginia state leaders ultimately voiced their objections through a committee of five men appointed to contemplate the issue of a separate women's organization for the support of missions. Their report, published in several state Baptist newspapers, first harkened to the fact that the church should be the nexus of mission work, not a distant board.

Men also discussed gender differences as a reason for limiting the women: "Furthermore, your committee think [*sic*] that it is to be feared that a separate and distinct organization of the women of the churches for independent mission work might have a tendency, in its ultimate results at least, to compromise that womanly reserve and modesty, and as Paul styles it, that 'shamefacedness,' which is . . . beyond all price. . . . We further fear that such an independent organization of women naturally tends towards a violation of the divine interdict against a woman becoming a public religious teacher and leader, a speaker before mixed assemblies, a platform declaimer, a pulpit proclaimer, street preacher."[19] Numerous men in positions of SBC leadership relied on traditional ideas of gender to stand against the women organizing. Many SBC men at all levels remained suspicious of the women's organization for decades to come.

Even though the creation of the national WMU continued to be met with fierce opposition, ultimately the women's talents for fundraising overcame multiple roadblocks. SBC leaders, faced with increasing FMB and HMB debt, desperate for the funds women's groups could contribute, and fearing an independent women's missions agency, convinced convention delegates to accept the organization and its auxiliary status.[20]

Growing a Centralized Organization

As an auxiliary, the WMU stood in a different relationship to the SBC than did boards such as the FMB and HMB. By calling the organization an "auxiliary" the women were agreeing to work alongside the SBC and support its programs. Yet the final result was somewhat ironic. Since the male SBC membership refused to allow the women to form a board within the SBC where male leadership could have exercised some control, the women were compelled to form their own "side" organization over which the men did not have total control. Ultimately, this would make possible the vast expansion of Southern Baptist women's skills in administrative leadership, institutional organizing, and careful financial management as they successfully developed and maintained their own complex, multistate organization.

In 1888, the women created the WMU with an executive committee headed by a president to direct the work of the new organization and a corresponding secretary to oversee the day-to-day workings of the staff. The committee consisted of women who each served their states as WMU state presidents. WMU society members in the various states annually elected women as their presidents. The first executive committee named Annie Armstrong of Baltimore the corresponding secretary, a term that would later change to "executive director." Martha McIntosh of South Carolina agreed to serve as president of the executive committee. The women chose to locate their headquarters in Baltimore, the location of the Maryland Baptist Mission Rooms, which had created and sent missions material to state and local groups since 1871. In the early years, Armstrong refused to accept a salary, and the FMB and the HMB covered the expenses of creating and distributing materials to local societies. Arguing that the union needed to be as professional as the male-led mission boards and recognizing their leader's unrelenting efforts to grow the organization, officers finally persuaded Armstrong to accept a salary in 1903.

Over time, the union's leaders implemented a corporate structure that mirrored several other women's organizations of the time. The WMU borrowed a system instituted by the Woman's Christian Temperance Union (WCTU) where state presidents served as vice presidents of the national WMU, constituting a board of trustees (also known as the executive committee).[21] Overall, during this period, Protestant women's organizations inculcated the ideas of democracy, even as women remained disenfranchised in politics, with local groups sending representatives to annual state gatherings to elect state officers who then represented them at the national level. Representation in the decision-making process tied local groups into directives of the national organization.

This structure did not translate into the national WMU's absolute or immediate control of local societies. The national organization expanded its power slowly as its leaders dealt with the Baptist concept of autonomous local churches. Local chapters' compliance with the directives of the national WMU occurred voluntarily, and the WMU lacked the power to dictate actions or to discipline local groups. This situation forced WMU national officers to make programs and services as attractive and compelling to local organizations as possible to assure cooperation. The national WMU used promotional and educational material to stir women to action and to centralize their efforts. Through nationally distributed publications that local members would purchase, such as *Our Mission Fields* (later renamed *Royal Service*), the WMU was able to engage Southern Baptist women with the work of missionaries and to encourage greater giving to the mission efforts.[22]

Gender roles in Asian countries, as described by mission publications, held a strong fascination for Southern Baptist women. Through the pages of national WMU publications, women were given stories of women in far distant lands who struggled with flagrant abuses because of their gender. The Chinese practice of binding girls' feet drew particular concern and often appeared in the literature. Women also read stories about *sati* in India and recoiled at tales of widows throwing themselves on their husbands' funeral pyres. WMU leaders wrote of the need to convert the nations to Christianity so that these practices would end and argued that female missionaries were the only hope for these "heathen" women.[23]

In expanding the women's sphere to include aiding women and children around the world, the WMU found that any direct connection to a female missionary helped pull churchwomen into mission support, which, in turn, drew the women more tightly into the efforts of the centralized organization. States that had native daughters serving on the mission field often published information on their work. Readers followed their single women missionaries with great interest. Tennessee was tied to Julia Meadows, North Carolina to Lottie W. Price, and Texas to Ida Taylor.[24] Alabamians claimed Willie Kelly as one of their own, even though she was born in Georgia, as she was educated in Alabama and had worked for the executive secretary of the Baptist State Board of Missions before her service in China began.

An article by Kelly in the "Woman's Work" section of the *Alabama Baptist*, the state Baptist newspaper, demonstrated the gendered nature of mission work and of the emotional appeal made to stateside women. Appealing especially to the sensitivities of mothers, Kelly's first concern in the article was regarding the health of a missionary's child, stating that twelve-year-old Joy Tatum had diphtheria and had to be taken to the hospital. She follows with the heart-wrenching information that the Tatum family had lost "one little girl with the cholera and one child [was] buried in Japan, so [Joy] was the only one left to them." Her letter went on to state that as a single woman she would not be allowed to go to a new area and live alone, begging for women in the states to send another single woman. Kelly's column continued with a description of the work needed to be done at the time, such as working with the girls' school at the West Gate Mission that she and another FMB missionary began in 1896.

In the late nineteenth and early twentieth centuries in countries such as India, China, and Japan, female missionaries found fertile ground for offering girls a formal western-style education, as Great Britain and the United States exerted considerable influence as global powers in this era.[25] It was also an opening for new ways to interact with native families, as most areas in the countries only provided education for boys. Missionary women used the stories of their interactions with girls and women in far distant lands to inspire Southern Baptist women to give to the mission effort and support the centralized WMU organization.[26]

If that were not enough to inspire local church women, both the FMB and the HMB regularly pleaded with them to become active in the WMU. In 1904, FMB Corresponding Secretary R. J. Willingham wrote each and every WMU member, reminding her of the biblical widow who gave all the money she had as an offering. Reflecting on the example, Willingham urged women to participate in the WMU's annual mission offering: "This work is for God and the advancement of His kingdom. May our sisters, redeemed through His Son, gladly give that others may know and be saved."[27] The work of missions, it seemed, had a magnetic pull for Southern Baptist women, many of whom felt an empowerment not experienced in other areas of life. Not only did missions provide opportunities to unmarried women to travel and work around the world, but also SBC and WMU leaders convinced ordinary churchwomen that through their offerings they were becoming an integral part of missionary work, even if they never travelled to a mission field themselves.

Centralizing Fundraising

The WMU's centralized organization led the way for denomination-wide SBC fundraising, including instituting the most iconic mission drive in the denomination, the annual Lottie Moon offering for foreign missions. All of this came out of the creativity and skill of WMU officers who worked tirelessly to increase contributions to the FMB and the HMB. Their enterprise focused on special or named offerings, centering on an annual offering for each board. The first year that the WMU was founded, leaders decided to call for an offering for foreign missions that local women's groups would collect during the Christmas season and forward to the FMB. The concept of worshiping through monetary gifts was important in WMU rhetoric, and Christmastime giving was a natural choice for a major offering.

Using their centralized structure, national WMU leaders established three steps in the offering process, directing the activities of church groups. First, the national office in Baltimore sent literature and collection boxes to state officers, who took the next step and passed these on to local organizations, a direct top-down funnel. During December, members used the boxes to collect money at home, inserting coins they could spare from household budgets. Finally, local members gathered during the first week of January, the "Week of Prayer," for daily meetings, collected the boxes, and sent the funds to the national WMU. In 1918, after several decades of successful WMU-led fundraising for foreign missions, the WMU leaders suggested that the FMB offering bear the name of Lottie Moon, a dedicated missionary to China famous in Southern Baptist circles.[28] Given the centrality of women to the missionary effort, it was fitting that the denomination's most significant annual offering was named after an unmarried missionary woman.

The success of the annual offering for foreign missions was recognized as early as 1895, spurring the corresponding secretary of the HMB to request a similar collection for missions conducted within the United States. In response, the corresponding secretary for the national WMU sent letters requesting that all women's missions groups observe the second week in March as the Week of Self Denial for Home Missions.[29] As with the Christmas offering for foreign missions, the national WMU sent information to the state WMU offices to be disseminated to local groups, including instructions on how the week should be conducted.[30] Though significant, this fund, ultimately named the Annie Armstrong Easter Offering after the WMU's first corresponding secretary, never reached as high a total as the Lottie Moon Christmas Offering. Nevertheless, the fact that both national SBC offerings for foreign and home missions were instituted by the WMU and named after Southern Baptist women involved in missions attests to the importance of women's work in creating a unified identity and centralized infrastructure for the Southern Baptist denomination.

With the success of these two major offerings, SBC leaders understood more completely the fundraising power of the WMU's centralized organization and sought to utilize it for other needs. For example, the HMB requested that the national WMU financially support the Tichenor Building Loan Fund, which provided low-interest loans for frontier churches and chapels to aid construction of church buildings. The centralized structure of the WMU allowed national officers to accept the Tichenor project as one of their official causes and then direct local groups to fulfill the commitment. The national WMU did not use annual offerings for the Tichenor fund but rather developed a monetary goal for the entire organization that they divided among the states. Each state in turn directed local groups to send money throughout the year for this fund.[31] Local groups then used either fundraising activities or individual donations to raise the money.

State WMU treasurers needed local groups to report their donations in order to prove the state met its goals. To set these goals, the national WMU's executive board determined goals, called "apportionments," for each state. The state WMU leadership then broke that goal down to arrive at goals for individual church societies. Report forms, which the state leaders created, provided a means for societies to report their progress toward monetary goals. Even though the national WMU worked to build a centralized organization, there still existed some reluctance on the part of local leaders to send in these forms, leading to frustration on the part of state leaders. A plea from the Alabama WMU treasurer demonstrated the frustration she felt: "The April reports should be in by the tenth. Tired of this announcement! Well, I am too, and it shall not appear again."[32] In an attempt to stimulate reporting, the Alabama WMU created Gold Star Certificates to be awarded to groups that reported every quarter of the year.[33] While local women could resist centralizing efforts as well as the male church leadership, state and national WMU proved skilled at instituting programs, awards, and competitions to win over local support for their causes.

Though the popular culture of the time often portrayed (and elevated) women as gentle and meek, the WMU's records pointed to a strong sense of aggressive, though good-natured, competition within the organization, which was one of the tools the WMU successfully employed to engage women at the local level with the central organization. WMU leaders used competition among the states as a tool to stimulate increased giving and reporting. During the annual WMU meeting, states received their yearly apportionment from the national WMU. State leaders published information throughout the year regarding their state's progress toward its goal. This information often compared collections between states. In a 1905 North Carolina Baptist paper, WMU state leaders printed a list showing their state ranked third in giving and asked, "Shall we overtake Georgia? Having done that, we may raise our eyes to Virginia."[34] The Tennessee WMU rejoiced that their young women's organization was third in giving in 1907 but added, honestly, that not all states had yet organized such groups and that, as the numbers grew, the competition would be more difficult.[35] Texas boasted in 1910 that for missions they had "led for years all the states in gifts."[36]

As the national WMU created channels through which funds would flow, it also took a more active role in standardizing programming and providing material for local groups to use during their monthly meetings. Relatedly, it expanded the national organization to include age-level departments to develop and publish various kinds of literature. This proved not only to bolster the denomination-wide unity of women involved in the WMU but to be yet another source of funding for the national organization. Early in the century, the national office began sending packets containing various articles to women's missions groups that paid a thirty-cent annual subscription fee.[37] National officers also encouraged members to subscribe to the *Foreign Mission Journal* that the FMB produced.[38]

Though it continued to endorse the FMB journal, in 1906 the national WMU began printing its own monthly magazine, *Our Missions Field*, which it renamed *Royal Service* in 1914. State officers encouraged local societies to subscribe and to use this material for monthly meetings.[39] *Royal Service* became the curriculum piece that extended the national WMU's uniform control over groups across the convention, effecting standardized and simultaneous programming. Through *Royal Service*, members studied the same topics each month; they contributed to the same named offerings; and they learned about the social issues that national, rather than state or local, leaders deemed necessary for consideration. The women had created a strong, centralized organization reaching from the national office down to the women in the local church. This structure would prove essential to the male-led SBC as it struggled to create the same type of organization.

Supporting the Seventy-Five Million Campaign

Though the officers of the WMU created a fundraising juggernaut, the SBC and its various agencies and boards had long suffered from a lack of funding, with no unified way to raise money. Early in its history, the FMB had attempted to finance its work by appointing agents who would spend time in designated areas in the South promoting the work of the SBC foreign missionaries and soliciting funds for their support. Some agents were paid positions, but others were volunteers.[40] Other SBC agencies followed this same model, leading to local churches being bombarded with requests for funding from each board or agency. The local pastor had the ability to decide which agent was given access to his congregation. Depending on the charisma of the agent and the message he was able to bring, funding skewed toward one board or another. The random nature of contributions caused the SBC to languish behind denominations with a more centralized structure.

With the help of the concerted efforts of the WMU, the convention attempted to rectify this disparity, launching the Seventy-Five Million Campaign in 1919 at the annual convention. The goal of the campaign was to centralize the funding of all mission, educational, and benevolent work of the convention, with the SBC Executive Board collecting the funds and disbursing them to the various agencies.[41] The results of the Seventy-Five Million Campaign were mixed. While the SBC did not succeed in achieving its fundraising goals, the Seventy-Five Million Campaign did spur the denomination to create centralized fundraising methods modeled after the WMU, which later enabled the SBC's success in launching the Cooperative Program.

During the Seventy-Five Million Campaign, church members pledged an amount of money they would give over a five-year time period. Local churches pledged a total of $92 million to be donated to the SBC by 1924—well beyond the $75 million initially sought. Of that total, WMU members pledged $15 million. In the end, only the WMU achieved its stated goal in contributing to the campaign, while the SBC fell far short of collecting the overall pledges from local churches and actually came out of the campaign in debt. The centralized organization the WMU had developed during the previous decades gave the women a clear understanding of how to determine and achieve their fundraising goals. WMU leaders carefully calculated prior giving and used conservative estimates to establish their goal. From that point, the national leadership passed down apportioned goals to the state WMU organizations.[42] The SBC had no such organization in place at the beginning of the Seventy-Five Million Campaign, and attempts to emulate WMU fundraising mechanisms came too late to salvage their fundraising efforts.

The WMU leadership was eager to prove the worth of their organization to the convention and became heavily involved in the Seventy-Five Million Campaign in three significant ways. First, WMU leaders served on SBC committees that directed the work of the funding program. Second, the women were able to promote the Seventy-Five Million Campaign and the Cooperative Program through their own national publications. Lastly, the WMU worked through its established, centralized network to aid the SBC in creating a similar structure. In essence, the WMU used its experience with motivating independent groups to submit voluntarily to a centralized organization as an example to the SBC of what could be done with autonomous local churches.

The male SBC leadership attempted to reproduce the centralized flow of information and funds that the women of WMU had already established. To begin the Seventy-Five Million Campaign in 1919, the convention chose L. R. Scarborough, president of Southwestern Baptist Theological Seminary, to be the campaign's general director. The leadership suggested an organization that would include state organizers, state publicity directors, associational or district organizers and publicity directors, local church directors (preferably the pastor), and local church organizers. The men also agreed to develop a group of "Baptist Four Minute Speakers" who would be available to speak in worship services and other church gatherings in support of the campaign.[43]

To organize these fundraising efforts, the SBC leadership created several committees, such as the Conservation Commission and the Headquarters Committee. Prominent WMU officials served on these national committees. In 1920, the SBC named Kathleen Mallory, the WMU's executive director, to the Conservation Commission of the Seventy-Five Million Dollar Campaign. The duties of this commission were to carry out the original plan for the campaign and to enlist churches in support.[44] Mallory possessed experience, particularly that of educating local groups to ensure their voluntary support. As a member of the Conservation Commission, Mallory made several proposals to help local pastors motivate church members. The WMU offered the use of its previously established Week of Prayer for Home Missions as a vehicle to communicate the convention's needs. The Conservation Commission and the WMU sent out a joint appeal urging Baptist pastors to preach sermons of self-denial in connection with the 1923 week.[45] The Conservation Commission also asked the WMU to develop a week specifically for the Seventy-Five Million Campaign, demonstrating the respect denominational leaders held for the women's format.[46] SBC leaders also encouraged state and local Baptist officials to include the WMU in all organizations created to support the denominational efforts.[47]

At the same time, Minnie Lou Kennedy James (Mrs. W. C. James in the minutes), national WMU president, served on the Headquarters Committee, which functioned as an executive committee for the Seventy-Five Million Campaign. James stressed the importance of mission study to the success of the WMU and urged pastors to begin mission study groups for men. She further recommended that pastors present a missionary program once a month at midweek prayer meetings, stating that churches conducting these meetings "led in spiritual power and in gifts to the Campaign."[48] WMU leaders recognized that no issue united Southern Baptists more firmly than the romantic image of the self-sacrificing missionary suffering in distant lands.

In addition to WMU women serving in leadership capacities in managing the campaign, the WMU supported the Seventy-Five Million Campaign through its own organization's extensive infrastructure and network of programs, functioning from the national office to state offices down to local societies. Mallory encouraged state WMU leaders to join her at the

Nashville campaign launch, demonstrating the support of the entire WMU organization. Fifteen of eighteen state WMU organizations had leaders in attendance at the meeting.[49] State leaders added paying campaign pledges as a requirement for the Standard of Excellence, a goal toward which WMU local societies strove, ensuring that groups would make every effort possible to meet the goal.[50] In the opening year of the Seventy-Five Million Campaign, the WMU used its main publication, *Royal Service*, to publicize the effort. Beginning in July when the campaign was accepted at the annual SBC convention until December before Southern Baptists were to make their pledges, article after article focused on the importance of the campaign. WMU groups accepted the new rhetoric of centralized funding for the SBC and made the campaign a part of their monthly meetings. Members heard regular reports of their progress toward financial goals.[51] The national WMU produced numerous fundraising aids through the five years of the Seventy-Five Million Campaign. Groups kept charts recording every member's pledge and her progress toward paying it.[52] *Royal Service* included blank pages for members to sign as a "pledge to redeem in full and increase if possible" their pledge to the campaign. In 1924, during the closing years of the Seventy-Five Million Campaign, an article appeared in *Royal Service* supporting a union-wide week of prayer that would encourage members to fulfill their pledges.[53]

The male leadership had no piece of literature that reached directly to the hands of male church members as the WMU had with *Royal Service*. To address this need, Scarborough followed the model provided by the WMU. He created the *Baptist Campaigner*, a monthly bulletin that included articles from various male convention leaders. SBC leaders also began publicizing the campaign in state Baptist newspapers, where many state WMU groups already had in place a column that shared information from the national WMU.[54]

SBC leaders worked to continue developing channels through which information could flow. The Sunday School Board sent publicity items to pastors to use, mirroring items the WMU often sent to its local societies. One such item was a short piece to use on the cover of a church Sunday bulletin entitled "Baptist Money in Easter Hats Would Meet Campaign Needs." This piece used figures showing that Baptist women spent $14,785,714 on Easter hats, while men spent $60,285,714 on cigars, cigarettes, snuff, and chewing tobacco, that could instead be given to the campaign. Another tool used by the leadership was form letters sent to the pastors. Men of standing in the convention such as Scarborough urged participation in the campaign.[55]

Although the WMU was fully supporting the Seventy-Five Million Campaign and the leadership of the SBC seemed to be accepting the aid of the WMU, there were indications that the system lacked complete mutual respect.

The women of the WMU were greatly concerned that they be seen as an integral part of the male-led SBC, as WMU leaders had fully committed the support of their organization to the fundraising efforts. The auxiliary status of the organization meant that this support was voluntary. It was clear that the WMU desired to aid the SBC, using their centralized network to the fullest, but they did not want their organization to be diminished in the process. WMU leaders had recorded the pledges of members from local societies for the Seventy-Five Million Campaign then kept a close eye on making sure that these donations, hence their money-raising ability, be recorded and acknowledged in SBC records. In the early years of the Seventy-Five Million Campaign, Mallory worked with Scarborough to encourage state convention secretaries to assist in the process by directing state treasurers to record all WMU donations separately.[56]

As the deadline for the campaign neared, the WMU became increasingly concerned that certain donations might not be credited to the organization, causing it to seem that the WMU had not met its pledged amount. In 1924, the WMU president stated that the WMU was aware of gifts given that were never recorded "on the books of the WMU because they [were] sent in as family gifts and no separate record could be kept."[57] At the end of the same month, Mallory attached an article to her report sent to WMU state leaders in which she stated that WMU efforts to reach their goal by August would be jeopardized if church treasurers forwarding their money did not clearly mark the percentage of funds that should be credited to the WMU. She urged WMU leaders on all levels to make this issue a priority.[58] Again in September, Mallory stressed the importance of WMU receiving credit for all funds donated by WMU members. Her skepticism over the correct flow of these funds was obvious: "You know that people will promise to do a lot of things with our money before they get it, and I am ever so anxious for us to train our church treasurers to see the justice of keeping careful records of our [WMU] gifts."[59]

Both SBC and WMU officials grew nervous as 1924 arrived and the total pledged was not transforming into actual donations. Each set of leaders responded differently. Male leaders of the SBC recognized that the local pastor was the "key man" needed to encourage local church members to redeem fully their pledges. In his local congregation, the pastor was the gatekeeper who had to be convinced to support the campaign. Some of these men, it was discovered, took money given to the church for the campaign and transferred it to local projects. It was imperative that the convention leaders reach these men and pull them into support of the Seventy-Five Million Campaign.[60]

Those speaking for the SBC offered both a carrot and a stick in their messages to the pastors. Materials coming from the SBC encouraged churches to establish budgets on which to function and through which to pay the Seventy-Five Million Campaign pledges. The message was that churches that lived on budgets would develop a stronger financial base and would ultimately be able to pay their pastors a higher salary. The "stick" took the opposite form. Pastors who did not support the Seventy-Five Million Campaign were warned they might see their salaries lowered or even might be removed as pastor all together. Scarborough used a biblical reference to call unsupportive pastors "the abomination of desolation." Relying on the images from the Great War, those not leading their churches to contribute were labeled "deserters."[61]

The female leadership of the WMU took a different approach. *Royal Service* articles, for instance, presented "tithing testimonials." These articles shared stories of women who found creative ways to raise the funds they needed to fulfill their pledges. Readers also found encouragement to be good stewards of all their finances and to give a tenth, a tithe, to the work of God. The female leadership had learned in their years of creating their centralized organization the best way to motivate the voluntary support of their members. Male SBC leaders, with little experience, struggled to find appropriate messages for the local pastors. As the Seventy-Five Million Campaign ended, the results were obvious. The women had succeeded and reached their goal. The men had not. The WMU had previously developed a successful way of motivating its female members. The SBC was still endeavoring to find effective ways to motivate the men of the denomination.

In the thrilling days of 1919, when Baptists pledged $92 million, the male leadership of the SBC had divided that amount among the boards and agencies. The leaders of these groups then planned their budgets on these amounts and then expanded their work accordingly, rather than waiting for the actual funds to materialize. These added up to a growing disaster for the convention. As each year passed, short-term giving goals were missed. Yet, the boards and agencies continued to borrow funds based on the pledged amounts, amassing disabling debt. By 1924, it was clear that the funds were not being donated, leaving the boards and agencies with a financial calamity. Of the $92 million pledged, Southern Baptists had actually contributed only $58 million. The male leadership and the channels of communication they had worked to develop had failed.

The WMU and the Cooperative Program

The SBC exited the Seventy-Five Million Campaign deeply in debt; though with the help of the WMU, the convention had begun to move toward a centralized structure that would allow for more financial control.[62] The male leadership of the convention worked to develop and implement a new funding program that would be an ongoing system, rather than a time-limited one. The WMU would again step in and use its centralized organization to support the new program, effectively guiding its members to participate in ongoing fundraising activities to benefit the SBC.

In 1925, SBC leaders created the Cooperative Program (CP). The CP built on the idea that each church should create an annual budget and, as a part of that budget, encourage percentage-based giving to state and national levels. Individual churches determined a set percentage of their budget and sent it to the state level. State leaders also determined a budgetary percentage to send to the national SBC. The executive committee then divided the funds among various entities, freeing them from the need to plead directly for funds.[63] This new system worked to solidify the tie between the local, state, and national SBC that the male leaders of the SBC had worked to create during the Seventy-Five Million Campaign, emulating the structure of the WMU. Success would create a modern, centralized denomination with a bureaucracy in place to direct the flow of the funds.

The WMU's president and its executive director, Minnie Lou Kennedy James and Kathleen Mallory—both of whom had worked on Seventy-Five Million Campaign—were centrally involved in the development and implementation of the CP. Mallory, for example, served on the committee responsible for the apportionment of funds to various SBC agencies and institutions.[64] In 1928, the Cooperative Program Committee agreed that its stewardship campaign should use "the same themes and terminology" that the WMU had chosen previously for its emphasis.[65] SBC leaders also publicly acknowledged the importance of the weeks of prayer for both home and foreign missions and noted how the WMU had used these weeks to encourage giving, first to the Seventy-Five Million Campaign and then to the CP.[66]

Mallory and James were often the only female members on these SBC committees, and their written records reveal the novelty at this time of women and men working together in this way. In a letter to I. J. Van Ness, who chaired the Cooperative Program Committee as well as served as executive secretary of the Sunday School Board, Mallory expressed disappointment after one meeting that more time had not been spent in prayer before the committee made its decisions. She also stated misgivings that the committee hurried through its work without sufficient consideration given to the "essentials."[67] Van Ness replied: "I think perhaps you misunderstand the masculine which comes to the forefront in our Commission meetings." He stated that the men had done their praying before they came to the meetings. He admitted that at times he too was disappointed at the lack of discussion but continued: "I think also there is the masculine tendency when a thing is clearly stated and everybody undertand [*sic*] it, not to talk any more about it." Van Ness, who maintained a cordial relationship with Mallory and James throughout their careers, concluded his letter by stating that Mallory held her position "in the midst of this masculine company very finely." The men on the committee maintained high respect for Mallory because she was willing, in the words of Van Ness, to "play the game with them." Van Ness ended his letter by assuring Mallory: "You bring us a very needed standpoint and have much greater influence than you sometimes imagine."[68]

Once SBC leaders established the CP, WMU leaders put their centralized program to work supporting the effort. WMU leaders included in their monthly magazine, *Royal Service*, articles stating biblical standards of giving.[69] Articles on stewardship regularly encouraged WMU members to give through their churches to SBC causes.[70] As it had earlier, the WMU produced items members could use in their efforts to increase giving. Tither cards facilitated the recording of WMU pledges and gifts. Those who followed through with their pledged tithe could purchase a tither's card for thirty-five cents. The national WMU also provided inexpensive Christmas cards for members. Mallory encouraged women to use these cards instead of more expensive ones and put the amount saved into the Christmas offering.[71] Again, the national office sent cardboard alabaster boxes to state WMU offices to be distributed to local churches.[72] These boxes recalled the biblical reference to the woman who broke an alabaster vase of expensive perfume to anoint Jesus' feet. The WMU did not hesitate to support the centralizing efforts of the SBC in the new funding program. However, as the women came to learn, this centralization would bring a threat to their own autonomy.

Fighting for Their Own

With the creation of the CP, WMU gifts to the convention were no longer counted separately. Church members, male and female, made their contributions to the church, which forwarded the funds to the national SBC. Church treasurers would list all giving from their churches in one budgetary figure, nothing separate for the WMU. Significantly, this meant that WMU leaders would no longer be able to point to fundraising figures to be able to prove their worth to the convention. However, WMU leaders demanded that their beloved Lottie Moon Christmas Offering and Annie Armstrong Easter Offering stand as separate symbols of their strength, fighting for those to be left separate from the national budget that the SBC Executive Board created.[73] The WMU Executive Committee urged the chairman of the CP, who in 1927 remained Van Ness, to write a letter stating his approval that the offerings be seen as separate "over and above" items from the new unified budget that was controlled by the SBC Executive Committee.[74] In a letter to Van Ness, Mallory reminded him of his promise to "watch out so that nothing would work against our plan" for the offerings.[75] The idea of "over and above" became a clarion call. While WMU leaders urged members to practice tithing to support the church budget and the CP, they also pressed the women to raise extra money for the missions offerings, "over and above" the tithe.[76]

WMU's defensive reaction to the new order was evident in the rhetoric of its leaders. In her report to the 1926 annual WMU meeting, Mallory began by stating that the WMU Christmas offering the previous year totaled almost half of what had been given by the rest of the denomination for a special Christmas clearing of the FMB's debt. She argued that once this comparison was publicized "then surely no discreet thinker or ardent friends of missions will again worry because the Union encourages its members to make alabaster, self-denial offerings."[77] Obviously, there had been "non-friendly, indiscreet" people who had challenged the use of the alabaster boxes to collect funds for WMU offerings, and Mallory reacted to this negative assessment. Articles in *Royal Service* also sounded a note of caution leading up to the WMU Easter offering. Women read that the WMU "would seek no gift that would interfere with [their] pledges to the 1926 Cooperative Program of Southern Baptists; but gratitude to God, like a bubbling spring, overflows, goes the second mile in giving."[78] The WMU felt compelled to support the CP because of its status as an SBC auxiliary. However, throughout the program's development the organization's leaders insisted on its right to retain previously developed mission funding methods. Nevertheless, the growing strength of a centralized SBC organization challenged the independence of the WMU.

This conflict reached a crescendo in 1929. That year the SBC Executive Committee developed a new financial plan. Leaders developed a pie-chart approach with each SBC entity being given various percentages of the total amount of funds churches gave to the CP. One point in the plan stated that any gift given to an agency from any source would be counted against that agency's percentage. This meant that the Lottie Moon and Annie Armstrong offerings for the FMB and HMB would count toward the percentage allotted for the FMB and HMB, making the offerings a de facto part of the CP and lowering the total amount of funding directed toward the mission boards.[79]

The national WMU reacted strongly against the proposal. Mallory sent a copy of the proposed financial plan to all state WMU leaders, urging them to study the document to be able to plan an action to "safe-guard the offerings . . . as well as any other gifts which might be made with the longing to increase by such 'over and aboves' the maximum allotted to any object included in the SBC Cooperative Program."[80]

At the SBC annual meeting where the new plan would be brought to the floor for a vote, WMU leaders in their report stated they were "radically opposed to any budget system which would preclude or discourage the offerings" to the mission boards. The women were standing up to the male leadership, and in the final wording of the plan it was obvious that the WMU had proven its clout. The approved plan included wording allowing the offerings to stand separate from the CP percentages.[81] With the offerings safe, and with local WMU women funneling their monies through church treasurers to the national SBC in addition to its mission funds, the CP became successful. The WMU continued to place the idea of regular tithing to their church budgets before the women through *Royal Service* and taught the idea that giving to the missions offerings were "over and above" commitments. Local pastors could rest assured that the women were adding to the church's budget. Through the CP, women could proudly point to state and national ministries they supported, along with their support of missions.

As its executive board now distributed funds coming through the CP, the SBC could finally call itself a modern denomination. This was largely because of the model of centralization set forth by the WMU and the WMU's insistence that the men follow the women's lead. The WMU was indeed "a greater influence than you imagined." But as the chapters ahead reveal, the WMU's victory proved short-lived. Centralization enabled the SBC to grow and expand in power as well as size. And women's support for the denomination, including its missions endeavors, often meant losing their independence. As a result, the WMU became more of an auxiliary than it was in these early years, its influence diminished and consigned to the margins of denominational life.

Notes

1. Ladies Aid Society Minutes, Jan. 6, 1902, Siloam Baptist Church, Marion, AL, Special Collections, Samford University (SCSU), Birmingham.
2. Ladies Aid Society Minutes, Jan. 20, 1902, Advertisement from "Democrate Print," n.d., included in Minutes.

3. Ladies Aid Society Minutes, Feb. 10, 1902.
4. Bill J. Leonard, *Baptists in America* (New York, NY: Columbia Univ. Press, 2005), 99–100.
5. C. Douglas Weaver, *In Search of the New Testament Church: The Baptist Story* (Macon, GA: Mercer Univ. Press, 2008), 164.
6. For examples, see Wayne Flynt, *Alabama Baptists: Southern Baptists in the Heart of Dixie* (Tuscaloosa: Univ. of Alabama Press, 1998); *Southern Baptists Observed*, ed. Nancy Tatom Ammerman (Knoxville: Univ. of Tennessee Press, 1993).
7. The histories published by Southern Baptist scholars rarely, if ever, have mentioned the importance of WMU to the centralizing efforts. In 1965, W. E. Grinderstaff gave a comprehensive timeline of the steps that led to the development of the Seventy-Five Million Campaign and the Cooperative Program. He mentioned the WMU only at the end of his discussion, stating that the "emphasis by Woman's Missionary Union, Brotherhood, Sunday School, Training Union, and church music led to uniform promotion." See Grinderstaff, *Our Cooperative Program* (Nashville, TN: Convention Press, 1965), 22–31. More recently, Jesse C. Fetcher's book commemorating the 150th anniversary of SBC's founding also downplayed the significance of the WMU. He did not mention any WMU involvement with either funding effort, only stating that by 1927, along with other SBC organizations, "a vibrant WMU organized a broad base of support for Southern Baptists' total program." See Fletcher, *The Southern Baptist Convention: A Sesquicentennial History* (Nashville, TN: Broadman and Holman, 1994), 146. Historians researching state Baptist organizations tended to include WMU activities in separate sections, rather than integrating it as a core organization in Southern Baptist history. In 2016, Andrew Christopher Smith examined the importance of the Interchurch World Movement and the reaction to fundamentalism in relation to the development of the Seventy-Five Million Campaign and the Cooperative Program, but he made no mention of WMU and its leaders in the development of these programs. See Smith, *Fundamentalism, Fundraising, and the Transformation of the Southern Baptist Convention, 1919–1925* (Knoxville: Univ. of Tennessee Press, 2016).
8. West End Benevolent Society Minutes, Oct. 14, Oct. 21, Dec. 30, 1890, Pendleton Street Baptist Church, SC (also known as Greenville Baptist Church), Furman University Special Collections, Greenville, SC.
9. Woman's Mission Society Minutes, June 19, 1891, Jan. 28, 1894, Records of First Baptist Church, Eden, NC (also known as Leaksville Baptist Church), North Carolina Baptist Historical Collection (NCBHC), Wake Forest University, Winston-Salem, NC.
10. Ladies Missionary and Aid Society Minutes, Jan. 1889, Records of Greensboro Baptist Church, Greensboro, NC, NCBHC.
11. Ladies Aid Society Minutes, Jan. 27–June 9, 1890, Records of Siloam Baptist Church, Marion, AL, SCSU.

12. Ladies Aid and Missionary Society Minutes, Oct. 2, 1905, May 5, 1901, Records of First Baptist Church, Terrell, TX, Texas Records, Texas Baptist Historical Collection, Baylor University, Waco, TX.
13. WMU Minutes, May 7, 1917, Records of First Baptist Church, Parsons, TN, Southern Baptist Historical Library and Archives (SBHLA), Nashville, TN; WMU Minutes, n.d. and Aug. 25, 1890, Pendleton Street Baptist Church; Ladies Aid and Missionary Society Minutes, Nov. 10, 1902, Records of First Baptist Church, Huntsville, AL, SCSU.
14. Smith, *Fundamentalism, Fundraising, and the Transformation of the Southern Baptist Convention*, 20–22.
15. Melody Maxwell, *The Woman I Am: Southern Baptist Women's Writings, 1906–2006* (Tuscaloosa: Univ. of Alabama Press, 2014), 5.
16. Maxwell, *The Woman I Am*, 27. For an interesting study focusing on these issues in China, see Wayne Flynt and Gerald W. Berkley, *Taking Christianity to China: Alabama Missionaries in the Middle Kingdom, 1850–1950* (Tuscaloosa: Univ. of Alabama Press, 1997).
17. William R. Estep, *Whole Gospel Whole World: The Foreign Mission Board of the Southern Baptist Convention, 1845–1995* (Nashville, TN: Broadman and Holman, 1994), 119–21.
18. Garnett Ryland, *The Baptists of Virginia, 1699–1929* (Richmond: Virginia Baptist Board of Missions and Education, 1955), 325–27.
19. *Western Recorder* (KY), Dec. 6, 1888, 2.
20. Catherine B. Allen, *A Century to Celebrate: History of Woman's Missionary Union* (Nashville, TN: Broadman Press, 1987), 33–46.
21. Dawn Michele Dyer, "Combatting the 'Fiery Flood': The Woman's Christian Temperance Union's Approach to Labor and Socialism" (PhD diss., Auburn University, 1998), 33–34.
22. For detailed information on the first one hundred years of WMU history, see Catherine B. Allen, *A Century to Celebrate.*
23. Maxwell, *The Woman I Am*, 31–33.
24. *Biblical Recorder* (NC), Jan. 29, 1902; *Baptist and Reflector* (TN), Aug. 21, 1902; Inabelle Graves Coleman, *One of Us: The Story of Willie Hayes Kelly* (Durham, NC: Christian Print, 1959); *Baptist and Reflector*, May 10, 1906, 6; *Biblical Recorder*, June 6, 1904, 10; *Baptist Standard* (TX), Feb. 15, 1906, 10.
25. See, for example, Jane Hunter, *The Gospel of Gentility: American Women Missionaries in Turn-of-the-Century China* (New Haven, CT: Yale Univ. Press, 1984); and Karen Seat, *"Providence Has Freed Our Hands": Women's Missions and the American Encounter with Japan* (Syracuse, NY: Syracuse Univ. Press, 2008).
26. *Alabama Baptist*, Jan. 14, 1903, 4.
27. *Alabama Baptist*, Oct. 21, 1903, 4 and Dec. 21, 1904, 6.
28. *Baptist and Reflector*, Dec. 10, 1903, 6; *Baptist Standard*, Feb. 1, 1906, 10.
29. Woman's Missionary Society Minutes, Mar. 6, 1895, Records of First Baptist Church, Darlington, SC, Furman University Special Collections.

30. *Biblical Recorder*, Feb. 26, 1902, 7.
31. Allen, *A Century to Celebrate*, 29.
32. *Alabama Baptist*, Apr. 9, 1902, 7.
33. Hermione Dannelly Jackson, *Women of Vision* (Montgomery, AL: Woman's Missionary Union, Auxiliary to Alabama Baptist State Convention, 1964), 40.
34. *Baptist Recorder*, Aug. 16, 1905, 10.
35. *Baptist and Reflector*, July 25, 1907, 6.
36. *Baptist Standard*, Apr. 7, 1910, 26.
37. *Baptist and Reflector*, Jan. 1, 1903, 6.
38. Woman's Missionary Society Minutes, Mar. 1903, Whiteville Grove Baptist Church, North Carolina Records, NCBHC.
39. *Biblical Recorder*, Dec. 19, 1906, 10.
40. Estep, *Whole Gospel Whole World*, 63.
41. Melody Maxwell, "'Planking Down the Cash': Woman's Missionary Union's Support of the Southern Baptist Convention, 1919–1945," *Baptist History and Heritage Journal* 45, no 1 (Winter 2010), 69.
42. Allen, *A Century to Celebrate*, 126.
43. "Suggested Program for Conference of Workers on Baptist 75 Million Campaign," Seventy-Five Million Campaign Collection, SBHLA.
44. Conservation Commission of the Seventy-Five Million Campaign Minutes, May 15, 1920, SBHLA.
45. Conservation Commission of the Seventy-Five Million Campaign Minutes, Jan. 24, 1923.
46. Conservation Commission of the Seventy-Five Million Campaign Minutes, June 3, 1924.
47. Conservation Commission and the Southwide Conference on the Program of the Seventy-Five Million Campaign Minutes, June 28, 1922, SBHLA.
48. Headquarters Committee Minutes, June 28, 1922, SBHLA.
49. Central Committee Minutes, June and July 21, 1919, North Carolina State WMU Office, Raleigh.
50. "Standard of Excellence for Woman's Missionary Society," WMU Yearbook, First Baptist Church, Abilene, TX, Texas Baptist Historical Collection.
51. Woman's MS Minutes, Feb. 2, 1920, West End Baptist Church, Birmingham, AL, SCSU.
52. Woman's MS Minutes, "Pledges to 75 Million Campaign" Chart, 1921.
53. Maxwell, *The Woman I Am*, 85, 74–75.
54. Scarborough to Van Ness, July 28, 1919, Van Ness Papers, SBHLA.
55. "Baptist Money in Easter Hats Would Meet Campaign Needs," Sunday Bulletin, Apr. 9, 1922, Records of First Baptist Church, Nashville, TN, SBHLA.
56. Mallory to F. S. Groner, Feb. 13 and Mar. 12, 1921, Mallory Files, Texas Baptist Historical Collection.
57. "Address of WMU President," WMU Annual Meeting, 1924, WMU Archives, National WMU Office (WMUA), Birmingham, AL.

58. Attachment to Corresponding Secretary's Report, WMU Executive Committee, May 28, 1924, WMUA.
59. Mallory to Ida M. Stallworth, Sept. 17, 1924, Alabama WMU Records, SCSU.
60. Smith, *Fundamentalism, Fundraising, and the Transformation of the Southern Baptist Convention*, 111–12.
61. Smith, *Fundamentalism*, 117–18, 123–27.
62. Smith, *Fundamentalism*, 188.
63. Chad Owen Brand and David E. Hankins, *One Sacred Effort: The Coorperative Program of Southern Baptists* (Nashville, TN: Broadman and Holman, 2005), 110–13.
64. Committee on Future Program of Southern Baptists Minutes, June 3–4, 1924, SBHLA.
65. Corresponding Secretary's Report, WMU Executive Committee Minutes, June 13, 1928, WMUA.
66. Corresponding Secretary's Report, WMU Executive Committee Minutes, Nov. 3, 1926, WMUA.
67. Mallory to Van Ness, June 17, 1926, Van Ness Collection, SBHLA.
68. Van Ness to Mallory, June 18, 1926, Van Ness Collection, SBHLA.
69. "Ways of Winning," *Royal Service*, Oct. 1925, 16.
70. "Biblical Commands for Tithes and Offerings," *Royal Service*, Mar. 1926, 31.
71. WMU Executive Committee Minutes, Oct. 6 and Dec. 1, 1926, WMUA.
72. Hannah Reynolds to Mallory, Aug. 11, 1924, Alabama WMU Records, SCSU.
73. Allen, *A Century to Celebrate*, 155. The WMU offering for the Home Mission Board was known as the Week of Prayer for Home Missions at the time, which included a "thank offering." The WMU renamed the week for Annie Armstrong in 1934. The current name, the Annie Armstrong Easter Offering for Home Missions, became official in 1969.
74. WMU Executive Committee Minutes, Jan. 26 and Feb. 25, 1927, WMUA.
75. Mallory to Van Ness, Nashville, May 4, 1926, Van Ness Collection, SBHLA.
76. Allen, *A Century to Celebrate*, 150.
77. Corresponding Secretary's Report, WMU Annual Meeting, 1926, WMUA.
78. "Viewing the Land," *Royal Service*, Mar. 1926, 4.
79. SBC Executive Committee Minutes, Mar. 5–6, 1929, SBHLA.
80. Report WMU Corresponding Secretary, WMU Executive Committee Minutes, Apr. 3, 1929, WMUA.
81. WMU Report, *Annual of the Southern Baptist Convention, 1929* (Nashville, TN: Executive Committee of the Southern Baptist Convention, 1929), 47.

Two

"I *CAN'T* GO IN ALONE"

A Frontier Girl's Transformation into a Southern Baptist Missionary

T. Laine Scales, Chelsea L. Cichocki, and Kari S. Rood

On May 13, 1909, from her room in the Woman's Missionary Union Training School in Louisville, Kentucky, twenty-five-year-old Jewell Legett wrote: "And now the day of all day[s] that I have dreaded most is almost at hand,—the day of examination before the Foreign Mission Board. It is the most serious step I ever have taken; but I am as light-hearted as a child could be. . . . If only mamma and papa were here to go into the room with us. I feel like I can't go in alone."[1] In spite of her anxiety, Jewell did go into the room to be examined. But while physically alone, she still carried with her the support and encouragement of many Baptist friends.

Most immediately, there were her training union peers, staff, and even fellow female applicants. In preparation for her exam, Jewell's roommate, Annie Sandlin, had rehearsed several questions with her, many based on the grapevine from former female candidates. Jewell notes in her diary, for instance, "You know Dr. Willingham [Foreign Mission Board secretary] always asks about your love affairs," so she had carefully rehearsed her response to the personal question for single women.[2] After an evening of such practice, and very little sleep, Jewell and three other missionary applicants from the school met for morning prayer in the rooms of the principal, Mrs. McLure. A China missionary returning to the United States for a year of furlough, Miss Willie Kelly, came by, says Jewell, "to tell us not to be afraid, and to squeeze our hands, before we left home."[3] As Jewell and the other students performed a choral piece in a morning session of the Woman's Missionary Union meeting, Jewell observed, "how lovingly those women watched us." Later that day, Rev. R. W. Lide, her friend Jane's father and a board examiner, came to escort Jewell and the other women applicants to the board room.[4] Each of these affirming gestures substituted for and expanded upon what her mother and father may have offered if they had been able to travel from Texas to Louisville for this special day.

Throughout her young life, then, Jewell benefited from a nurturing network of Baptists. Growing up in a minister's home, with her family's heavy involvement in a local church congregation, attending a coeducational Baptist college, and then transitioning to the Baptist's flagship training school for missionary women allowed her to weave a web of support. In fact, the moment of Jewell's examination and acceptance into the Southern Baptist missionary force provides a vignette that raises significant questions about women missionaries of the early twentieth century. How did young Southern Baptist women hear and accept the call to be a missionary? How did Jewell's childhood experiences shape her concepts of calling and of missionary work? What role did gender expectations play in the shape of her calling? While we cannot draw complete conclusions from one case study, Jewell Legett's story helps us to imagine the formative childhood and adolescent experiences that prompted and enabled young Southern Baptist women to become missionaries at the turn of the twentieth century.[5] More specifically, she provides a window into understanding how frontier life shaped gender in this era.[6]

Our claim is twofold. First, a triad of family, church, and community nurtured the growth of Jewell as a mission-minded young girl, and, second, the gendered constructions within this triad (Jewell's own parents, her local Texas Baptist church, and her frontier community) proved somewhat more elastic than many Southern Baptist families and churches in different regions and locations. The role that Jewell assumed was not necessarily "radical" for Southern Baptists, as, after all, other girls and women successfully pursued missionary status. But as we will demonstrate, the affirmation and support she received along the way proved more progressive than in other Southern Baptist families, churches, and local and regional communities. Finally, as we will indicate, there is a comparative nature to this account. Young men aspiring to mission work often followed a more defined path of seminary training and preaching experience before applying to the Southern Baptist Foreign Mission Board. In contrast, the pathway for Jewell's generation of girls and women was more ambiguous as they sought to participate in the denomination's evangelical mandate to "share the gospel." While the words of the popular hymn "We've a Story to Tell to the Nations" cultivated a sense of God's call to overseas missions in both boys and girls, following that call proved more difficult for women.

A Frontier Family

Jewell's mother and father met and married in Buffalo Gap, Texas, in 1881, shortly after their parents migrated into the area. Thomas Riley (T. R.) Legett's family pushed west from Monticello, Arkansas, while Alice's parents, William and Bettie Herring, hailed from the east, starting their journey from their home in North Carolina. They stopped in Llano County, Texas, where Alice was born, on their way to settle in Buffalo Gap. Westward migration occurred for many reasons. Evangelizing the frontier motivated many Southern Baptist families, such as the Legetts, and in becoming a preacher, T. R. followed in the line of many Southern Baptist men known for their pioneer spirit and missionary zeal.[7]

Jewell Legett (born 1884) and her younger brothers Carey (born 1887) and Tom Jr. (born 1892) grew up in an evangelical Southern Baptist home, where the Bible was read often, the family prayed together, and their "Mama and Papa" lived to "serve the Lord." T. R. was thirty and Alice barely twenty when Jewell, their first child, was born. T. R.'s religious devotion, his love for his daughter, and his sense of the fragile nature of frontier life were all apparent in the letter he wrote to Jewell on her first birthday.

> Buffalo Gap, Texas
> August 15, 1885
> To my Dear Daughter Jewell. This your First Birthday, you do not now know, but should God spare your life you will know, that by this Birthday Card and this note, that you are ever present in my mind and that with each returning year, I shall pray, as I have prayed, for God to bless my darling child. And Should I dye [*sic*] before you, know what a father is, Strive to meet me in Heaven where I pray to Go.
> Your Father, T. R. Legett.[8]

During Jewell's early childhood, T. R. Legett served as pastor of the First Baptist Church of Buffalo Gap, and Alice Legett used her nursing skills to assist in their family-run drugstore. Alice also volunteered in the church and managed the household. The Legetts lived within visiting distance of their extended family, and in later years, Jewell recorded many memories of childhood days visiting her grandparents, aunts, and uncles.

As for Buffalo Gap, the town was merely twenty-seven years old in 1884, the year of Jewell's birth, and had been established as part of the Center Line Trail used to run cattle from Texarkana to El Paso. Named for the gap through which buffalo traveled to reach the high plains, it originally functioned as an early winter camp for hunters, with easy access to trade centers. By the time the Legetts arrived, Buffalo Gap had already experienced major fluctuations in population and town activity. When Abilene was founded in 1881, as a result of the new Texas and Pacific Railway headquarters, Buffalo Gap underwent a sharp decline in residents, dropping from twelve hundred to four hundred in just four years.[9] The preacher's young family then moved in 1891, when Jewell was seven, to Sherwood, Texas, and four years later to Arcadia, Texas, near the Gulf Coast, staying there less than two years.[10] The family mourned the deaths of five infants throughout these moves, leaving five small graves spread across the frontier as they moved from place to place preaching the gospel.[11]

The Legetts finally settled on the Gulf Coast at Port Lavaca in 1897, where T. R. and Alice would rear their children and remain the rest of their lives. Port Lavaca had been devastated by two hurricanes (1875 and 1886) within the two decades before the Legetts arrived. The population doubled between 1890 and 1896, growing from four hundred to eight hundred residents. Named *La vaca,* the Spanish word for "cow," the town functioned as a hub for cattle shipments. However, the progression of the railroad system through Texas bypassed Port Lavaca, and it never regained its prestige for cattle shipment. The seafood and tourism industries helped to revitalize the town in the early twentieth century, which may have prompted the Legett's relocation.[12]

Missions-Minded Parents

Many women missionaries grew up in a minister's family. According to the historian Jane Hunter, over 40 percent of the women missionaries appointed to serve in China by the American Board of Commissioners of Foreign Missions had fathers and mothers who participated in church work as either missionaries or ministers. Hunter notes that these women were in some sense emulating both parents; nevertheless, they had derived their vocational inspiration from a stronger identification with their fathers. This identification informed or provided girls with a certain strength and assertiveness that led them to pursue a mission career.[13] And Jewell proved no exception.

T. R. desired for his oldest child to be a missionary from the time she was born. His evangelical spirit fueled his own ministerial work throughout Texas, and he hoped his own daughter would do the same. On the day of

Jewell's birth, he lifted her high in his hands and prayed that God would call her to serve as a missionary. He did not tell this story to the young Jewell, carefully guarding his hope and dream, until after she made a formal commitment to missions when a student at Baylor University. "I wanted you to be God-called, not Dad-called," he quipped, explaining his secrecy.[14]

T. R.'s support of Jewell's missionary calling indicated his confidence in the young Jewell; he even invited her along on weekday trips to visit the sick and weekend excursions as he rode on horseback through the region, preaching at churches in small towns about ten or fifteen miles away.[15] For example, in July of 1900, T. R. was busy in nearby Seadrift with a wedding and a "protracted meeting," a revival of several days resulting in six baptisms.[16] In addition, he occasionally preached at the Port Lavaca Church (later called First Baptist Church) and represented the church as a delegate or "messenger" for the Colorado Baptist Association in 1900.[17] T. R. would later be remembered by Port Lavaca Baptist Archie Kirkland as "a strong pillar of both the Baptist Church and the Masonic Lodge, [who] served as chaplain, preacher, and priest to many many people of all faiths throughout Calhoun County."[18]

T. R. could not support the Legett family on preaching alone, so during the week he ran a drugstore with the family name in Port Lavaca, just as he had done in Buffalo Gap. Legett's carried a variety of goods: "We have Roach paste, Perfume, Fly Paper, nice Dressing Cases, Patent Medicines, any kind of a Brush, Pencils, Dolls, Etc. Come and see for yourself."[19] Alice Legett helped in the drug store and was known locally for her nursing skills and as a "companion to the whole community."[20] Although the local newspaper recognized T. R.'s religious activities, Alice Legett's religious leadership went undocumented. Archie Kirkland, the Southern Baptist church clerk at Port Lavaca, recorded in his diary that Alice was one of the principal workers in a "Cottage Prayer Meeting."[21] However, other than this one indication, Alice's work remains difficult to discern. Of course, women's work was often overlooked and unreported. The Texas women's historian Patricia Summerlin Martin called the mission activities of Baptist women "hidden work" as it involved care for the poor and sick, an activity not valued in the same way as men's evangelistic endeavors.[22] Women's church-related pursuits are most often revealed through private documents, such as diaries and letters, rather than through formalized meeting minutes.

Having seen her mother take on many roles in the home, church, and with children, Jewell learned how to serve. Alice Legett's model of volunteer service in the community encouraged young Jewell toward religious faith, hard work, and helping others. Her father's paid service as a preacher, though not enough to support the family, showed Jewell the importance of sharing the gospel message as one's primary vocation, even when poorly compensated. The models of both her mother and father likely influenced Jewell's sense of obedience to God's call and her readiness for the hard life of a missionary woman in China.

Home Life

Although we lack diary accounts of Jewell's early childhood, we can piece together an impression of her adolescent life in Port Lavaca from a 1904 diary of her summer visit home from college, during which she resumed many of the daily activities of her childhood and early adolescence. The Legett children spent significant time in the nearby bayou and bay. Jewell and her cousin Lander enjoyed rowing in his boat, while she often went "bathing" (swimming) in the bay with her female cousins and friends.[23] Her brothers, Tom and Carey, went fishing daily and on one occasion caught ten fish, "enough for dinner and supper."[24] The Legetts were also a family of readers and writers, and after sundown, they enjoyed reading aloud to one another. They regularly perused the *Texas Baptist Standard*, the newspaper for Texan Southern Baptists, which originated under the name *Baptist News* in 1888. The paper featured a column just for children, engaging young readers in tales about missionaries and inviting them to send money for orphaned children and mission work.[25] It is likely that Jewell learned stories about foreign missionaries from reading articles such as "A Bundle of Letters from China," which translated and published messages from Chinese converts to a returned missionary.[26]

Letters from "Papa," written for Jewell regularly from the time she was one year old until her father's death a few days before her thirty-eighth birthday, modeled the importance of the written word in maintaining relationships between family and friends. Jewell began writing a diary at age sixteen and would continue sporadically writing diaries and unpublished memoirs for the rest of her life. She used her writing skills later to publish articles in *The Lariat* (Baylor's student newspaper), the *Baptist Standard*, and brochures for the Woman's Missionary Union (WMU).

In addition to highlighting her reading practices and writing skills, Jewell's diaries indicate her love of music, a passion that she would develop further at Baylor and in the WMU Training School. A musical family, the Legetts often entertained themselves and their friends accordingly in the evening. T. R. played the violin, Jewell sang and played the piano, organ, and flute, and brother Carey also played the flute. They performed not only for home entertainment but in church services as well.[27] At age seventeen, Jewell then learned to move outside the comfort of her home, playing the piano at a revival in her grandparent's church.[28] Whenever she visited aunts and uncles, music was an important part of the visit, as she recorded in her diary: "We sat out on the gallery [porch] in the moonlight for a long while. Aunt Dick and Uncle Frank on one quilt on my right and Aunt Lillie on one [quilt] on my left. I sang a few old songs for them."[29] Music functioned as a vital skill for missionaries, particularly women, and in later years Jewell would attract potential converts in China by playing the organ and singing for a group of men, women, and children.[30]

A frontier home required constant upkeep, and mothers and grandmothers trained young girls in domestic work from an early age. In fact, Jewell's first chore was washing dishes, assigned "as soon as [she] was old enough to do anything."[31] T. R. and Jewell's two younger brothers participated in household chores, thereby challenging our assumptions of traditionally gendered tasks and domestic spaces in frontier and Texan life and culture. Tom scrubbed the gallery (porch), and one day, when Jewell was busy making her own dress, her father took on her assigned responsibilities for cleaning the house so she could have more time to sew.[32] Perhaps the blurred lines between women's and men's chores in the Legett household also provided a flexibility that would shape Jewell's perceptions of women's education and church work: women and men worked together to accomplish the common goals of evangelizing others. Although the work was never complete, the entire Legett family took time for napping. Jewell reported an especially long nap from 1:00 to 4:00 p.m., perhaps due to the heat of an August day in Texas in 1904.[33]

In her teen years, Jewell and her family received a very special gift from a group of WMU members in Louisville, Kentucky. It was the practice of WMU associations to send "missionary boxes" or "frontier boxes" filled with gifts to families "serving in the Lord's work" and living on meager incomes. The resourceful women would find out the sizes and descriptions of the family members and cut and sew garments and bedding.[34] Finally, they would tuck in some toys or cash to bring extra joy to the servants of the Lord. The box for the Legetts contained a large overcoat for T. R., coffee, sugar, marbles for the boys, and some dresses for Jewell as she anticipated the needs of college life.[35] The gift of a missionary box demonstrated to the Legetts, and to Jewell especially, that mission work, while poorly paid work, was still highly esteemed. Mission-minded women supported the cause as co-laborers with missionaries, not only praying for their needs but trying to supply and meet those practically. Jewell would have an opportunity in later years to personally thank the women who sent the box when she visited the Chestnut Street Baptist Church in Louisville. From a young age, then, she could not help but feel that the Baptist community of support was far-reaching as she had experienced its nurturing here and in numerous other spaces beyond home.[36]

Church, School, and Paid Employment

The weekly routine for the Legetts included and indeed prioritized church. Alice and the children attended the Baptist church in Port Lavaca while T. R. traveled by train to preach in nearby towns. After visiting neighbors in the community or entertaining guests at their house, the family returned to church for Sunday evening service.[37] In her earliest extant diary from 1901, the sixteen-year-old Jewell described a visit to her aunt's place of worship. The country church service was an all-day affair, with a morning sermon followed by dinner on the grounds, a baptizing four miles away, and an evening sermon. In her diary, Jewell recorded the main points of the sermon for later reflection, a practice she would continue throughout the rest of her life. She then demonstrated her evangelical zeal by noting how happy she was to see those she loved publicly acknowledging her Lord: "Oh how mine and Aunt Jo's hearts thrilled when Aunt Lillie and Uncle John gave their hands to be prayed for! Young as I am, carefree as I am, I could not live without my Savior!"[38]

During the week, Jewell and her brothers attended the local school, and her missionary records indicate completion of high school in Port Lavaca.[39] She was studious, as evidenced by her graduation from Baylor University in 1907 in an era when few women attended, and even fewer completed, college or university.[40] Her interest in learning may have contributed to her choice to teach school after college, though in this era women's career choices were limited. She would also take charge of several girls' schools in China in later years. While there is little information available about Jewell's high school work in Port Lavaca, we do know her school was a coeducational public school.[41] Consistent attendance of school alongside both males and females may have contributed to Jewell's decision to pursue a coeducational experience at Baylor.

Jewell attended school daily, except during the summer, until she went away to college. But her mother, Alice, worked outside the home in Legett's, the family-owned business, in addition to the variety of responsibilities she assumed at home such as cleaning, cooking, and sewing. In the latter nineteenth century, a time when many white middle- or upper-class women did not work outside the home, Texas women turned to employment outside the home: by the time Jewell turned sixteen, about 15 percent of Texas women were in the paid labor force. Women like Alice may not have been recorded in this statistic because presumably she did not earn a formal salary, but she worked, as she was able, to keep the family drugstore afloat. We have no information about Jewell's employment until she became a teacher at Goodnight Academy for a few months after graduating from college. However, her attitude toward women's employment was favorable as she makes clear in an essay she wrote at age twenty-two for *The Lariat*. The young Jewell argued that it was acceptable, reasonable, and honorable for young women to work for pay in order to put themselves through college.[42] The fact that such an editorial would be written indicates that some students at Baylor, *The Lariat's* primary audience, may have thought it unacceptable for women to earn a salary. Jewell would use persuasive writing throughout her life to educate and recruit readers to embrace her point of view, particularly related to missions.

A Frontier Community

While Jewell's early family life provided an environment in which a missionary could grow, the frontier communities in which she lived cultivated a particular notion of womanhood. Jewell was born toward the end of the frontier era, which spanned from 1800 and 1900, when travelers settled the sparsely populated prairies, mountains, and deserts west of the Mississippi. While our image of the frontier settler may call to mind families in covered wagons driving through dusty lands, settlers' experiences and motivations were diverse. People who settled had various reasons for heading west. Some sought economic opportunity; some craved adventure. But for people like the Legetts, the driving force was mission work—applying that evangelical mandate to share the gospel with those who were settling the West. While Jewell's grandparents and parents were among those traveling in covered wagons, and her family moved around several Texas towns in her childhood, the family had settled in a coastal town by the time she was twelve. Her daily life on the Texas coast may have been somewhat different from that of the frontier settlers in prairie or mountain communities as it blended the lifestyles of rural farming and the sea. As the historian Sandra L. Myres reminds us in her book *Westering Women and the Frontier Experience, 1800–1915*, frontier women were "not any one thing." They experienced a range of motivations, lifestyles, and responses to frontier living.[43] However, one common experience of "westering women" was a shift in gender expectations that provided new freedoms, along with new chores and duties that had previously belonged only to men.

Western life required women like Alice Legett and her daughter Jewell, whose families relocated from the Southeast, to reimagine the image of the "Southern lady." Patricia Summerlin Martin notes that frontier women with rural lifestyles were typically members of the lower and middle classes in Texas. These women did not fit the characterization of the "woman on a pedestal," and they bristled against any ideal of Victorian womanhood. In fact, Texas women, with their own daily and strenuous physical tasks to accomplish, "experienced a growing sense of equality with men."[44] As a young girl on the Texas frontier during the 1880s, Jewell was likely to encounter other girls and women who fulfilled expectations for their gender that were different from those back east. In her analysis of diaries from women traveling west in the mid-nineteenth century, the historian and literary scholar of the American West Lillian Schlissel concludes that women on the frontier worked hard and sometimes in roles that others might consider to be men's work: "Women crossing the frontier," she writes, "asked for no special help or treatment. . . . They were as knowledgeable as men about the qualities of grasses for the animals. They understood what was expected of them and endeavored to do their share of the work each day."[45]

Yet in spite of the toughness of the frontier woman's experience and the elasticity of gender expectations, Summerlin Martin argues that Texas women still valued the Southern lady ideal and "looked at it with romantic longing," but "Texas simply did not provide circumstances where that kind of existence could be realized."[46] In spite of her humble circumstances, Jewell grew up admiring the Southern lady ideal as held up and embodied by WMU leaders. A few years later, when she described her experience as a server for a WMU reception in Kentucky, her childhood admiration was evident: "They [the WMU women] were beautiful to see. Most of them were wealthy and of course richly dressed . . . I met women I have heard of always . . . such noble women they were, too."[47]

Although none of the diaries or letters from Jewell's childhood outline her own conceptions of womanhood, the young Jewell may have had similar ideals to other frontier Baptist women, especially regarding hard work. An article clipping from the *Baptist Standard*, November 14, 1895, provides a description of the aspirations of Texas young women and girls: "to be a gentlewoman who shows by her every word and action a sweet and gentle dignity. . . . A lady thinks no work derogatory, and no one is deemed too low to receive courtesy and kindness."[48] Unlike the few Southern women of the WMU's elite top leadership, who left physical labor to the servants, the Texas woman could still call herself a lady while valuing hard work and a democratic spirit of equality: no person was too low to receive kindness.[49]

Fannie Heck, darling of the North Carolina Southern Baptist elite and member of the "WMU royalty," spoke admiringly of the hard-working frontier women of the "lower classes." When she described Jewell's childhood in her book *In Royal Service*, Heck emphasized gendered expectations of Baptist women in Texas including hard work and sacrifice: "She [Jewell] took her place in the family life, doing her share in the heavy work which must be done by the frail hands of mother and children during the preacher's long absences."[50] Jewell's reality informed Heck's description as she also learned by observing her mother's hard work in the home and community: "Mamma is always doing something for people. I wish I could do as much for her as she does for me, so she wouldn't always be so tired."[51]

Texas Baptist Women

Hard work, "doing for others," and self-sacrifice characterized Texas Baptist women like Alice Legett who took the lead in educating children and adolescents about missionary work. During the 1860s and 1870s, for Baptist families like the Legetts moving across the frontier, money was scarce. The Old South remained the hub of Southern Baptist culture, and Texas itself was still a mission territory to be "tamed." Though Southern Baptist women had very limited leadership roles in their Texas churches, particularly regarding preaching, they began creating church societies to raise money, accomplish mission work of their own, and promote religious education as early as the Civil War. Through these "aid" or "industrial societies," women raised the necessary funds to address the needs of soldiers and their families "by means of socials, box suppers, and other entertainments."[52] The societies continued to grow in the wake of the war's devastation. However, this growth was not without controversy. Some women's organizations struggled to survive in conservative places less accommodating of women's expanding roles. In East Texas, for example, "disapproval formed on the general basis of their presence representing 'innovation' and for the specific cause that women were overstepping their God-given boundaries."[53]

In 1886, when Jewell Legett was two years old, women representing seventy distinct mission groups in Texas met to consolidate their efforts and form the Baptist Women Mission Workers of Texas (BWMW), which had previously been named the Woman's Missionary Union (not to be confused with the national WMU created in 1888).[54] As the new women's organization in Texas grew throughout the 1890s, women learned to participate in church life in fresh and innovative ways, and it is likely that Jewell's mother, Alice, would have been an integral part of this process. Although the women's meetings were simple, with prayer, a song, a scripture reading, and business transactions, they imparted and honed important skills. Women's missionary work provided occasion for their public speaking. A visiting missionary might give a report, or a group leader could make an appeal for a collection. In this way women forged a special type of public speaking distinct from the preaching offered by the pastor. Even though the content may have been similar, "preaching" was performed by a man who had been called and ordained, and it took place in a pulpit. "Teaching" was provided by women who explained the Bible to other women. They were "giving a Bible talk" or "delivering an address," rather than preaching.[55] The young Jewell would have been exposed early to these models of the distinctive types of feminine public speech offered in Texas.

In addition, the Texas women of the BWMW used innovative ways to evangelize in the frontier environment. Borrowing a model from foreign missionaries, they employed "Bible women" to travel and present the gospel to women and children, particularly immigrants, in their own language. In 1893, the BWMW employed four Bible women to work around Texas: in Austin with Swedish immigrants, in Corpus Christi and El Paso with Mexicans, and in Dallas with "The Americans."[56] The practice of working with Bible women to spread the gospel would become an integral part of Jewell's China mission experience.

Missions Education

In later years, Jewell described how God called her to be a missionary at the same moment, when twelve, that she accepted Christ and was baptized. This calling would be confirmed many times as she moved through Baylor and her WMU Training School education. For many years she kept this calling a secret from her family, fearing that they would not want her to go far away. In the early nineteenth century, a single woman may not have considered missionary work because it was reserved for men only, along with preaching. In fact, marriage was the only means to mission service. But in the mid-nineteenth century, Southern Baptists followed other Protestant mission boards and opened the field to single Baptist women. The famed missionary Lottie Moon, who served in China from 1873 to 1912, became an impetus and inspiration for many girls like Jewell who went to the very part of China where Moon herself had labored.

Jewell's call to mission work came at a time when Southern Baptist women were organizing for missions fundraising and missions education. The national WMU eventually became a major supporter of Jewell's education for mission work, particularly through its training school in Louisville, Kentucky, which she attended just before sailing to China. As an adult Jewell would fully embrace WMU practices of a personal approach to evangelism and sacrificial giving to missions even as she nurtured new WMU groups among Chinese women. As a child and adolescent, Jewell learned these values through the missions education groups in which her mother and other women of her church would participate.

To feed her desire to go overseas as a missionary, the young Jewell would have listened to many stories about missionaries and their work. The historian of missions Joan Jacobs Brumberg describes a "culture of evangelicalism" that relied on revival meetings, missionary stories, and college organizations to encourage and move young people to respond to a call to mission service.[57] All three of these elements converge in Jewell's story. She was converted in a revival meeting of the Methodists, participated in missions education offered by Baptist women's groups, and eventually joined a missionary volunteer organization at Baylor. Women's missions organizations most likely had a decisive influence on Jewell's commitments during her childhood and adolescence, especially her early sense of calling.

Southern Baptist women emphasized training and education in missions for both males and females through their mission organizations. Sharing the gospel story, otherwise known as evangelism, was at the heart of Southern Baptist life and culture and thus informed the training of children. Women equipped both boys and girls with the tools of evangelism from a very early age. While men preached from the pulpit, women had the special task of teaching the children. Although her activities are not documented, it is likely that young Jewell participated in a number of learning activities through the Port Lavaca Baptist Church. Baptist children learned about the Bible in Sunday Schools and in "mission bands" organized by the women. Financial stewardship was emphasized, and children were taught to give systematically by such methods as setting aside an egg in a missionary basket to be sold for a contribution to missions.[58]

Beginning in the late nineteenth century, the WMU organized children's Sunbeam Bands in churches across the South and certainly in Texas. Led by women in local church WMU groups and societies, Sunbeams raised money for missions, memorized Bible verses, and sang songs. The official colors of the organization were gold and white, and their rally cry emphasized the sacrifice and determination needed for evangelization:

> Sunbeams! Sunbeams! Sunbeams!
> To climb the mountains steep
> To cross the waters deep
> To carry the light
> That makes the world bright
> Sunbeams! Sunbeams! Sunbeams![59]

Although it is not clear whether Jewell's own church had a Sunbeam Band, we do know that Sunbeam Bands were organized around Texas. By 1899, there were 115 such bands in the state and a statewide Sunbeams superintendent to encourage and coordinate them.[60] Whether they were a part of her own upbringing and childhood, Jewell still replicated these models as she worked with Chinese children in the Sunday Schools and mission bands of Shantung.

Public Speaking, Testimony, and Teaching

When she turned twelve, shortly after moving to Port Lavaca and while visiting a Methodist church meeting, Jewell decided to formally declare herself a follower of Christ. She returned to her own Baptist congregation to make public her profession of faith. Afterwards, she was baptized in the Gulf waters and recognized as a formal member of the church.

Her story followed Baptist protocol of the time. Baptists based church membership on a person's conversion experience and subsequent baptism, which could happen at any age. The individual converted spoke of his or her experience to the congregation publicly in a form of testimony and answered any questions posed by members. The church then voted on whether to approve the baptismal candidate and welcome him or her as a new member. During this period, some Southern Baptists wanted to restrict the practice of public testimony to men, limiting women to affirming statements made on their behalf by the male pastor. However, as Summerlin Martin notes, Texas Baptists were less restrictive generally and encouraged women to make their own confessional statements even beyond the point of baptism.[61]

In other parts of the South, particularly during Jewell's childhood, Southern Baptist leaders forbade public speaking for women. One of the most outspoken critics to women speaking in public was John A. Broadus, who was highly influential in shaping nineteenth-century Southern Baptist views on women's proper place.[62] In his widely circulated essay "Should Women Speak in Mixed Assemblies?" Broadus used biblical texts such as the letters of Paul to argue that women should speak only before other women and children and never to "promiscuous audiences" that included men.[63] Broadus's position as professor of biblical studies at the flagship Southern Baptist Theological Seminary in Louisville, also home to the WMU Training School, provided him a wide audience and high status in the denomination.

In contrast to their eastern counterparts, Texas Baptists were generally more lenient on the issue of women speaking in public. One public incident in 1895, when Jewell was eleven, demonstrated differences in the Texas attitude. Mina Everett, a Texan hired by the national SBC mission boards to raise money among Texas Baptist women, began speaking to mixed audiences largely because some men actually requested to attend her gatherings. To demonstrate opposition, the SBC mission boards immediately docked her pay. As a result, the Texas Baptist WMU women raised money to cover Everett's salary, showing their support for her methods, while also writing to seek the advice of the national office. Annie Armstrong of Baltimore, the WMU's corresponding secretary, advised them to silence Everett and other women in order to preserve their reputations among the SBC and WMU leaders. The next year, Everett resigned to remove herself from the controversy.[64]

Jewell's Texas upbringing, with the comparative freedom of women to speak publicly in church services with male congregants present, differed from the more traditional protocol in Kentucky even more than a decade after the incident with Mina Everett. Jewell's Kentucky diaries indicated that women there were still forbidden to testify in church to their conversion or calling. While a student at the training school in Louisville, Jewell spoke publicly at the end of a church service when she went to the altar to declare her intention to go to China as a missionary. In the emotion of the moment, she told her story and later that afternoon realized her mistake with shame: "I've disgraced the training school and Dr. Doolan's church, and myself. I forgot in my happiness that women never speak in mixed audiences in Kentucky . . . but on reflection I was glad I had done it, and I knew Dr. Doolan knew conditions in Texas and knew I really did forget."[65] Such regional differences indicate the variety of practices among Southern Baptists, with Jewell having additional opportunities in childhood and beyond to express herself in speech and writing more freely than some other Baptist women. Relying on her friend Dr. Doolan to interpret her Texas upbringing and minimize her shame, Jewell actively claimed the support she would need for the rest of her life as she served in the SBC.

The Commission: A Network of Support

In May of 1909, a few days after Jewell's dreaded interview with the Foreign Mission Board, she experienced a concrete expression of support from her denomination, including her Texas Baptist friends. Following a successful interview, the new appointees would be presented to the Southern Baptist Convention as members of a global missionary force.[66] Four months later, Jewell would travel from Texas to Shantung, China, to begin her life's work.

At the formal presentation, Jewell recognized that this was a rare opportunity for women missionaries to attend the session as guests, since women were not allowed on the convention floor until a decade later.[67] She expressed her admiration of the SBC men: "They called us to take the rostrum at the beginning of the service, and during the two hours before our part of the program came off, I had an opportunity to see the Southern Baptist Convention in session. And a mighty host they are, and God's kingdom can't keep from coming while such men as compose that convention manage affairs."[68] Jewell, the youngest of all who were presented, felt particularly moved when the men of the SBC stood to honor the missionaries "and a sea of snowy handkerchiefs were waved. [Dr. Willingham] knew every [missionary], the history of each, his struggles while in the home land and in the field, and how he did tell the tale! And those great strong men all over the house wept like babies."[69] Upon introducing each missionary, Dr. Willingham asked the messengers present, "Men, who will pledge themselves with me to stand by these?" Jewell was again touched by the show of hands as she looked down from the rostrum, five or six feet above the crowd. "As long as I ever, ever live, if it is forever, I will not forget those thousands of uplifted hands."[70]

While Jewell was impressed with the size of the crowd, she had established an intimacy with several supporters from her Baylor days and her Texas church community. And as she stood on the stage to be introduced to her Southern Baptist supporters, substitute "family" from Texas and Kentucky attended. "Mrs. Hill waved to me from the gallery, and Mr. Bob Coleman, from Dallas, who I did not know was here, smiled such a glad smile."[71] Moreover, after the service, well-wishers greeted the new missionaries, adding a further sense of intimacy. Jewell mentions renowned Baptist statesmen, like George W. Truett, who personally promised to pray for her. Many cherished friends, such as her Baylor roommate, Mattie Curtis, likewise congratulated and wished her well. "Many an earnest 'God help you,' 'I'll stand by you,' 'God bless you, my child' I heard."[72] While Jewell certainly wished her parents were there, her father's prayer at her birth, that she would one day serve as a missionary, had been answered.

Conclusion

Jewell's childhood and adolescent experiences, which we have explored here, planted the seeds that would continue to grow through her college days at Baylor and her formal missionary training at the WMU Training School in Louisville. As we have noted, during this time, women's church work was simply assumed and rarely celebrated. At the commission service, at least, male messengers waved their handkerchiefs in unison to pledge their support for her missionary service. And yet, we hear little of Jewell and her female missionary compatriots of that day afterwards in the formal annals of the SBC. Nor do we find them cited as anything more than statistics in the denominational histories. Indeed, women's work as missionaries has remained hidden and buried, scarcely touched or recognized. While the denominational history and literature concentrates on the exploits and deeds of one, Lottie Moon, hundreds of women served as Southern Baptist missionaries over the twentieth century, informing and shaping the denominational mission force, which became something more akin to an empire after World War II. Jewell's story provides a significant case study, pivotal to reimagining Southern Baptist history from the standpoint of women. Unlike the journey men took to missionary and ministerial appointment, women like Jewell had to forge alternative and often circuitous paths. As for Jewell, a creative and particular combination of frontier freedom and pioneering spirit, familial backing with mission-minded parents, and an upbringing in a church in which women educated, testified, and taught, as well as support from the Woman's Missionary Union, enabled her to follow in the footsteps of the legendary Lottie Moon, whom she had admired since early girlhood.

Notes

1. Jewell Legett Diary, May 13, 1909, Jewell Legett Daniel Papers, Box 1, Texas Collection, Baylor University, Waco, TX.
2. Legett Diary, May 10, 1909.
3. Legett Diary, May 13, 1909.
4. Legett Diary, May 13, 1909.

5. For more on Jewell Legett's college experiences, see T. Laine Scales and Craig Clarkson, "Preparing College Students for Mission: The Role of the Student Volunteer Movement in the Calling and Formation of a 'Baylor Girl,' 1903–1907," *Baptist History and Heritage* 46, no. 3 (Fall 2011): 43–59. On her missionary training at the WMU Training School in Louisville, KY, see T. Laine Scales, "Jewell Legett and the Social Curriculum: The Education of a Southern Baptist Woman Missionary at the WMU Training School, 1908–1909," *Baptist History and Heritage* 41, no. 1 (Winter 2006): 77–90.
6. Our methodology involved extensive use of Jewell's diaries and memoirs. Legett's friend sent a few pages of her writings to the Woman's Missionary Union Archives in Birmingham, and her descendants generously donated her diaries to the Texas Collection at Baylor University. In researching and writing about Jewell, we explored the nature of biography and the feminist methodology of "vocational kinship" in women's history and literature, which argues for biographers to create new methods for writing about women's lives while also acknowledging the relationship that often develops between (women) biographers and their subjects, thereby affecting the writing process. As feminists and followers of Christ writing about a woman who shared our institutional affiliation, Baylor University, where we wrote this piece, we three authors experienced a profound identification with Jewell. Laine is also connected to Jewell through churches and Baptist institutions in Louisville, most notably Southern Baptist Theological Seminary. This idea of vocational kinship not only spoke to our experiences but shaped the ways we approached this chapter as a case study for other Southern Baptist women and girls from a similar frontier culture. Rosemary Keller defined and outlined this concept as she concentrated her scholarship on the religious lives and spiritual practices of American women. For a definition, see Keller, "Women's Spiritual Biography and Autobiography," in *Encyclopedia of Women and Religion in North America*, ed. Keller and Rosemary Radford Reuther (Bloomington: Indiana Univ. Press, 2006), 68–69. For those interested in this idea of vocational kinship, and the relationship between biographer and subject, also helpful are the essays in Sara Alpern, Joyce Antler, Elisabeth Perry, and Ingrid Scobie, eds., *The Challenge of Feminist Biography: Writing the Lives of Modern American Women* (Urbana: Univ. of Illinois Press, 1992) as well as "The New Academic Hagiography: A Roundtable Conversation," *Fides et Historia* 49 (Summer/Fall 2017): 37–56.
7. Legett's ancestry is recorded in "Baby's Book scrapbook," circa 1915, Jewell Legett Daniel Papers, Texas Collection. For more on frontier preaching in the early days of Texas, see the memoir of Z. N. Morrell, *Flowers and Fruits in the Wilderness*, 3rd ed. (St. Louis, MO: Commercial Printing, 1882). For a daughter's view of Southern Baptist frontier ministry, see Opal Leigh Berryman, *Pioneer Preacher* (New York, NY: Thomas Crowell, 1948); and chapters 8 and 9 of Robert A. Baker, *The Blossoming Desert: A Concise History of Texas Baptists* (Waco, TX: Word Books, 1970).

8. T. R. Legett to Jewell Legett, 1885, Jewell Legett Daniel Papers, Texas Collection.
9. *The Handbook of Texas Online*, Texas State Historical Association, 2010. Last modified June 12, 2010.
10. J. M. Carroll, Texas Baptist Statistics (Houston, TX: J. J. Pastoriza, 1895), 106.
11. Fannie Heck, *In Royal Service* (Richmond, VA: Foreign Mission Board of the Southern Baptist Convention, 1913), 152–53. In describing the Legett's ministry, Heck writes:"Five little graves! Five little graves of five little sisters. Not lying close together where the mother [Alice] might come to cover them with flowers, but weary miles apart, each one farther toward the ever moving frontier." Although Heck claims that all of the deceased infants were girls, we know of one male child, Milo, who lived to age four and died after the family settled in Lavaca, indicating that the information on the children's sex cited by Heck may not be accurate.
12. *The Handbook of Texas Online*, Texas State Historical Association, 2010.
13. Jane Hunter, *The Gospel of Gentility: American Women Missionaries in Turn-of-the-Century China* (New Haven, CT: Yale Univ. Press, 1984), 32–33.
14. "Jewell Daniel 100 Remembers Service with Lottie Moon," *Baylor Line*, Feb. 1985.
15. Legett Diary, July 13, 1901.
16. "Seadrift," *Calhoun County News*, July 31, 1900.
17. Archie Kirkland, "Autobiography and Diary" in *Karankawa Kountry Quarterly*, vol. 8 (Port Lavaca, TX: Calhoun County Genealogical Society, 1986).
18. Archie Kirkland, *Shifting Sands of Calhoun County* (Port Lavaca, TX: Calhoun Co. Historical Commission, 1980), 192.
19. *Calhoun County News*, Oct. 28, 1902.
20. Kirkland, *Shifting Sands*, 192.
21. Kirkland, *Karankawa Kountry*, 7.
22. Patricia Summerlin Martin, "Hidden Work: Baptist Women in Texas, 1880–1920" (PhD diss., Rice University, 1982), 103.
23. Legett Diary, Aug. 1, 1904.
24. Legett Diary, Aug. 15, 1904.
25. Legett Diary, Aug. 5, 1904. See, for example, *Baptist Standard*, July 25, 1895, 6.
26. *Baptist Standard*, July 25, 1895, 7.
27. Legett Diary, Aug. 28, 1904.
28. Legett Diary, Aug. 4 and 5, 1901.
29. Legett Diary, July 26, 1901.
30. Legett Diary, n.d., circa Apr. 1912.
31. Legett Diary, Aug. 31, 1904.
32. Legett Diary, Aug. 31, 1904.
33. Legett Diary, Aug. 6, 1904.
34. Catherine B. Allen, *A Century to Celebrate* (Birmingham, AL: Woman's Missionary Union, 1987), 121–22.
35. Legett Diary, Mar. 20, 1909.
36. Heck, *In Royal Service*, 152–53. In 1895, when Jewell was eleven years old, the

WMU members sent 358 "frontier" boxes containing clothing and supplies to missionary families serving in the West and Southwest. See Joe Westbury, "HMB Heritage: Missionaries, Volunteers, Evangelism & More," Mar. 12, 1997, *Baptist Press*. See also Legett Diary, Mar. 20, 1909.

37. See, for example, Legett Diary, Aug. 21 and 22, 1904.
38. Legett Diary, Aug. 4 and 5, 1901.
39. Jewell Legett Application, Feb. 4, 1909, International Mission Board Archives and Record Center, Richmond, VA.
40. The historian Barbara Miller Solomon reports that, in 1900, only 2.8 percent of American women age eighteen to twenty-one years old attended college; *In the Company of Educated Women: A History of Women and Higher Education in America* (New Haven, CT: Yale Univ. Press, 1985), 63–64.
41. In her diary entries from the summer of 1904, Jewell reflects upon her acquaintance in sixth grade with a young man named Joe Hancock with whom she later crossed paths; Legett Diary, Aug. 23, 1904.
42. Jewell Legett, "How a Girl Can Make Her Way through College," *The Lariat*, 1906, 1–2.
43. Sandra L. Myres, *Westering Women and the Frontier Experience, 1800–1915* (Albuquerque: Univ. of New Mexico Press, 1982), 11.
44. Martin, "Hidden Work," 233.
45. Lillian Schlissel, *Women's Diaries of the Westward Journey* (New York, NY: Schocken Books, 2004), 13.
46. Martin, "Hidden Work," 280.
47. Legett Diary, May 12, 1909.
48. *Baptist Standard*, as cited in Martin, "Hidden Work," 225–26.
49. *Baptist Standard*, as cited in Martin, "Hidden Work," 225–26.
50. Heck, *In Royal Service*, 152–53.
51. Legett Diary, Aug. 15, 1904.
52. L. Katherine Cook, "Texas Baptist Women and Missions, 1830–1900," *Texas Baptist History*, no. 3 (1983): 34.
53. Martin, "Hidden Work," 107.
54. Mrs. W. J. J. Smith, *A Centennial History of the Baptist Women of Texas* (Dallas: Woman's Missionary Union of Texas, 1933), 136.
55. Martin, "Hidden Work," 176–77.
56. Martin, "Hidden Work," 130.
57. Joan Jacobs Brumberg, *Mission for Life: The Story of the Family of Adoniram Judson, the Dramatic Events of the First American Foreign Mission, and the Course of Evangelical Religion in the Nineteenth Century* (New York, NY: Free Press, 1980), 21–43.
58. Allen, *A Century to Celebrate*, 101–3.
59. Allen, *A Century to Celebrate*, 101–3.
60. Allen, *A Century to Celebrate*, 101–3.

61. Martin, "Hidden Work," 168. As Martin indicates, a *Baptist Standard* editorial from 1897 noted the openness to women telling their experiences at prayer meetings. Although there is no surviving record of Jewell's statement to her congregation, we may assume from this editorial, written in the same year Jewell was baptized, that such experiences were common in Texas.
62. Patricia S. Martin, "Keeping Silence: Texas Baptist Women's Role on Public Worship, 1880–1920," *Texas Baptist History*, no. 3 (1983): 22.
63. John A. Broadus, "Should Women Speak in Mixed Assemblies," in *Feminism: Woman and Her Work,* ed. J. W. Porter (Louisville, KY: Baptist Book Concern, 1923), 45–52.
64. Cook, "Texas Baptist Women," 40; Martin, "Keeping Silence," 20.
65. Legett Diary, Jan. 14, 1909.
66. Legett Diary, May 13 and 14, 1909. See also the "Proceedings" of the 1909 convention; *Annual of the Southern Baptist Convention, 1909* (Nashville, TN: Marshall and Bruce, 1909).
67. For descriptions of the first women messengers to the SBC, see Allen, *Century to Celebrate*, 307–8.
68. Legett Diary, May 14, 1909.
69. Legett Diary, May 14, 1909.
70. Legett Diary, May 14, 1909. The "Proceedings" of the 1909 convention indicates this session took place in the afternoon of the second day. Although it seemed to Jewell that thousands of hands were raised, there were only 1,547 representatives at the convention. All attendees would have been male as women were required to hold their own sessions separately. See *Annual of the Southern Baptist Convention, 1909.*
71. See Legett Diary, May 13 and 14, 1909. Although the exact identity of the Mrs. Hill indicated here is not known, Jewell mentioned the support of a Mr. and Mrs. Hill several times in her diaries, noting on Dec. 29, 1908, that "Mrs. Hill and I had such a comforting talk. She surely has faith in God, unlimited faith." On Jan. 14, 1908, she wrote that the Hills hosted a supper for the students from Texas.
72. Legett Diary, May 13 and 14, 1909.

Three

"THE MAMMY SUES ARE SCARCE IN THE SOUTH NOW"

Southern Baptist Women, Domestic Workers, and Progressive Era Racial Uplift

Joanna Lile

Novelist Isla May Mullins presented her fictional Carters as the ideal white Southern family. The wife of Southern Baptist Theological Seminary President E. Y. Mullins, Isla Mullins published four Carter family novels, together called the Blossom Shop series, from 1913 to 1918.[1] Mullins crafted the Carters as a blended family, brought together by the marriage of Alabama widower John Carter, a father of two girls, and Alice Grey, the widow next door and mother of one daughter. Their shared values and faith in God brought them an abiding affection for one another. John Carter was a successful lawyer, and Alice was a wise and gentle confidant for the three little girls: Anne, May, and Gene. However, other individuals lived in the Carter household. While Uncle Sam and Mammy Sue were the oldest persons in the home, Mullins described these African American employees as acting more like "old children" than mature adults. They were also fiercely loyal to the Carters, for they belonged to a "lost era" of faithful servants who gained joy entirely from serving their white families.

While Mullins portrayed these two loyal servants as adoring and protecting the three Carter girls, another character often attempted to lead the children astray. Mullins's second Blossom Shop novel told of the arrival of a third domestic worker, Cahaba, the "cornfield darky." Young, wild, and never entirely the family member that the Carters considered Uncle Sam and Mammy Sue to be, Cahaba almost always confounded the Carter girls' quest to become Christian ladies. Literally lurking in the shadows, eavesdropping, and spreading gossip, Cahaba tempted the oldest girl Anne and often thwarted Anne's efforts to prove her maturity to her family. In fact, as Anne's final act of growing up she had to defy Cahaba and resist the feelings of jealousy and resentment Cahaba attempted to incite in her with her gossip. In these vivid depictions of African Americans, Mullins offered both encouragement and warning about domestic servants, race relations, and racial uplift in the Progressive Era South.

As scholars have noted, "racial uplift" during the Progressive Era (1890–1920) carried a variety of meanings for white Southerners. Southern Baptists were conservatives when it came to uplift. Like the majority of white Southerners at this time, they rejected the notion that African Americans had the potential to attain intellectual equality with whites. At the same time, they dismissed the idea that African Americans and whites would never coexist peacefully.[2] Instead, they embraced a vision of uplift based on a belief in two possibilities as well as a caveat. As to the former, they maintained both the possibility of African American social and cultural advancement and the possibility of harmonious, albeit hierarchical, race relations. Neither, though, could occur in the absence of social controls imposed on African Americans by white Southerners.[3] Inherent in this conservative view was the conviction that the unprecedented social freedoms African Americans had enjoyed after emancipation had driven many to lawlessness, sexual immorality, and laziness.[4] As a result, the reforms associated with racial uplift frequently centered on behavioral change. In addition, Southern Baptists believed that uplift should begin with evangelism, stressing the importance of educating African American clergymen who would then help lead the race's advancement.[5] Moreover, Southern Baptist women tied racial uplift to the home, viewing the white home as a mission field to the African American domestic worker, who would then transform her own home according to white standards.

Although historians have demonstrated that home life and domesticity were important components of uplift ideology, those scholars considering Southern Baptist efforts at racial uplift, namely denominational church historians, have frequently limited their research to convention programs that offered ministerial training for African American men.[6] Indeed, Southern Baptist leaders insisted that these educational efforts were essential to racial uplift. And yet this narrow examination of Southern Baptist race relations obscures other denominational efforts, especially those that involved women, to achieve the conservative vision for African Americans in the post-Reconstruction South. In contrast to other populations the SBC sought to missionize, African Americans were the recipients of mission work whom Southern Baptist laypersons were most likely, sometimes very likely, to encounter on a daily basis. Hiring domestic workers in this era was a sign of middle-class respectability, freeing white women to engage in works of piety. Of course, Southern Baptists during this era were comprised of a broad spectrum of whites in the South, not all of whom employed domestic servants. Nevertheless, Southern Baptist women highlighted the significance of white women's interactions with African American domestic workers and pointed to those relationships as opportunities for white women to engage in racial uplift.[7]

In this chapter, I address this gap in the scholarship by turning to the overlooked writings on racial uplift written by and for Southern Baptist women during the Progressive Era and 1920s. Writing about their experiences with and prejudices against domestic servants allowed Southern Baptist women a greater voice in denominational publications. Since the topic of domestic servants related to home life, Southern Baptist women were able to discuss race relations without stepping outside of the domestic sphere. Women's publications on race sometimes appeared in state denominational newspapers, usually within the pages designated for women's writings on home life. More frequently, though, Southern Baptist women published their writings on race in pamphlets and articles printed by the Southern Baptist Woman's Missionary Union (WMU). Created in 1888, the WMU played a vital role in raising funds for Southern Baptist missions, educating women and children about denominational work, and involving women in local missions. The WMU published two successive magazines during this era and beyond, *Our Mission Fields* (1906–1914) and *Royal Service* (1914–1995), which kept Southern Baptist women informed of the denomination's work overseas and in the United States. These magazines were also critical avenues through which leaders of the WMU challenged their readers to support evangelistic efforts in their own communities and, in the case of work with African American women, in their own households.

Southern Baptist women persistently asserted in these publications that they were missionaries to African American women, particularly the domestic servants they employed. They viewed their efforts to uplift their domestic workers as a form of lay piety through which they believed they could live out the teachings of the Gospel. Though their efforts contrasted with that of their male counterparts, working with African American domestic servants not only gave Southern Baptist women a critical role to play in racial uplift, it affirmed their notions of religious and moral superiority over African American women and rested solidly on white supremacy. In the end, Southern Baptist women saw in their contact with domestic workers an opportunity to reinstate something they, and most white Southerners, believed had been lost. By calling upon their white middle-class sisters to become missionaries to their domestic servants, Southern Baptist women attempted to restore the imagined interracial harmony they believed had defined the era of slavery.

This chapter, then, is not about on-the-ground realities of what race relations were actually like during this era but about how Southern Baptist women imagined their mission work to African American domestics and how they shaped narratives about race in the Southern Baptist Convention (SBC). The writings of Southern Baptist women provided two-dimensional caricatures of the African Americans they employed, and thus my examination of these writings provides a window into white women's race narratives rather than a window into the experiences of African American domestic workers themselves. Noticeably absent from white women's writings was any recognition of the struggles of African American communities during this era, including restricted employment opportunities, low wages, or the injustice of disfranchisement. Instead, Southern Baptist women's complaints about their domestics' supposed depravity only strengthened systematic racism since, as Michele Mitchell observes, "notions of racial degeneracy vitally informed the concurrent erosion of black civil rights."[8] This study foregrounds white women's contributions to Southern Baptist race narratives and how Southern Baptist women as well as men were agents in perpetuating what Kevin Gaines calls the post-Reconstruction "assault on black citizenship and humanity."[9]

Before moving to the story of Southern Baptist women and racial uplift, it is necessary to note the contestation around the term "uplift," particularly the differences in how white Southerners understood and used the term in contrast to how African Americans themselves understood it. The vast majority of white Southern progressives maintained that uplift could not be achieved without changes in African Americans' behavior, including the embrace of Victorian notions of sexuality and home life and the ability to provide more efficient service to whites as laborers.[10] White Southerners were also convinced that uplift hinged on the preservation of white supremacy, with white Southerners, including most Southern Baptists, leading and exemplifying "proper" behavior for African Americans.[11]

Like white Southern progressives, African American progressives often emphasized behavior and conduct as paths to uplift but for very different reasons. With political participation severely limited or completely denied them, African Americans recognized that the home was an institution they could still control and mold. Reformers believed that adopting Victorian notions of family life would allow African Americans to claim "moral authority," respectability, and prove their worthiness of citizenship to white Americans.[12] In contrast to white Southern progressives' notions, then, African American uplift ideology existed to dismantle white supremacy.

Creating "the Old-Time Sympathy" through Ministerial Training

Male SBC officials were convinced that the Gospel demanded that they evangelize African Americans and train their religious leaders. Like many Southern evangelicals, Southern Baptists believed that divine providence had brought Africans to the United States, and so the Southern Baptist Home Mission Board (HMB) often portrayed African Americans as the greatest test of their commitment to missions and evangelism. Despite the many slaves who had eventually joined their churches, Southern Baptists felt that the work of evangelizing African Americans remained unfinished and was even, by the Progressive Era, floundering.

There were many reasons for this opinion, which Southern Baptist men and women shared. First, following emancipation, many African Americans established their own Baptist churches. But Southern Baptists rejected African American Baptist churches and ministers as filled with errors and falsehoods. Second, although the Northern American Baptist Home Mission Society (HMS) had worked among African Americans in the South following the Civil War, Southern Baptists dismissed their activities as ineffective in preventing the moral and religious regression of the race. While they occasionally affirmed the HMS's work as noble, many Southern Baptists remained convinced that the HMS's emphasis on founding schools did not meet African Americans' spiritual needs. They concluded that African Americans had declined religiously, despite the good intentions of the HMS, because African Americans had been removed from the spiritual care of their antebellum Southern white pastors. The dismal results of this separation were obvious to denominational leaders. In 1900, the HMB warned that the new generation of African Americans was a decidedly baser generation than the one brought up in slavery. "If any one doubts the truth of this statement, let him compare the morals and the religion and the reliability of the average old ante-bellum Negro with the morals of the average new generation," the board's report concluded.[13] In short, Southern Baptists wanted, as in previous generations, to be intimately involved in the religious instruction of African Americans. Like Southern progressives, Southern Baptist leaders imagined that friendship rather than oppression had informed antebellum race relations and insisted that the passing of these relationships had been disastrous for African Americans.[14]

There were other reasons why denominational officials heartily supported ministerial education. For one thing, Southern Baptists were convinced that proper religious education had not and would not cause blacks to agitate for social equality. Victor I. Masters, publicity superintendent for the HMB, assured Southern Baptists that an educated African American would be "careful not to impose himself on whites in a way that might suggest social aspirations or invite rebuff."[15] The SBC could remedy its "loss of control" by steering African American churches and ministers. In turn, African American ministers could teach their congregations to accept white supremacy.[16]

As the HMB explored the establishment of seminaries and schools to train African American ministers, it held that white Baptists must directly oversee their operation. Other Southern Baptists supported this move. For example, in 1912, the prominent Texas Baptist editor and seminary professor James Gambrell wrote that African American ministers would be successful leaders of their own people only if they were first "encouraged, strengthened, and aided by the whites."[17] Similarly, an SBC committee created for exploring the possibility of sponsoring a "Negro theological seminary" explained that "the need of the seminary to train their preachers and other religious workers among them is daily increasing." The need for a seminary placed a burden on whites as "the stronger 'big brother'" to provide theological education for African Americans.[18] In the same way, the HMB created New Era Institutes to train African American ministers and deacons. Some African American leaders were reluctant to entrust white ministers with the responsibility of educating their ministers, while Southern Baptists worried that the institutes would embolden African American ministers to agitate for social equality.[19] As a result, New Era Institutes were short-lived.

The ultimate goal of ministerial education was to grant Southern Baptists greater control over the teachings being presented in African American churches and to educate African American ministers so that they would be "fit" to lead their congregations. While it signaled that Southern Baptists believed educated African Americans were capable of becoming effective religious leaders, ministerial training was the result of a suspicion that the race was declining religiously and morally and needed to be more closely guided by white Southern leaders. Southern Baptists wanted, as in previous generations, control over African Americans' religious instruction. They looked forward to an era when African Americans would have a more educated clergy that could guide their race toward morality, especially along the lines of thrift, obedience to the law, and sexuality. Southern Baptists also hoped that trained clergy would not encourage their congregations to agitate for social equality. At the same time, they looked back to the era of slavery, when white ministers exerted greater influence over African Americans. Drawing upon romantic notions of antebellum interracial relationships, HMB officials then concluded that greater involvement in African American religious training was necessary so that "the old-time sympathy and fellowship between the races may be restored."[20]

"We Become Almost Hopeless": Southern Baptist Women and the Modern Domestic Worker in the White Home

Southern Baptist women sought to restore the "old-time sympathy" through missions too but with a portion of the African American population they believed held greater sway over the moral improvement of the race than ministers. While many Southern Baptist male denominationalists argued for teaching doctrinal purity to clergymen, Southern Baptist women maintained that, as keepers of the black home, black women needed reforming more urgently. Because domestic workers composed the group of African American women whom white women encountered most frequently, they often bore the brunt of Southern Baptists' criticism. And female writers, such as Mullins, lamented the perceived decline in morals and home life among the women they employed, sometimes reflecting on past days when, they insisted, their servants exhibited more pleasing behavior. Before examining Southern Baptist women's notions of white women as missionaries, it is necessary to consider how Southern Baptists viewed the role of the domestic worker in the white home and the concept of home itself.

Scholar Michael Harris discusses mammy figures such as Mullins's Mammy Sue as the "fantasy" servant. Even though many whites recalled such childhood mammies, her description is mythic.[21] As a symbol of "the ideal of black womanhood," she was neither young nor attractive by white standards. She was never provocatively dressed and was instead "covered from neck to ankle with clothing" with her hair wrapped in a bandana.[22] Mammy Sue embodied all the qualities of this ideal servant with Mullins portraying her as "harmless, witless," and ever faithful.[23] Mullins's sentimental reverence for the mammy of bygone days was widely shared by other prominent individuals in the denomination. In 1918, Victor I. Masters, publicity superintendent of the HMB, praised the character of antebellum slaves, explaining that many white Baptists had been taught the Christian faith from their "mammy."[24] For Southern Baptists of Masters's day, however, images of faithful mammies were little more than memories. For them, the disappearance of the antebellum mammy had been disastrous for white families.

Throughout the early twentieth century, the WMU warned of a trend that many Southerners and Southern Baptists had sensed for years: "The splendid old mammy with the worthless or degraded son or daughter is so common a sight that we become almost hopeless," one author lamented in the organization's periodical *Our Mission Fields*.[25] Indeed, the image of the harmless mammy of antebellum days was "fast fading from memory," and her granddaughter, the modern domestic servant now responsible for raising white children, was considered dishonest, promiscuous, and rash. As one Southern Baptist woman noted in the pages of *Royal Service*, her "artificial airs and flapper dress" represented the worst aspects of modern society.[26]

Southern Baptist men and women alike followed much of the cultural reasoning of the time in explaining such a downfall. First, they commonly assumed that since the abolition of slavery, those African Americans "who had never felt the civilizing effects of slavery" had retrogressed in the absence of close contact with white society.[27] Second, female domestics' living situations may have also raised questions about their loyalty to their employers as well as their morality. Early twentieth century domestics began "living in" with their employers less frequently, opting for the increased autonomy that accompanied "living out." The move towards living out may have contributed to white women's suspicions that their domestics were less loyal to their families and more likely to engage in sexual promiscuity than previous generations.[28]

But the potentially dishonest or inefficient worker in the white household was only one problem that Southern Baptists, particularly Southern Baptist women, perceived. WMU writers also alleged that the contemporary African American woman was not fulfilling her obligations to her own home and family. To understand their reasoning here, it is important to consider the larger meanings that home life held in the minds of Southern Baptists. Just as Southern Baptist writers, namely WMU women writing about missions, presented the state of "heathen" homes overseas as indicators of their inhabitants' moral progress, they often made the same assumptions about

African Americans, using their homes too as evidence of the state of their morals and spiritual health.[29]

Not only did WMU writers consider African American homes physically dirty and unkempt, they also correlated African American housing with low morality. In the pages of *Royal Service*, writer Mary Faison Dixon reminded her readers in 1917 that "the question of negro health and housing is a moral question." She complained of African Americans: "His present mode of life is such as to render it well nigh impossible for him to be moral, and his present immorality makes him an inefficient laborer, an expensive criminal, a distributor of infectious diseases, and a moral plague."[30] In this instance, the writer was referring to the effects of poor housing on both African American women and men. White female writers did not often specify the varieties of "immorality" that were supposedly rampant in African American homes. WMU women likely followed white cultural assumptions that sexual immorality, including incest, was common among families living in cramped, crowded dwellings. African American reformers' own writings implied that incest was a concern for them as well.[31] While Southern Baptist women worried about their domestic workers' immoral behavior, they also worried that maids and nurses coming from disease-ridden homes would infect the white children in their care. Historian Tera Hunter notes that although domestics were blamed for being carriers of a number of diseases, tuberculosis was the one ailment most regarded as a "Negro disease." Many white Southerners believed that servants were singularly responsible for carrying the dreaded illness into their neighborhoods and homes.[32]

If filth and disease were problems inherent in African American men and women alike, perceptions of motherhood, home, and family life applied more specifically to African American women. Southern Baptist women held African American women more culpable, as mothers, for the state of African American homes. And Southern Baptist women's writings focused on the "American Negro Mother" as the source of the South's racial problems because of her inability to raise her children according to proper moral standards. The race could only improve if white women intervened and exemplified proper mothering to their domestic workers. If not, African Americans would continue to be "a curse" to white Southerners.[33]

Although reflections on contemporary African American families and home life were frequently bleak, Southern Baptist women identified ways to influence, or missionize, their domestic servants and thereby help transform African American home life. Most apparent here is the way WMU writers pleaded with their readers to develop personal relationships with their domestics. Combining scriptural commands with commonly held notions of white women's piety and African American women's immorality and ignorance, they argued that utilizing their relationships with African American women was essential to following the Gospel. This was also in keeping with the WMU's concept of personal service, which wedded evangelism and missions to social service.[34] Through personal service work, women might lay the foundation for long-term missionary service to African American women.

Denominational officials encouraged personal service as it related to African American women because it complemented their own work with African American men. Southern Baptist women's approaches to racial uplift supported the overall notion that African Americans ought to look to whites for guidance, so their emphasis on transforming home life would have appeared natural, rather than radical or even threatening, to denominational leaders who held women responsible for the home. Most important to them, women instructing female domestics were not instructing men, and they remained in the household.

Women's missions would have complemented male leaders' efforts in other, more practical ways too. As many scholars have noted, the work of the boards and agencies of the convention at this moment was floundering, particularly in comparison to the WMU. In fact, both mission boards often found themselves short of the funds necessary to cover expenses and missionaries already on the field. Already reluctant to expend more on "negro missions," denominational leaders surely found women's home-based missions to domestic servants to be inexpensive and expedient. After all, this "mission" front was paid for by the individual white families who employed domestic servants; the domestic servant in turn freed up the time of white women to missionize them. James Gambrell pointed to the convenience of using white homes to accomplish racial uplift: "Cleanliness, truth, virtue, industry, care of children, honesty—all these can be inculcated while the work goes on."[35] To be sure, men such as Gambrell quickly saw that denoting every white woman as a missionary made use of relationships and structures already in place.

Relatedly, they may have also viewed women's home-based missions as having the potential to last much longer than HMB programs such as New Era Institutes, thus ensuring a more expansive influence. As corresponding secretary of the HMB, Isaac Taylor Tichenor greatly supported the work of the WMU here and believed that successfully influencing African American women would, more than any other factor, determine the moral and religious future of African Americans in the South. "To reach the negro women of the South and uplift them morally, socially and religiously is essential to the progress of their race," Tichenor explained, adding that "no permanent good can be found in any people which does not base itself upon the character of its women."[36]

For Southern Baptist women, the call to evangelize their domestic servants hardly represented any radically new challenge. After all, as a report of the HMB noted, in antebellum days the slaves' "moral and religious training" had been instigated by "the wives and daughters of the white people in whose home he was a servant."[37] Southern Baptists romanticized these relationships and appealed to contemporary Baptist women to replicate these former ties in their current households. Without formal records of such work, it is difficult to discern how many women answered the call to assume the role of missionary to their domestics, but the existence of instructions for this type of work demonstrates that it was a critical concern of Southern Baptist women, particularly leaders of the WMU.

"Her Example Is the Rich Property of the Negro Woman of the South": Southern Baptist Women as Missionaries to Domestic Workers

Writing for Tennessee's *Baptist and Reflector* in 1897, Laura Dayton Eakin portrayed her childhood home as a mission field where she read the Bible to her beloved Aunt Barbara. In testifying to her missionary calling, she remembered climbing into Aunt Barbara's lap every Sunday afternoon to read scripture aloud to her illiterate "aunt." She added, "I did not know it was 'missionary work' . . . I was only doing it because I loved dear old Aunt Barbara, my grandmother's cook." Based on Eakin's age when she wrote this piece, roughly fifty-two, Aunt Barbara would have been a slave when young Laura climbed into her lap. From her narrative, it appears that Eakin regarded Aunt Barbara as a faithful servant who exemplified the steadfast loyalty that, in many white Southerners' minds, typified that former generation of African Americans and now needed reviving. Eakin described her in the beloved terms Mullins used in presenting the Carters' relationship to Mammy Sue. Eakin then urged her fellow female readers to emulate her act of evangelism by sharing the Gospel with the domestic workers in their own homes. "I want you . . . each one, everyone, to say it over earnestly and to answer it in the fear of God," Eakin pleaded. "What can I do to bring the negroes here in our own homes to know what real religion is? How can I help them to better lives?"[38] Eakin was not alone. Her testimonial reminiscences and call to evangelism echoed similar pleas for Southern Baptist women to teach the Gospel to their domestic workers. After all, as Eakin asked her readers a week later, "How many of us even know whether the cook is a Christian or not?"[39]

In addressing exactly how Southern Baptist women were to serve as missionaries to their domestics, rarely did authors such as Eakin or those penning the WMU's literature look to guidance from African American religious leaders, even those trained by their white male counterparts. In fact, both white and African American ministers failed to play any significant role in women's narrative instructions. Instead, Southern Baptist women primarily limited their writings to discussing the spiritual transformations they envisioned taking place inside their own homes and for which they were personally responsible.

The literature of the day, primarily written by Southern Baptist women to Southern Baptist women, highlighted several ways for women to achieve evangelism and missionary status. As the Eakin piece demonstrates, Southern Baptist women were encouraged to give Bible lessons and combine scriptural study with discussions of conduct. One pamphlet instructed white women to discuss "some scripture text, some spiritual truth" along with "neatness and thrift."[40] Thus, "good conduct" often went hand-in-hand with being a "good servant." And just as Southern Baptist women combined evangelism with discussions of conduct, they likely also combined evangelism with "good servant" lectures, teaching Christianity alongside efficiency and honesty, and reminding their domestics that their place was that of the "humble subordinate" in the household.[41]

Writers also cautioned that women employers must not discuss passages or teachings that might be too complicated for their domestic servants to understand. To that end, some writers even suggested that white women invite their domestics to listen to children's Bible stories, arguing that they might be able to better comprehend these simple lessons. "Let Molly hear the stories read to the children," Laura Dayton Eakin suggested.[42]

Relatedly, Southern Baptist women writers argued that their evangelistic efforts would matter little if their domestic servants did not pass these teachings on to their own children. A WMU author writing for *Baptist and Reflector* advised her readers to purchase for their maids and cooks Joanna P. Moore's paper *Hope,* which contained Bible lessons for African American families. The author of the article explained that the "plain" and "practical" teachings in Moore's paper would be suitable for domestic servants to grasp. The author also praised *Hope* because it encouraged readers to train their children in the Bible twice a day.[43]

And yet, this same *Baptist and Reflector* author admitted that the typical servant was too exhausted from her daily domestic work to instruct her children in the faith "unless some kind of assistance and encouragement is afforded her."[44] Southern Baptist women believed they had been given a unique opportunity to evangelize and teach their domestics about motherhood, yet this woman conceded that the very work that domestic workers performed, if they performed it well, prevented them from devoting themselves to their own homes and families.[45]

Southern Baptist women might also become missionaries by modeling Christian homes and demonstrating the appropriate maternal qualities therein. Writers frequently encouraged women to seize opportunities to counsel African American women on their role in creating such a home. Denominational leaders perpetuated the myth of the aggressive African American female who lacked the nurturing qualities of the white woman. Unlike the Christian white woman, she was viewed as "aggressive, immoral, and slovenly."[46] Writers suggested that there were numerous opportunities for white women to demonstrate Christian motherhood and nurture for their servants. Southern Baptist women were told, for example, to follow the lead of one wealthy Southern woman who cared for an ill African American child because the little girl's mother was too ignorant to know how to nurse her back to health. Unlike the white mother, the African American mother "lacked skill and tenderness" and was therefore unable to take care of her own daughter.[47] The writer considered this deed a modern-day equivalent of the lowly New Testament act of foot washing and a fulfillment of the commandment to take care of "the least of these."[48]

A Christian home was likewise tied to cleanliness. Although many African American women worked as domestic servants, Southern Baptist women authors still maintained that white women might even demonstrate homemaking for them. One issue of the *Alabama Baptist* highlighted the story of a young woman who assisted a local African American family. The story described a white Southern family who had taught their daughter to be kind to the poorer neighboring African American family. The writer explained that the white family lived "in a very fine country home" that was run by a "good father" and a "faithful mother." When the daughter of this "gracious country home" learned that a young African American neighbor would soon marry and bring his bride to live in a "humble cottage," she decided to prepare a proper home for the couple. While the groom was away, she cleaned his house, delivered new linens, and hung new pictures on the walls so that the cottage would be "home-like for the new colored housekeeper."[49] This "unusual" girl had learned Christian ideals in her elite white home and had now helped establish a new Christian household for a black family. Her act of stepping out of her household and entering the African American household was presented as a dramatic example of servanthood, which other white Southerners should strive to emulate.[50]

Finally, Southern Baptist writers fretted over African American women's supposed sexual immorality and prompted their readers to seek opportunities to discuss their servants' sexual relationships. It was not uncommon for employers to lecture or criticize their domestics for their dating practices and/or out-of-wedlock pregnancies.[51] At the same time, and in contrast, African Americans tended to view white women's households as environments in which they might fall victim to sexual exploitation by white men. Although white women viewed their homes as near sanctuaries in which African American women could be guided toward a better life, domestic workers were more likely to view these homes as spaces where they were vulnerable to sexual assault.[52]

On the subject of African American women's sexuality, Southern Baptists promoted the notion that African American leaders likewise longed for white women to lecture their domestic workers on sexuality. Newspaper editors occasionally published pieces by African American authors that affirmed the notion that white women ought to monitor their domestic workers' behavior more closely. Moreover, such pieces assured Southern Baptist men and women that African Americans were not seeking social equality. Two examples are indicative here. In 1922, the *Christian Index*, Georgia's Baptist newspaper, printed a piece that was intended to be a powerful call to the white Baptist women of Georgia to talk with their domestic workers about their private lives. In this case, the *Christian Index* printed a speech that an unnamed African American woman delivered at a WMU meeting earlier that year. The speaker urged her white listeners to encourage their maids to attend church, to maintain high standards of personal morality, and to keep them accountable for their social activities. They ought to ask them how they spent their free time. Did they attend church or stay out late at night?[53] This plea reinforced the notion that employers carried the weighty yet all-important spiritual responsibility of teaching their domestics how to resist temptation. The speaker also noted that maids who followed their employers' moral examples would become better workers. She remarked that "setting a higher standard of living and Christian service" would make maids "more efficient in your homes, rendering you better service, morally, intellectually, and industrially."[54]

That same year the *Alabama Baptist* printed portions of an address by "Negro Orator," educator, and racial accommodationist William Hooper

Councill. He first argued that African American women's tendency towards sexual promiscuity was one weakness that their white employers might remedy. In spite of her "weakness and temptations," the African American woman had "the white woman's chastity held up before her" as an example of virtue. Councill then reminded his audience that it was in their best interest, and in the best interest of the entire white race, that African American women look to white women for guidance. Indeed, it was natural that African American women should look to white women for direction. After all, Councill noted, it was "a fact as clear as the noonday sun" that "the white woman in the South is the highest type of pure, spotless womanhood in the recorded history of man." Moreover, Councill reminded his audience, the stakes were extremely high. In fact, "the highest welfare of the white South" was at risk when the promiscuous, dishonest, or otherwise immoral domestic worker entered the white home. After all, "half a million" domestic workers "hold in their pure or impure arms, half a million white children, who in some measure are pure or impure as their nurses affect them." His conclusion drove home the point. White children could not truly be raised in a Christian home if "impure" hands held and raised them.[55]

While the WMU encouraged women to instruct domestics through Bible study, informal lectures, and daily discussions, the organization did, at times, use formal institutes and meetings to educate working-class African American women on what it perceived as Christian womanhood. One example was the organization's Mothers' Industrial Schools, which were sometimes called Sewing Schools. While scholar Michele Mitchell notes that middle-class African American women commonly met among themselves to "exchange ideas about baby health and attend talks on heredity or morality," white women directed the WMU's Mothers' Industrial Schools.[56] They provided religious instruction and also gave the participants the opportunity to acquire new clothing. Listening to a Southern Baptist woman present a lesson on the Christian faith, African American women worked on a garment that they could keep once it was completed. The WMU enticed women and their children to attend with the promise of new clothes and even forbade the women who attended the Industrial Schools from working on their garment outside of the school.[57] Significantly, the schools targeted mothers, who, the WMU hoped, would repeat the lessons they had learned to their children. Writings from the WMU on these schools also suggested that children often accompanied their mothers to these schools, making these meetings a way of instructing African American children directly. After all, the WMU insisted, their efforts would have little meaning if they were unable to impact the next generation.

"My People Are Becoming Land Owners, We Are Painting Our Houses"

But what did racial uplift look like, more exactly, in the minds of Southern Baptist women? Southern Baptist women did not fail to recognize the work of educated and elite African American women and at times showed interest in cooperating with African American female leaders who they believed shared their goals of uplifting working-class African American women and transforming African American home life. Significantly, these African American women showcased uplift and thereby represented white women's successes. At the same time, for Southern Baptist women, uplift did not mean equality. Racial uplift, they insisted, did not threaten white supremacy.

The prime example here would be the friendship of the WMU's first corresponding secretary Annie Armstrong and later WMU writer Una Roberts Lawrence with the prominent National Baptist Convention (NBC) leader Nannie Helen Burroughs.[58] Burroughs's famous training school for black women and girls, which operated under the motto "the Bible, the bath, and the broom," educated its students in keeping house as well as maintaining "womanly virtue."[59] Burroughs also helped found the Woman's Convention of the National Baptist Convention in 1900. Southern Baptist women, particularly WMU leaders, believed the creation of this organization was a needed step in beginning a moral transformation among African American Baptist women and uplifting African American home life. After visiting the Woman's Convention meeting in 1902, a group of representatives from the WMU happily reported that one of the African American speakers had discussed Christian home life in her speech. The African American speaker had argued that the teachings that began at "the fireside" could plant the seeds for greater missionary work in the future.[60] Another WMU report approved of the women's movement within the NBC yet reminded Southern Baptist women that it remained "the duty of the stronger to aid the weaker."[61] While the work of the Woman's Convention might bear fruit among working-class African American women, white women should not neglect their duty to guide the African American women they encountered.

In 1924 the WMU published a fictional account of an educated African American woman traveling by carriage with two white gentlemen. During the course of the journey, the two men expressed their surprise that their fellow traveler was such a polite and well-spoken African American. "I thought you seemed different from most Niggers," one of the passengers told her. She responded that she was, in fact, representative of her race and that the "lowest class" of African Americans had given all African Americans a bad name. She explained that, as a home demonstrator, she was on a quest to educate African American women. To prove to the gentlemen that her race had made moral and social progress, she discussed the material advancement that could be found within African American households. "My people are becoming land owners, we are painting our houses, putting screens into our windows, carpeting our floors and educating our children," she explained.[62]

This story was intended to elicit sympathy for elite African American women, arguing that they deserved recognition for keeping homes that were modeled after white middle-class households. Significantly, this story implied that African Americans' progress could be measured by the character of their women and the quality of their homes. Improved homes signified more than economic progress to the Baptist women who read this story. After all, they viewed the home as the most significant shaper of families' and children's faith and morals. Those who took pride in the construction and design of their homes surely possessed high standards for personal behavior as well.[63] Based on this story, much of the credit for African Americans' advancement was owed to the women, like the central character in this story, who kept Christian households, as well as the white women whose homes served as their example. The account went further than others in showcasing the abilities of African American mothers to achieve respectability in the eyes of white Baptist women.

But the author of this story also made a point of assuring her readers that African American women such as the home demonstrator were not seeking social equality. The rest of the story, like Councill's message, echoed the Atlanta Compromise by arguing that economic progress did not cause elite African Americans to demand social equality. After discussing the progress of her race, the home demonstrator concluded her conversation with the two white men by assuring them that elite African Americans did not pose a threat to the racial hierarchy of the South. "You think we want social equality. We don't," she told them. "We only want a fair chance to better our own people. You think we want to ride with you on trains. We don't. We only want decent cars to ride in," she insisted.[64]

The white writer behind this tale believed that African Americans ultimately desired nicer homes, not social equality. Such a story assured readers that they should not feel threatened by educated and middle-class African Americans, as even the "uplifted" African Americans were not seeking social equality with whites. In the end, Southern Baptist women assumed they were progressive on racial issues because they supported African Americans living in cleaner and more spacious homes. But their concept of racial uplift was limited to establishing homes with books on shelves and curtains in windows. In short, they held that African Americans should strive to have middle-class households through the limited economic means available to them in the segregated South. And as the WMU indicated here, they believed African American reformers ultimately sought this end, with its inclusion of white supremacy, as well.

The juxtaposition of this article with less optimistic articles on the decline of African American home life seen earlier in this chapter illustrates the complicated attitudes Southern Baptist women held toward African American women during the Progressive Era. On the one hand, Southern Baptist women were willing to grant respect to educated and elite women, such as those in the Woman's Convention of the NBC, because they believed they shared their goals of advancing and bettering African American home life rather than seeking social, economic, or political equality. On the other hand, other Southern Baptist women warned that working-class African American women were declining morally, despite the good faith efforts of the NBC. Thus, when the above story was published in 1924, some Southern Baptist women continued to view African Americans as "perpetual children," while other voices in the denomination declared that modern African Americans were in fact "no longer a child race."[65] The conflict resulted from the underlying tensions around racial uplift and fears regarding the South's future. In this way Mullins's character Cahaba, in her fictive journey toward transformation and uplift, embodied this conflict.

Conclusion

In the first two installments of the Blossom Shop series, Cahaba stood for much that was wrong with the "New Negro." But by the third installment, *Anne's Wedding*, she had completed courses at a normal school and had become a respectable teacher in her African American community. Of course, in Mullins's world, Cahaba did not pull herself out of poverty and ignorance on her own. She was able to escape living in squalor because of the Carter family, especially its women. First, according to Mullins's narrative, the three Carter sisters demonstrated patience and kindness with Cahaba; second, they presented themselves as examples of Christian womanhood and provided for her a model of respectable conduct and behavior; and finally, a female member of the extended Carter family took pity on Cahaba and financed her education.[66]

This might seem a likely conclusion to the Carter family and their work of racial uplift. But Cahaba's education was not her ultimate redemption. In the end, Cahaba's education was merely one component on the way to full redemption, for as she became less the "cornfield darky," she became increasingly loyal to the Carter family. In fact, when the Carters experienced a reversal of fortune, Cahaba abandoned the classroom to assist the family as a domestic worker. In a dramatic show of loyalty and affection, she donned the mammy's kerchief "in the old-time negro way."[67] It was likewise important to Cahaba that the rest of the community see where her loyalties lay. The last thing she wanted, she exclaimed, was for the town to think she "was one of these here niggers that when they look twicet into a spellin' book an' 'rithmetic, jes' unwrops their wooley hair, switches a trailin' dress around . . . an' is too triflin' to bake a hoecake!"[68] Once Anne Carter's nemesis, by the time of Anne's wedding, Cahaba became her lady's maid. At the same time, and despite her education, Cahaba still demonstrated her former childlike superstition and hot-tempered fits with Anne musing, "Oh Cahaba, no amount of schooling can tone down your imagination."[69] In the end, Cahaba still needed the Carters as much as if not more than they needed her.

For Southern Baptist women like Mullins or the WMU writer behind the fictive carriage tale, something greater was at stake. As Mullins put it, "the Mammy Sues are scarce in the South now," and their disappearance was threatening to white households.[70] A careful examination of Southern Baptist women's writings during the Progressive Era shows that their portrayals of racial uplift and advancement, most obviously as embodied in African American women, hearkened back to the figure of Mammy Sue in her beloved white household. Indeed, for Southern Baptist women, her restoration ensured the persistence of white supremacy and ultimately the salvation and redemption of their Old South.

Notes

1. See Isla May Mullins, *The Blossom Shop: A Story of the South* (Boston, MA: Page, 1913); *Anne of the Blossom Shop, or: The Growing Up of Anne Carter* (Boston, MA: Page, 1914); *Anne's Wedding: A Blossom Shop Romance* (Boston, MA: Page, 1916); and *The Mt. Blossom Girls, or, New Paths from the Blossom Shop* (Boston, MA: Page, 1918). Mullins does not give the years or decade in which the books are set, but the stories are likely set in the 1890s. Mammy Sue's and Uncle Sam's ages indicate that at least one generation had passed since the end of the Civil War.
2. Joel Williamson, *A Rage for Order: Black-White Relations in the American South Since Emancipation* (New York, NY: Oxford Univ. Press, 1986), 70–86. Joel

Williamson calls this first group Liberals. The latter, termed Radical Racists, believed that emancipation had and would continue to lead to African Americans' permanent moral decline.

3. "Conservatives" believed in peaceful race relations and African American advancement while also championing white supremacy. See Williamson, *Rage for Order,* 70–71.
4. William Link, *The Paradox of Southern Progressivism,* 1880–1930 (Chapel Hill: Univ. of North Carolina Press, 1992), 63, 70.
5. Keith Harper, *The Quality of Mercy: Southern Baptists and Social Christianity, 1890–1920* (Tuscaloosa: Univ. of Alabama Press, 1996), 89–111.
6. See, for example, Robert Baker, *Southern Baptist Convention and Its People* (Nashville, TN: Sunday School Board, Southern Baptist Convention, 1974), 264–90; John Lee Eighmy, *Churches in Cultural Captivity: A History of the Social Attitudes of Southern Baptists* (Knoxville: Univ. of Tennessee Press, 1988), 37–40; Harper, *The Quality of Mercy*, 89–110; and Paul Harvey, *Redeeming the South: Religious Cultures and Racial Identities among Southern Baptists, 1865–1925* (Chapel Hill: Univ. of North Carolina Press, 1997), 33–99, 180–86. Some important exceptions include Bill Sumners, "Bridge Builders: Baptist Women and Race Relations at the Turn of the Century," *Journal of African-American Southern Baptist History* 2 (June 2004): 4–17; and Carol Crawford Holcomb, "Mothering the South: The Influence of Gender and the Social Gospel on the Social Views of the Leadership of Woman's Missionary Union, SBC, 1888–1930" (PhD diss., Baylor University, 1999), 107, 226–38. Sumners examines WMU leaders' friendships and cooperation with prominent women in the National Baptist Convention such as Nannie Helen Burroughs. Holcomb also examines WMU leaders' involvement in interracial cooperation and WMU publications on race relations.
7. The Southern Baptist writers I examined did not consistently employ a single term to describe their domestic workers. They often used the word "servant" to describe any female domestic worker and at other times used specific terms such as "cook" or "maid" to denote the exact nature of the individual's work. Recent scholars favor the terms "domestic" and "domestic worker." Additionally, Elizabeth Clark-Lewis notes that the word "servant" usually referred to a live-in domestic worker. Since it cannot be assumed that the writers I examined limited their discussions only to live-in servants, I use the more general terms "domestic" and "domestic worker." See Rebecca Sharpless, *Cooking in Other Women's Kitchens: Domestic Workers in the South, 1865–1960* (Chapel Hill: Univ. of North Carolina Press, 2010); Tera Hunter, *To 'Joy My Freedom: Southern Black Women's Lives and Labors after the Civil War* (Cambridge, MA: Harvard Univ. Press, 1997); and Elizabeth Clark-Lewis, *Living In, Living Out: African-American Domestics in Washington, D.C., 1910–1940* (Washington, DC: Smithsonian, 1994).
8. Michele Mitchell, *Righteous Propagation: African Americans and the Politics of Racial Destiny after Reconstruction* (Chapel Hill: Univ. of North Carolina Press, 2004), 123.

9. Kevin K. Gaines, *Uplifting the Race: Black Leadership, Politics, and Culture in the Twentieth Century* (Chapel Hill: The Univ. of North Carolina Press, 1996), xiv.
10. Link, *Paradox of Southern Progressivism*, 75–77.
11. As William Link points out, uplift ideology was indeed "a strange combination of ideas: a fervent belief in white supremacy along with a belief in the necessity of black progress." See Link, *Paradox of Southern Progressivism*, 63–68.
12. Gaines, *Uplifting the Race*; Mitchell, *Righteous Propagation*; and Stephanie Shaw, *What a Woman Ought to Be and Do: Black Professional Women Workers during the Jim Crow Era* (Chicago, IL: Univ. of Chicago Press, 1996).
13. *Annual of the Southern Baptist Convention* (Nashville, TN: Marshall and Bruce, 1900), 128.
14. Link, *Paradox of Southern Progressivism*, 63–65; and Natalie Ring, *The Problem South: Region, Empire, and the New Liberal State, 1880–1930* (Athens: Univ. of Georgia Press, 2012), 189.
15. Victor I. Masters, *The Call of the South: A Presentation of the Home Principle in Missions, Especially as It Applies to the South* (Atlanta, GA: Publicity Department of the Home Mission Board of the Southern Baptist Convention, 1918), 59.
16. Paul Harvey argues that Southern Baptist leaders were haunted by a sense of "loss of control" over African Americans in the post-Reconstruction South. See Harvey, *Redeeming the South*, 3.
17. James B. Gambrell, "The Race Question in the South," in *The Home Mission Task* (Atlanta, GA: Home Mission Board of the Southern Baptist Convention, 1912), 187.
18. *Annual of the Southern Baptist Convention, 1917* (Nashville, TN: Marshall and Bruce, 1917), 86.
19. Rufus Spain argues that the institutes were short-lived due to Southern Baptists' paternalistic attitudes toward black ministers, who desired to "break the bonds of subservience to the whites." See Spain, *At East in Zion: A Social History of Southern Baptists, 1865–1900* (Tuscaloosa: Univ. of Alabama Press, 2003), 64. See too Harvey, *Redeeming the South*, 184.
20. *Annual of the Southern Baptist Convention, 1910* (Nashville, TN: Marshall and Bruce, 1910), 32.
21. See Michael Harris, *Colored Pictures: Race and Visual Representation* (Chapel Hill: Univ. of North Carolina Press, 2006).
22. Harris, *Colored Pictures*, 101, 92.
23. Harris, *Colored Pictures*, 135.
24. Masters, *Call of the South*, 70.
25. "City Missions," *Our Mission Fields*, Nov. 1910, 38.
26. *Royal Service*, Mar. 1929, 14.
27. Williamson, *A Rage for Order*, 78–79. Williamson identifies the belief in retrogression as a characteristic of Radical Racists (see n. 2). Radicals endorsed violence for maintaining white supremacy and could not envision blacks and whites living together in the United States for very long. While many Southern Baptists

accepted the Radicals' belief in retrogression, they did not share with Radicals the belief, as quoted in Williamson, that "there would be no place for blacks in the South or in America."

28. On living out, see Clark-Lewis, *Living In, Living Out*; and Sharpless, *Cooking in Other Women's Kitchens*, 91.
29. Melody Maxwell discusses WMU leaders' depictions of "heathen" home and family life in *The Woman I Am: Southern Baptist Women's Writings, 1906–2006* (Tuscaloosa: Univ. of Alabama Press, 2014), 28–33.
30. Mary Faison Dixon, "The Uplift of Two Races," *Royal Service*, July 1917, 9.
31. Mitchell, *Righteous Propagation*, 145.
32. Hunter, *To 'Joy My Freedom*, 74–97, 195, 196.
33. Homer Lamar Grice and Ethel Harrison Grice, *Daily Vacation Bible School Textbooks: Intermediate Book One* (Nashville, TN: Sunday School Board of the Southern Baptist Convention, 1925), 45.
34. One of the first WMU leaders to use the term "personal service," and the woman responsible for creating the Personal Service department of WMU, was Fannie E. S. Heck. A progressive and sometimes controversial leader of the WMU, Heck believed social service and evangelism ought to complement one another. She urged Southern Baptist women to bring this understanding of personal service to their work with black women. Heck argued that cultivating personal, individual relationships with African American domestics could lead to racial advancement. See Holcomb, "Mothering the South," 119, 228–29.
35. Gambrell, "The Race Question in the South," in *The Home Mission Task*, 187.
36. Tichenor, as quoted in Woman's Missionary Union, *Plain Words on a Duty*, 3.
37. *Annual of the Southern Baptist Convention, 1909* (Nashville, TN: Marshall and Bruce, 1909), 231.
38. *Baptist and Reflector*, Jan. 21, 1897.
39. *Baptist and Reflector*, Jan. 28, 1897.
40. Woman's Missionary Union, *Plain Words*, 8.
41. Clark-Lewis, *Living In, Living Out*, 101.
42. *Baptist and Reflector*, Jan. 28, 1897.
43. *Baptist and Reflector*, Jan. 21, 1897; and Joanna P. Moore, *"In Christ's Stead": Autobiographical Sketches* (Chicago, IL: Women's Baptist Home Mission Society, 1902), 217–19.
44. *Baptist and Reflector*, Jan. 21, 1897.
45. In addition, Elizabeth Clark-Lewis's research convincingly demonstrates that domestics were unable to attend church as often as they would have liked due to their work for white women. See Elizabeth Clark-Lewis, *Living In, Living Out*, 125.
46. Mitchell, *Righteous Propagation*, 57.
47. Charles L. Graves, "Doctrinal and Practical Teachings: The Relation of Greatness and Service," *The Convention Teacher*, Nov. 1919, 56–57.

48. Matt. 25:40.
49. *Alabama Baptist*, Jan. 13, 1927.
50. *Alabama Baptist*, Jan. 13, 1927.
51. Sharpless, *Cooking in Other Women's Kitchens*, 160–62.
52. Clark-Lewis, *Living In, Living Out*, 46–49.
53. *The Christian Index*, Jan. 5, 1922.
54. *The Christian Index*, Jan. 5, 1922.
55. *Alabama Baptist*, Feb. 16, 1922.
56. Mitchell, *Righteous Propagation*, 96.
57. Woman's Missionary Union, *Plain Words on a Duty*, 10–11.
58. See Sumners, "Bridge Builders"; Holcomb, "Mothering the South," 107, 225; and Harvey, *Redeeming the South*, 240–41.
59. Harvey, *Redeeming the South*, 242–43.
60. *Report*, Woman's Missionary Union, Southern Baptist Convention, 1902, 16–17.
61. *Report*, Woman's Missionary Union, Southern Baptist Convention, 1898, 17–18.
62. "The Law of Kindness," *Royal Service*, Aug. 1924, 15.
63. Southern Baptists' cultural heritage included a Victorian "material Protestantism" that encouraged the use of furnishings, artifacts, and decor to signify a family's religious devotion. Colleen McDannell, *Material Christianity: Religion and Popular Culture in America* (New Haven, CT: Yale Univ. Press, 1998), 57–98.
64. "The Law of Kindness," *Royal Service*, 15.
65. Ella Broadus Robertson, "The Negro Pro and Con," *Home and Foreign Fields*, Feb. 1919, 22.
66. Mullins, *Anne's Wedding*, 24.
67. Mullins, *Anne's Wedding*, 159.
68. Mullins, *Anne's Wedding*, 57.
69. Mullins, *Anne's Wedding*, 24.
70. Mullins, *Anne of the Blossom Shop*, 119.

Four

SAVING SOULS AND SOCIETY

The WMU and Social Reform in the Progressive Era

Carol Crawford Holcomb

In 1913, Fannie Exile Scudder Heck, president of the Southern Baptist Woman's Missionary Union (WMU), published *In Royal Service*, a history of Southern Baptist women's mission work. In the pages of the book, Heck traced the progress of Southern white women from the pampered antebellum "girl" of the 1830s to the modern woman of her day. She described women before the Civil War as sheltered and protected from life. At the end of the book, Heck celebrated the expanded opportunities for the women of her generation and was optimistic that a new day had dawned. "How shall we sketch the woman of today?" she asked. "Shall we typify her in cap and gown; with the thermometer and scalpel; with book and globe; with ledger and adding machine; with cuffs and apron; with notebook and typewriter; before a flying loom?"[1] Heck envisioned educated, confident Southern women becoming doctors, teachers, writers, and mathematicians. Her comments were bursting with hope for both women and the economy of the South. Fannie Heck was certain that the world was changing for the better and that Southern Baptist women could participate in ushering in a new social order. Her unbridled optimism that people could create opportunities and institutions to change society placed her at odds with her more conservative Southern Baptist peers. Heck represents a notable example of a Southern Baptist progressive.

Historians of the American South have accurately described the vast majority of white Southern Protestants at the turn of the twentieth century as rural traditionalists, protective of local autonomy, suspicious of government interference, and fiercely independent. They were committed to biblical authority, evangelism, missions, white supremacy, and the status quo.[2] Southern Baptists have been consistently characterized as quintessential conservative Southern Protestants. In his social history of Southern Baptists, John Lee Eighmy, while acknowledging some progressive influences, affirmed that Southern Baptists were, in general, "captive to their culture."[3] However, when the Progressive Era (1890–1920) is viewed through the lens of women's activities in the denomination, starting with women like Heck, we find that progressivism made greater inroads into Southern Baptist circles in the first decades of the twentieth century than previous scholarship has recognized.

There were a number of key Southern Baptist women, including Heck, who can be numbered among Southern progressives. Some of these women endorsed the Social Gospel, the theologically liberal wing of the Progressive movement. While we should be cautious not to overestimate their numbers, we should be equally careful not to underestimate their influence, especially within the WMU. Progressivism ran counter to the prevailing patterns of Southern evangelical history, yet WMU records from this era demonstrate that Southern Baptists were not theologically homogenous. Social Gospel theology challenged Christians to expand their vision of salvation beyond individual conversion in order to deliver their communities from the bondage of social sins, such as child labor, poverty, and the sale of alcohol.

Even the most conservative Southern Baptists did express "social concern," but most firmly believed individual conversion to be the solution for societal ills.[4] They insisted that if individuals are transformed then they will, in turn, transform institutions and structures. Conservative Southern Baptists expressed their social concern through ministry programs aimed at dealing with the effects of harmful social conditions, helping individuals with programs such as orphanages and food pantries.[5]

Southern Baptist "progressives" likewise affirmed the necessity of individual salvation and appealed to the Bible as their highest authority. Moreover, similar to most Southern Baptists, conservative and otherwise, they believed that the South had a special mission in the world, which included perpetuating racial hierarchies. At the same time, these Southern Baptist progressives differentiated themselves from conservatives by their attempts to identify and remove the *causes* of social problems. They advocated for social reform legislation and developed programs aimed at eradicating, rather than simply alleviating, social ills such as poverty. In line with the Progressive movements of the era, they possessed a profound sense of optimism that the modern tools of professional organizations could change and improve society and insisted that systematically addressing social problems was central to the mission of the church.[6] As I demonstrate in this chapter, this progressive approach to society was most evident in Southern Baptist life through the Personal Service department of the WMU.

The WMU and Southern Baptist "Progressives"

The ideals of the Progressive Era were introduced to Southern Baptist communities in part due to the work of individual leaders of the WMU who promoted progressive ideas to Southern Baptist women through WMU literature and shaped WMU programs using progressive methods. These WMU leaders studied the social teachings of Methodist women, visited social settlements like Jane Addams's Hull House, embraced the work of the Woman's Christian Temperance Union (WCTU), and participated in the foremost expression of Southern progressivism: the Southern Sociological Congress (SSC). They not only studied social reform, they institutionalized it. In 1909, WMU President Fannie Heck established a department called Personal Service and named Lulie Pollard Wharton as director. The department's purpose was to apply the "religion of Jesus Christ" to the "social problems of the day," thereby introducing a new emphasis on social action into the WMU agenda.[7] Personal Service leaders insisted that social reform and social work fit within the historic mission of the WMU, even as they introduced new concepts of "salvation." Women had organized the WMU specifically to support the work of Southern Baptist mission boards whose singular goal was the salvation of individuals' souls through conversion to Christianity. While Personal Service leaders argued that their department supported this conversion model of salvation, Personal Service objectives simultaneously pointed toward "social salvation" by challenging Southern Baptist women to consider social reform as religious work. Personal Service published manuals, pamphlets, and monthly magazine columns to educate Baptist women about social problems. These writings undermined the conservative theology supporting individual conversion and, at times, openly endorsed the Social Gospel.

These publications of the Personal Service department provide most of the resources for this chapter. Fannie Heck's book, speeches, essays, and personal correspondence also help paint a portrait of Southern Baptist progressives. Heck emerges as the most prominent progressive in the WMU, perhaps because she left so many records. Lulie Pollard Wharton (director of the Personal Service department), Maude Reynolds McLure (principal of the WMU Training School), and Emma Leachman (director of the WMU Settlement House in Louisville, Kentucky) were mentioned frequently enough in the Personal Service records to suggest that they were also key players in WMU efforts to promote social reform during this period. After considering the intersections between WMU leaders and progressivism, the chapter outlines the early years of the Personal Service department. Finally, the chapter turns to theological concerns. There are threads of the Social Gospel woven into the fabric of the Personal Service department. They do not dominate the pattern, but they are present. The references to the Social Gospel provide the best evidence that Southern Baptist women not only borrowed the rhetoric of the Progressive movement but also understood and—at times—appropriated its theological framework.

Progressive Influences

During the Progressive Era, leaders of the WMU made a concerted effort to study the social service activities of other denominations and organizations.[8] Southern Methodist women, many of whom advocated the Social Gospel, appeared in WMU correspondence and publications regarding progressive activities more than any other outside group.[9] WMU leadership often quoted from Methodist publications and frequently copied their social service programs.

Methodist women began social ministries in Southern cities around the turn of the twentieth century.[10] They were the first denomination in the South to establish social settlements, a program designed to accomplish urban reform by establishing a permanent presence in impoverished neighborhoods. Prior to the establishment of settlement work preparatory education at the WMU Training School, Southern Baptist students learned methods for conducting city missions at the Methodists' Wesley House in Louisville.[11] When the Personal Service committee began preparing a manual to help local women establish Baptist settlement houses in cities across the South, which they would call Good Will Centers, they turned to the *City Mission Manual of the Methodist Episcopal Church, South*. The WMU adapted this manual for their needs and wrote an acknowledgment to the Methodists in the bibliography.[12] This exchange of ideas occurred on the local level as well. The Superintendent of Missions for the Birmingham Baptist Association WMU lamented in 1913 that she had not accomplished all she wished because "to attend the meetings of our Executive Board, visit three societies, and take one visit to investigate the work which the Methodist women are doing at Avondale [was] the best [she] could do."[13]

Beyond their interactions with Methodists, the WMU encountered progressive ideas through their contacts with leading social reformers. The work of Jane Addams at Hull House was of particular interest to WMU leadership. In notes for a speech, Heck praised two women, Jane Addams, the "first citizen of Chicago," and Mrs. Barrett of London, not because they were "suffragists" or "society women" but because they were women "putting their hearts and lives below the lowest and lifting."[14] In 1912, Heck wrote to Wharton and described her favorable impressions of Addams's book, *Seventy Years at Hull House*.[15] WMU leaders McLure and Leachman toured Hull House as well as the Baptist and Presbyterian settlement work in Chicago.[16] They borrowed a few of Addams's ideas for their social ministry. "In one of the clubs at Hull House we heard them planning for gardens in the outskirts of the city where small plots were to be rented at $1.50 a season," they relayed to Heck. "Later we may be able to get the city to let us use some ground in this way."[17]

The Woman's Christian Temperance Union served as a third major influence because the WMU shared the WCTU's passion for abolishing alcohol. As the WCTU increased its focus on legislative changes to curb drinking and other vices, so too did the WMU. Texas state WMU leaders resolved: "We must heartily endorse the W.C.T.U. and Anti-Saloon League, the two organizations whose nonpartisan and nonfactional work commends them to every anti-saloon Texan."[18] Speakers for the WCTU often appeared on the programs of both national and state WMU meetings. The national WMU commended the work of the WCTU and recommended its pamphlets to their membership.[19] Annie Armstrong, one of the WMU's earliest leaders and corresponding secretary from 1888 to 1906, was an ardent supporter of the WCTU and kept copies of their publications in her notebooks. She filed pamphlets from the WCTU's Department of Social Purity—one of the more progressive plans of the WCTU aimed at eliminating prostitution.[20] The WCTU Social Purity department presented prostitution as problem affecting evangelical women because of the danger of sexually transmitted diseases. At first, the department sponsored programs to rescue individual women. In the 1890s, the Department of Social Purity began lobbying to raise the legal age of consent that remained in some states as low as ten years old.[21] WMU writers incorporated the rhetoric of the Purity Department into their programs and admonished Baptist women to keep abreast of the issues. In 1925, Wharton listed WCTU as an example of the "awakening" of social service in the nineteenth century.[22] Wharton wrote that Frances Willard, president of the WCTU from 1879 to 1898, "rallied women to fight the forces of King Alcohol. . . . This delicate, womanly woman of clear brain, loving heart and powers devoted to the cause of uplift and the eradication of evils that slay manhood and womanhood is proudly claimed by us all as a compatriot."[23]

State and local WMUs also embraced the WCTU. Southern Baptist members of the WCTU were typically members of the WMU.[24] The WMU of Woodlawn Baptist Church of Birmingham, Alabama, for example, advertised WCTU meetings in their own gatherings. Often the organization met in the same room of the church as the WMU and listed its meetings on the church calendar. Many state and local WMU leaders also accepted leadership roles in the WCTU.[25] The first secretary of the Tennessee WMU traveled across the South with WCTU President Frances Willard.[26] The founder of the Mississippi WMU was one of the founders of the Mississippi chapter of the WCTU.[27] Texas WMU matriarch Fannie Breedlove Davis commented in an unpublished memoir that she had been "president of the local WCTU work" in San Antonio "for five years."[28] Although Southern Baptist women never occupied any of the prominent leadership roles in the national WCTU, they did serve on the state and local levels and were visible members of the Southern WCTU.

Finally, WMU leaders were shaped by the work of the Southern Sociological Congress (SSC), a conference founded by Southern governors that met annually from 1912 to 1920 "to study and improve social, civic, and economic conditions in the South."[29] In March of 1913, WMU president Heck was commissioned by the governor of North Carolina to attend the SSC and was elected second vice president of the SSC in 1914. The experience with the SSC led her to establish a corollary organization in her own state: the North Carolina Conference for Social Service. Other WMU leaders were involved in the SSC as well. Wharton and the secretary of the Louisiana WMU, Elizabeth J. Falvy, also attended the SSC. McLure served as a delegate from the state of Kentucky and was a member of the Race Relations Committee in 1915. SSC meetings featured lectures by leading figures in the Social Gospel movement and addressed some of the most progressive issues of their day. The WMU magazine *Royal Service* printed reports from the meetings and quoted their resolutions concerning such issues as child labor, poverty, urban housing, health, literacy, and recreation.[30]

The Personal Service Department

Local Southern Baptist women were introduced to Southern progressivism primarily through the work of the WMU Personal Service department. Although the name of the department presented the work as "personal," the broad agenda of Personal Service was designed to alleviate social problems. The department promoted progressive values to Southern Baptist women through training manuals, handbooks, study guides, and monthly articles in WMU magazines *Our Mission Fields* and *Royal Service*. Heck and Wharton guided the department through its fledgling years with the help of a committee, and the primary writers for Personal Service columns from 1909 to 1930 were Heck, Wharton, Leachman, and McLure. These women were also the leading contributors to the *Handbook for Personal Service* and for the training courses. But they were not the only voices represented. Other WMU workers contributed to the Personal Service column in *Royal Service* during these years. Unfortunately, the columns and monthly studies rarely included an author attribution. It is difficult, therefore, to determine precisely how many women influenced or endorsed the more progressive policies of the department.[31] A large number of the Personal Service publications in the Heck and Wharton years favored a holistic concept of salvation that included both souls and society.

The organizational structure of Personal Service mirrored that of the broader WMU. Heck and Wharton encouraged local WMUs to establish Personal Service committees and to send detailed reports of their activities to national headquarters.[32] They urged societies to adopt a standard pattern of organization consisting of a state chairman, associational chairman, and society chairman of Personal Service.[33] State organizations began to form Personal Service committees in 1911. Soon WMU societies from Corpus Christi, Texas, to Norfolk, Virginia, began to organize for Personal Service.[34] By 1912, ten out of sixteen states affiliated with the WMU had Personal Service committees.[35] Personal Service was added to the Standard of Excellence for the WMU that year, requiring societies to participate in order to meet a rating of "excellence" in WMU work.[36] The national office soon prepared training pamphlets and a handbook for local societies to follow. In 1913, Personal Service was highlighted as part of the twenty-fifth anniversary celebration of the WMU.

The WMU's press consistently presented Personal Service information to local women to help them define the work. Beginning in 1913, *Our Mission*

Fields conveyed the Personal Service message directly into the homes of thousands of Southern Baptist women through articles and weekly columns.[37] The leading resource for Personal Service work was *A Manual of Personal Service*, later revised as the *Handbook for Personal Service*.[38] The initial pamphlet not only provided local societies with information on forming Personal Service committees but also offered detailed instructions for hospital work, prison work, work with "shop and factory girls," and organizing Mothers' Clubs, industrial schools, cooking schools, boys clubs, night schools, day nurseries, playgrounds, and even neighborhood entertainment. Heck and Leachman prepared the first manual. In the revision, with significant contributions from McLure, the handbook explicitly described its material as a blueprint for Southern Baptist "settlement work."[39]

Wharton and the Personal Service committee took great pains to articulate the purpose for their department. *A Manual of Personal Service* plainly stated that the "end and object" of Personal Service was "full salvation" for individuals, which they described as a salvation that included progressive ideals: "the betterment of the physical conditions, the development of the mental powers, the culture of the moral sense, in a word, making men better citizens because they are conscious citizens of the Kingdom of Heaven, whose laws are justice, peace and righteousness for all the world in all relations of life."[40] In the 1916 annual report, they explained: "In laying the foundation for this department the aim has been to make it broad and comprehensive, to line up with the most progressive thought and movements of the day and to seek those methods most conducive to the carrying out of our purpose—'to fight for prohibition, for observance of the Sabbath, for the sanctity of the home and the fight against crime, disease and poverty.'"[41] The "progressive thought of the day" meant social science methods and themes drawn from the Social Gospel and other Progressive Era movements. Under the banner of the "fight against crime, disease, and poverty," Personal Service leaders were interested in a comprehensive program to improve numerous aspects of society, such as housing, sanitation, health, education, and recreation; the condition of jails, orphanages, county homes, and other local institutions; as well as church and Sunday School membership and attendance. An annual report asserted: "We cannot express the aim of this new department in better terms than to say it is social service upheld by grace."[42]

WMU publications continued to use the phrase "social service" to describe their missionary methods even though there were strong sentiments against it among some Baptists. As late as 1920, a committee of Virginia Baptists pronounced that "right Gospel preaching will send nine-tenths of these special social service organizations to the scrap heap."[43] In contrast, the

Handbook for Personal Service stated: "The Founder of Christianity was the greatest social worker the world has ever known."[44] The 1913 WMU mission study program pronounced: "Christ enjoined social service and plainly taught that His treatment of men in the last day would depend on their treatment of each other here."[45]

Personal Service writers admonished workers to seek out the causes of social problems. "Too long God's people have endeavored with self-sacrificing but short sighted charity to help the victims of crime and want by dealing with the effects always more apparent than the deep seated and often unrecognized causes," declared the 1913 Personal Service annual report. In 1914, Wharton published an article in the Personal Service column of the *Royal Service* arguing that social problems could no longer be ignored: "The time for indifference and palliation is past. Causes must be found and dealt with."[46] As late as 1921, *Royal Service* emphasized that poor families needed more than "haphazard donations of food and clothing." Charity would not alleviate the serious social problems that plagued Southern society: "Soup and jelly to the sick are not solving the health problems that kill the babies in your town."[47] In a rare statement, the *Handbook of Personal Service* placed responsibility on the government for progressive social change: "The state which punishes vice should remove the causes which make men vicious."[48]

The Personal Service department encouraged formal, systematic neighborhood studies with the publication of *The Survey*—a broad-based program for analyzing local communities on issues ranging from sexual immorality to economics. Workers were instructed to take a map of the community, divide it into grids, and ascertain the demographics of each section. According to the plan, Southern Baptist women would go door to door with the list of questions, including: "Is there any sex immorality? What is being done to teach purity and the dangers of disease from an immoral life?" Regarding labor, women conducting the survey were to ask: "What is the chief industry? Any factories or mills? Is the work regular? Any seven day work? Any women or children employed? What is the lowest wage paid to men? to women? Is it a living wage? What proportion of wages has to go for rent? How many own homes? Is the safety of the factory or mill workers properly protected?"[49] Organizers hoped that the information would allow the surveyors to identify and solve social problems. Southern Baptist women were not alone in the optimistic belief that "whatever facts were collected by a survey would be put to good use"; this assumption was typical of the larger "survey movement" that emerged during the Progressive Era, of which these Southern Baptist women were a part.[50] Advocates believed that if ordinary citizens had the correct information, they would be able to solve the problems they encountered.

In addition to the *The Survey*, the Personal Service column in *Royal Service* urged WMU societies to take advantage of other resources to study their communities. "The Russell Sage Foundation and the American Red Cross . . . will give information on social services," explained a Personal Service column, "so will your State Board of Charities or Welfare, your state university and all the great denominational publishing houses."[51] The same column offered veiled criticism of local WMUs for their lack of "study of fundamental principles of social work" or "thorough knowledge of the conditions and needs of our own communities."[52]

Personal Service leadership hoped to monitor local WMU activity by providing a reporting form in the WMU yearbook. The form asked societies to identify their work with specific programs such as Good Will Centers, Mission Sunday Schools, Homemakers' Clubs, Cottage Prayer Meetings, Cheer-All Clubs, Boys' Clubs, Industrial Schools, Rescue Work, Sewing for Poor, Work for Negroes, Work for Foreigners, and Work for Prisoners. In addition to programs, there were categories for Visits, Services, Conversions, Bibles Distributed, Good Literature, Garments Made and Distributed, and Baskets Sent. In 1918, the categories expanded to include such programs as Americanization, Kindergartens, Day Nurseries, and Daily Vacation Bible Schools. Also in that year a category for Red Cross and War Relief efforts appeared, which was later simply called Nursing. Star Classes, focused on adult education, were added in 1921. WMU societies were expected to report on a wide range of activities, from standard missionary activity focused on individual conversion to more progressive programs designed to produce social change.

Personal Service writers worked to help local women across the South embrace a social reform agenda while persistently arguing that their goals were in keeping with historic objectives of the WMU to promote home and foreign missions. WMU leaders did have difficulty overcoming the reality that the application of the gospel to social problems was, in fact, a new concept for most Southern Baptist women. Local women usually conceived of missions exclusively in terms of evangelism to individuals. The older and more urban the WMU society, the greater the likelihood it would embrace the full agenda of Personal Service. Occasionally rural societies exposed to urban issues such as industry or immigration also embraced Personal Service. Many societies, however, gravitated toward simple missionary service and were uncertain about the meaning of Personal Service. Many WMU societies tended to include almost any "Christian act," such as "a smile" or "a word of encouragement," under the department of Personal Service.[53] One WMU association included contributions to a ministerial relief fund in their

Personal Service report. The national committee bemoaned the fact that "in many places the women have no very clear conception of what is meant by Personal Service."[54] WMU writers reminded women that individuals should certainly pursue "Christ-like living with regard to those around us" but organized Personal Service should be defined as work "for the uplift of the community of which the society is a part, carried on by its own members, and reported to the society."[55] The national committee persistently urged women to undertake more challenging forms of work.

Part of the problem was that the aims of Personal Service represented a new way of understanding the gospel, even though WMU leaders often insisted it was not. The original agenda of the WMU had been crystal clear: Southern Baptists aimed to save souls at home and overseas. The WMU had been formed to support these efforts through the Southern Baptist Home Mission Board (HMB) and Foreign Mission Board (FBM). The Personal Service department was formed to study and eradicate social problems. The new department of Personal Service faced a critical challenge: how could it find its niche within these clearly defined goals of the WMU?

Personal Service leaders studiously avoided placing the new department into competition with missions, but struggled to help women understand exactly how Personal Service fit into their organizational structure. While promoting Personal Service, the WMU committee endeavored to reassure local women that their focus on missions had not changed. Personal Service literature proclaimed that the "Gospel was its motive and conversion was its aim." Still, it was not a typical program of evangelism designed for individual salvation. Heck emphatically insisted that missions were a priority for the WMU. "It must be distinctly understood that [the activities of Personal Service] in no way interfere with or overlap the work the societies are now doing and the far larger things they expect to do for home and State missions," explained Heck. "To these two agencies [the HMB and FMB] the Union as a whole, and the State Central Committees as parts of the Union, have shown and will ever maintain the deepest allegiance."[56] Heck insisted that mission work was central, but also argued that Personal Service and mission work did not "overlap."

Heck and Wharton did not believe they were advocating a *new* gospel but instead believed they were promoting the *whole* gospel. Just as Walter Rauschenbusch contended that the Social Gospel was not an innovation but the "old message of salvation," Personal Service writers insisted they were recovering elements of the gospel that had been neglected. Heck sincerely believed that the church should be saving souls at home, saving souls overseas, *and also* saving society.

WMU Progressives and Race Relations

Race issues were unavoidable for WMU leaders who focused on addressing social problems. Although progressive Southern Baptist women discussed issues of race, made efforts to aid black Baptist women in forming mission societies, and sought to improve African American communities, they largely turned a blind eye to the systemic oppression and racial violence that permeated the South. Despite the optimistic language of social progress, Progressive Era articles in WMU magazines never openly endorsed racial or social equality. Even the most socially minded Southern Baptist women in this period remained firmly entrenched in white Southern culture.[57] While adopting progressive ideals, many continued to believe that racial peace and social order could only be achieved through segregation and disfranchisement. Thus the "progressivism" of many Southern Baptists reformers often led them to promote solutions for social ills that were far removed from the goals of racial justice activists.

The attitudes about race expressed in WMU magazines ran the gamut from blatant white supremacy to "romantic racialism," which embraced spiritual equality while defending segregation.[58] One pamphlet circulated by the WMU during the last decade of the nineteenth century endorsed "spiritual equality" in this way: "Our bodies are diverse in color, but our souls, if they have any color, are by nature equally dark, and by the blood of the lamb, may be made equally white."[59] Such statements likely seemed progressive to white Southern women, who also regularly published and read articles in WMU magazines highlighting African Americans' supposed moral deficiency as a root cause of the challenges they faced in the South. In a 1910 issue of *Our Mission Fields,* for example, a writer lamented the moral failings of "Negroes in the Cities": "There is in every Southern town of any size a large element of the colored population who live either from necessity or idleness just above the starvation line, crowded in ill kept houses and disregardful of many of the fundamental laws of decency and morals."[60]

WMU magazines often approached racial discussions under the topics of household management. The majority of references to African American domestic workers in WMU magazines were overtly racist. A representative discussion of the "negro maid" in one *Royal Service* issue included a series of questions designed to challenge African American domestic servants to higher Christian principles. "Does the colored girl realize that it is not fair to expect full pay for services when she has not rendered full service? . . . Does the colored girl understand she is obligated not to be wasteful or dishonest with the belongings placed in her care?"[61] The nature of these questions assumed moral deficiency in domestic servants, and the corresponding questions for the white women merely suggested that "mistresses" be good moral examples and friendly guides to their employees.

Some of the more positive comments about race came from other denominational publications that WMU leaders simply reprinted. In 1912, WMU president Heck wrote Wharton, chairman of Personal Service, recommending the publications on race relations by Methodist women: "[Southern Methodist Women's] recent publication . . . on work among colored women (a most difficult subject) has interested me."[62] *Royal Service* later published a number of these Methodist reports.[63] An anonymous author indicated that the Woman's Missionary Council of the Methodist Episcopal Church, South, had prepared a leaflet called *Plan for Cooperating with Negro Women* that contained "valuable suggestions, some of which we quote." None of the suggestions challenged segregation, but they instructed women to monitor the "equal" component of the "separate but equal" ideology of *Plessy v. Ferguson* (1896), the US Supreme Court ruling that had upheld racial segregation laws. One recommendation proposed "looking into the needs of the negro public schools, requiring of the public authorities that their premises be kept sanitary, helping to secure colored teachers of a high grade, and favoring the introduction of industrial training." Another promoted "looking after the recreation (or lack of it) of negro children and young people; endeavoring to interest the Christian women of all denominations in securing for them opportunities for clean play in playgrounds." Still another urged school boards to allow the use of black schools as community centers. White women were admonished to visit jails and courts to ascertain "the measure of justice accorded negroes in the local courts, and by creating a sentiment for justice to youthful criminals whom wise treatment may reform." Mission-minded women should "study negro housing conditions and their bearing on sickness, inefficiency, and crime . . . insisting that local authorities enforce in the negro district the sanitary regulations of the community."

The final recommendation encouraged women to create "in the local white community higher ideals in regard to the relation between the two races; by standing for full and equal justice in all departments of life; by endeavoring to secure for the backward race not only the full measure of development of which they are capable but the unmolested possession and enjoyment of all legitimate rewards of honest work; by standing, in short for the full application to the negroes and to ourselves of the Mosaic law of justice, 'Thou shalt love thy neighbor as thyself.'"[64] These statements, published in *Royal Service* in 1915, represent the most advanced thinking on the issue of race produced by white Southern progressives—despite the reference to African Americans as "the backward race" and the implication that there might be a limit to the level of development to which they were "capable." It is telling that the most progressive article in a Baptist publication was borrowed from Southern Methodist women, and the material they borrowed left plenty of room for the continuation of segregation and white privilege while doing the work of "social progress."

The programs for African American women and their families recommended by the Personal Service committee paralleled those they sought for other women and children. The Personal Service committee urged local Southern Baptist women to establish Good Will Centers, Vacation Bible Schools, day nurseries, and missionary societies among "negroes" of the South, and the committee asked local societies to report their work among African Americans. These were included with the other Personal Service statistics. Since the WMU's Personal Service department grouped the efforts on behalf of the black population under one general title of "work for the negroes," it is impossible to tell from the national statistics exactly how many of the various kinds of programs were conducted on the local level. From 1915 until 1925, an average of 9.7 percent of the local WMU societies reported "work for the negroes." The number seems large compared to the 5 percent of societies involved in settlement work. The definition of "work with negroes" varied from state to state and society to society. The December 1922 issue of *Royal Service* reported five states offering courses in mission study for "colored women." Oklahoma women appointed two members to their state Interracial Commission. South Carolina supported a "domestic science" teacher at Morris College. Texas invited "negro leaders" to attend the state convention and made contributions to the "negro Training School and Orphan's Home." In that same year Virginia merely communicated with their societies to "promote good feeling" between the races.[65]

Southern progressivism did introduce a more humane tone to racial rhetoric and led the WMU to include the improvement of African American social conditions among their goals. However, WMU leaders walked in lock step with Southern progressives in their support for segregation. There is no evidence to suggest that WMU leaders publicly challenged the system of segregation during the Progressive Era. Even the most theologically liberal wing of the progressivism, the Social Gospel theologians, did not promote full equality for African Americans. As the twentieth century unfolded, however, some Southern Baptists committed to progressivism did begin to advocate rethinking their approach to race issues; a 1923 editorial in WMU's *Royal Service*, for example, opined, "For though we have often been kind to them [African Americans], we have seldom been just."[66]

Personal Service and the Social Gospel

Despite their failure to challenge segregation and to fully confront other racial injustices of the Jim Crow South during the Progressive Era, WMU progressives nevertheless used their magazine as a conduit for the liberal theology of the Social Gospel movement that conservative Southern Baptists feared. Personal Service department writings endorsed the Social Gospel obliquely and directly. In 1915, the Personal Service committee published a pamphlet series *Our Duty to the Community* designed to provide guidance for local women in Personal Service, which was full of Social Gospel citations.[67] Lesson five concluded with a quote from the noted Social Gospel theologian and northerner Shailer Mathews: "And this is the social Gospel! the joyful message that the power of Jesus Christ, the Son of God, is sufficient to regenerate the social order which tends to express itself in individuals; that the Gospel is the power of God unto salvation not to the individual or society, but to the individual *in* society. And thus the individual gospel and the social gospel are seen to be the same glad news of the saving power of God in Christ."[68] The study ended with a bibliography for further reading comprised of books by Mathews and other liberal Social Gospel theologians.[69]

Similarly, the editors of *Royal Service* regularly referenced, quoted, and reprinted materials from Social Gospel writers and speakers. For example, a March 1916 issue of *Royal Service* quoted at length a speech made at the 1915 Southern Sociological Congress by Samuel Zane Batten regarding the responsibility of the church to address public health. Batten's words were resplendent with the Social Gospel message.[70] "First," according to Batten, "the churches must teach people the wide scope of redemption and must make them know that health is a Christian duty."[71] He continued with an admonition for the churches to go beyond the "results and deal with causes": "Thus far we have been content to feed the hungry, to nurse the sick, to rescue the perishing, to lift up the fallen. It is all very well to rescue the outcast, but it is better to abolish the white slave traffic. It is well enough to take the sickly child out of the slums; but it is more sensible to abolish the slums. It is well enough to feed the hungry family; but it is more Christian to create an industrial order where every man can earn and eat his daily bread without scantiness and anxiety."[72] Batten's words, endorsed by WMU leaders, strike at the heart of conservative Christianity. Batten dared suggest that the "industrial order" was to blame for poverty and want. Batten clarified his position even further: "It is well enough to build an orphanage," he implored, "but it is more religious to protect machinery and keep the fathers alive. The time has come for us to find the causes of poverty and sickness and deal with these. . . . There is something as foolish as it is un-Christian in nursing sick people and running a hospital when you can keep people well by abolishing bad housing and providing pure water. . . . We must realize that this work of preventing social evils is religious and spiritual work."[73]

Again and again in the pages of *Royal Service*, Southern Baptist women found a solid endorsement of the work of the Southern Sociological Congress and approval of the Social Gospel. The 1915 Personal Service report to the Annual Meeting of the WMU opened with a quote from Social Gospel writer Graham Taylor, the first chair of Christian Sociology in the United States at the Chicago Theological Seminary and founder of the Chicago Commons Settlement.[74] The mission program for August 1917 in *Royal Service* contained a two-page section taken directly from Social Gospel leader Josiah Strong's book *The Challenge of the City.* Mary Faison Dixon, who prepared the program, said that Strong was "a careful student of city problems and knows whereof he speaks."[75] Even when the first WMU report on Personal Service sought to assure readers that the new department would not stumble into an "overemphasis on social service," a Social Gospel theologian was referenced to make the point. The author of the report used the words of Mathews to voice her caution: "Dean Shailer Mathews, president of the Federal Council of Churches in America, issues a warning against the substitution of social service for spirituality in the church. He says: 'picnics are not the equivalents of prayer-meetings and Sunday-school baseball leagues have not yet developed into revivals.'"[76] Here the writer voiced caution about social service while legitimizing the teachings of Shailer Mathews and the Federal Council of Churches. She could have chosen any number of Southern Baptist leaders to issue a word of warning about social service, but she chose a Social Gospel leader, and a noted liberal theologian at that.[77]

WMU writers also quoted from Charles Sheldon's 1897 Social Gospel novel *In His Steps.* The novel described the influence of a small congregation who began to order their lives around the question, "What would Jesus do?" That question and the notion of walking "in his steps" became signal phrases for Christian-based social justice efforts and watchwords for the Social Gospel movement. The leadership of the WMU indicated their familiarity with the novel in several instances. Transcripts of speeches and articles in *Royal Service* had direct quotes from Sheldon, demonstrating the significance of this Social Gospel writer's influence. In a speech by Heck to the North Carolina WMU one year after the publication of the novel, her written manuscript climaxes with a direct quote of Sheldon's famous refrain, "if in your place, 'what would Jesus do?'"[78] As late as 1923, twenty-six years after the publication of the novel, a writer in *Royal Service* points again to Sheldon's work with a direct quote: "As Personal Service is a sacred trust committed into our hands by One who fed the multitude, prepared breakfast for weary, hungry disciples, healed the sick, changed home life by His presence and gave the peace of God in the forgiveness of sins, we can but follow with humility 'in his steps.'"

Personal Service writers also employed phrases such as the "Kingdom of God" in ways that would have pleased Rauschenbusch. Mary Livermore of Tennessee encouraged Southern Baptist women to cooperate with the secular movements for reform so that "their splendid humanitarian service" might help to "bring in the Kingdom of God in our midst."[79] The *Handbook of Personal Service* stated: "Until the whole church is thus enlisted for the whole world, the kingdom of God cannot wholly come in any part of the earth."[80] These statements expressed the WMU's acceptance of the Social Gospel premise that human participation could usher in God's reign on earth.

Social salvation was a crucial theme in Social Gospel theology. WMU writers often defended the idea of social salvation while acknowledging the importance of individual salvation. It was not unusual for a writer to quote a Social Gospel theologian, or an anonymous "social thinker" of the day who advocated the Social Gospel, then add a disclaimer by indicating support for individual salvation. In a 1913 pamphlet, the Personal Service committee presented their answer to the basic question: "What is the Personal Service work of Woman's Missionary Union?" The committee responded: "[Personal Service] is social service whose high ideal is not alone the lifting of mankind to better living conditions, to Christian business standards, especially regarding women and children employees, to proper and adequate opportunities for play, to social and cultural advantages, to educational privileges, but salvation for the life beyond through faith in Jesus Christ."[81] The phrase "not alone" suggests that human needs in the present life and spiritual well-being in the afterlife were both included in the goals of Personal Service. In the 1913 report to the annual meeting of the WMU, the Personal Service committee raised the issue of social salvation: "'When a man loves God he is saved; when he loves his neighbor society is saved,' says one of the leading social teachers of the day. These two great needs—the need for personal salvation and the need for Personal Service in the interests of society are embodied in the intention and design of religion."[82] The committee report did not expound on the implications of social salvation but rather indicated that society was an element of religion that must not be neglected. It could be the writers simply did not realize the theological import of the "social teacher's" words. Regardless, the report announced to all who heard it that salvation could apply to society.

In another reference to Social Gospel leader Josiah Strong, a column in *Our Mission Fields* discussed salvation in the context of urban problems, stating, "We are told by that deep student of our country's conditions, Dr. Josiah Strong, that 'already one-fourth of the people of the United States live in the cities, and three-fourths of the wealth is there.'"[83] The column went on to make the point that something had to be done to bring salvation to the multitudes in the cities. In typical Southern Baptist fashion, the writer first affirmed individual salvation: "The saved city would be just a community of people in right relation to God through faith in the Savior; and nothing else, we know, can ever take the place of that truth." But to this truth, she insisted, must be added an awareness of the social dimensions of sin: "But in seeking the salvation of the individual we need to take account of some of the forces that draw him away from the influence of righteousness, and to see how our own Christian life may help negatively by removing these forces as well as by supplying the positive force of a saving knowledge of Christ."[84] In other words, social forces can inhibit or support individual salvation. Although Personal Service writers approached the subject of social salvation with some hesitancy, they challenged claims that the church's responsibility to society ended with individual, spiritual regeneration.

This more holistic perspective of salvation can be found throughout Personal Service materials of the era. One of the plainest presentations of the Social Gospel appeared in Wharton's 1915 annual report to the WMU. Wharton placed the Social Gospel statement on the lips of an anonymous missionary: "With every year of missionary experience the conviction has grown that the Gospel of Christ is a Gospel for all life—here not less than hereafter—and for all departments of life." The missionary continued with an even more specific claim for the regeneration of social conditions, making a direct attack on conservatives' primary emphasis on conversion: "The reformation of earthly life is indeed the preparation for the heavenly citizenship, and should be not the selfish saving of individual souls alive, but a work as broad and inclusive as is the Love that 'so loved the world'; so that no physical, social, governmental or intellectual obstacle to man's truest and highest development is too secular for the spirit of Christ and His Gospel to strike at through its missionaries."[85] In addition to defending social service against attacks that it is more "secular" than spiritual, the missionary undermines the notion that salvation consisted only of a verbal assent to propositional truths. It is more than the "selfish saving of individual souls alive." In the cultural context of Southern Baptist life, the missionary's words are startling, and the message of the missionary would have been abundantly clear to WMU women in the local church. Salvation applied to every aspect of human existence. The gospel included anything that helped human beings in this world and the next. Taken together, these ideas expressed the spirit of the Social Gospel.[86]

Conclusion

References to the Social Gospel, endorsements of social work, and glowing reports of social reformers are woven through WMU literature in the Progressive Era. These threads of progressivism complicate our history of Southern Baptists, as they nuance the image of the denomination as impervious to liberalizing influences. Influential women introduced progressive ideas and Social Gospel theology into the heart of Southern Baptist life—the missionary enterprise.

What fruit did WMU progressivism produce? What difference did it make? The structure of the WMU itself is a testament to the professionalization of nonprofits that characterized the Progressive Era. The systems they developed to gather data, create budgets, promote programs, and organize volunteers epitomized progressivism. Even if local women did not fully endorse the Social Gospel, they overwhelmingly applied other emphases of progressivism such as scientific methods, efficiency, professionalism, democracy, and data gathering to their missionary organization. Even though there is little evidence to indicate that large numbers of Southern Baptist women expanded the definition of missions to include the salvation of institutions or society as a whole, WMU workers were enthusiastic about creating a professional missionary enterprise, an efficient organization with seamless communication from the national body, through the state, down to the local church. WMU leaders themselves unreservedly embraced what they called the "new sociology," the systematic analysis of social conditions and social problems that would eventually lead the WMU to train women in church social work and to establish a Baptist version of settlement houses across the South.

Baptists historically prized democracy and local church autonomy. These values have often proven to be a double-edged sword. One the one hand, the democratic structure gave local and national WMU workers some freedom to set their own agendas. Institutional autonomy made space (albeit separate from the central organizations of the SBC) for women to hone leadership skills through the WMU, from public speaking to financial planning. The national WMU exercised this freedom to participate in social reform organizations, promote progressivism in their publications, and support a platform of social reform. It speaks to the power of the WMU that some local Baptist women participated in Personal Service and became conversant with progressivism at all. On the other hand, this same decentralized congregational structure ensured that local women could choose not to cooperate with national WMU agendas if they wished. And time again, Southern Baptist women as well as men employed the commitment to autonomy and independence in service of maintaining the status quo, eventually closing this little-known chapter of Progressive Era reform within the denomination.

Notes

1. Fannie Heck, *In Royal Service* (Richmond, VA: Foreign Mission Board of the Southern Baptist Convention, 1913), 298.
2. Dewey Grantham, *Southern Progressivism: The Reconciliation of Progress and Tradition* (Knoxville: Univ. of Tennessee Press, 1983), 16. See also Kenneth Bailey, *Southern White Protestantism in the Twentieth Century* (New York, NY: Harper and Row, 1964); Samuel Hill, *Southern Churches in Crisis Revisited* (Tuscaloosa: Univ. of Alabama Press, 1999); and Anne C. Loveland, *Southern Evangelicals and the Social Order, 1800–1860* (Baton Rouge: Louisiana State Univ. Press, 1980).
3. John Lee Eighmy, *Churches in Cultural Captivity: A History of the Social Attitudes of Southern Baptists* (Knoxville: Univ. of Tennessee Press, 1972). In his 1977 work examining the social views of Southern Baptists at the end of the nineteenth century, Rufus Spain characterized the denomination as "relatively unconcerned about the problems of society during the period," or "at ease in Zion." Eighmy then built on Spain's argument, and together they tell a tale of Southern conservatism and localism. See Rufus Spain, *At Ease in Zion: A Social History of Southern Baptists* (Nashville, TN: Vanderbilt Univ. Press, 1967). The title is a reference to Amos 6:1, in which the prophet criticizes the powerful and elite for being comfortable with social injustice.
4. Here I am using the term "social concern" as defined more broadly by Robert D.

Linder to mean "a general interest in society's problems." He further defined "social ministries" as those activities carried out by Christians to "help . . . individuals harmed by adverse social conditions." Finally, "social action" was an "organized effort at any level—personal, nonpolitical, and political—which seeks to change social and economic conditions to conform more closely to principles laid down in the Bible." See Linder, as quoted in Eighmy, *Churches in Cultural Captivity*, xi.

5. For an analysis of the ways that Southern Baptists attempted to aid individuals, see Keith Harper, *The Quality of Mercy: Southern Baptists and Social Christianity, 1890–1930* (Tuscaloosa: Univ. of Alabama Press, 1996).
6. Patricia Summerlin Martin, "Hidden Work: Baptist Women in Texas, 1880–1920," (PhD diss., Rice University, 1982).
7. *WMU Annual Report* (1912), 51. Catherine Allen believes WMU avoided using the term "social service" directly in connection with personal service to avoid "antagonizing opponents of the social gospel." See Allen, *A Century to Celebrate: History of Woman's Missionary Union* (Birmingham, AL: Woman's Missionary Union, 1987), 215.
8. *WMU Annual Report* (1917).
9. John Patrick McDowell demonstrates that Southern Methodist women embraced the Social Gospel in its entirety. See McDowell, *The Social Gospel in the South: The Woman's Home Mission Movement in the Methodist Episcopal Church, South, 1886–1939* (Baton Rouge: Louisiana State Univ. Press, 1982), 3.
10. For descriptions of early Methodist settlement houses, see Sara Estell Haskins, *Woman and Missions in the Methodist Episcopal Church, South* (Nashville, TN: Methodist Episcopal Church, 1920), 202.
11. Carrie Littlejohn, *History of Carver School of Missions and Social Work* (Nashville, TN: Broadman Press, 1958), 64.
12. *The Handbook of Personal Service*, nd., Personal Service Notebooks, Woman's Missionary Union Archives, Birmingham, AL. There is a great deal of debate over whether or not the Baptist Good Will Centers should be categorized as social settlements. T. Laine Scales has made an excellent argument that they functioned more as missions than settlements. However, the WMU leaders at the time called them social settlements, and it is significant that they believed they were aligning themselves with progressives like Jane Addams. See Scales, *All That Fits a Woman: Training Southern Baptist Women for Charity and Missions, 1907–1926* (Macon, GA: Mercer Univ. Press, 2000).
13. *Proceedings of the Birmingham Baptist Association* (1913), Southern Baptist Historical Library and Archives (SBHLA), Nashville, TN.
14. Unpublished notes, Heck Papers, North Carolina Baptist Historical Collection, Wake Forest University (NCBHC), Winston-Salem, NC.
15. Fannie E. S. Heck to Lulie Wharton, c. 1912, WMU Archives, National WMU Office (WMUA), Birmingham, AL.
16. M. R. McLure to Fannie E. S. Heck, Feb. 8, 1915, Heck Papers, NCBHC.

17. M. R. McLure to Fannie E. S. Heck, Feb. 8, 1915, Heck Papers, NCBHC.
18. *Proceedings of the Twenty-Fifth Annual Meeting of the Baptist Women Mission Workers of Texas* (Nov. 21–22, 1911), 34.
19. Allen, *Century to Celebrate*, 238.
20. Annie Armstrong Notebooks, WMUA. For more detailed discussion of the WMU's attitude toward temperance, see Allen, *Century to Celebrate*, 238–41; and Rosalie Beck, Kay Shurden, and Catherine Allen, "The Impact of Southern Baptist Women on Social Issues: Three Viewpoints," *Baptist History and Heritage* 12 (July 1987): 29–49.
21. Ruth Bordin, *Woman and Temperance: The Quest for Power and Liberty 1873–1900* (Philadelphia, PA: Temple Univ. Press, 1981), 110.
22. *Royal Service*, Aug. 1925, 29.
23. *Royal Service*, Sept. 1925, 27.
24. Carolyn Weatherford insisted that "Woman's Missionary Union and women in Southern Baptist life are synonymous. If women had leadership roles outside of Woman's Missionary Union, history is silent." Carolyn Weatherford, "Shaping of Leadership among Southern Baptist Women," *Baptist History and Heritage* (July 1987): 15; and Charles W. Deweese, "Deaconesses in Baptist History: A Preliminary Study," *Baptist History and Heritage* (January 1977): 26–36. See also Elizabeth Flowers, *Into the Pulpit: Southern Baptist Women and Power since World War II* (Chapel Hill: Univ. of North Carolina Press, 2014).
25. This is unpublished research noted in correspondence between historians Ruth Provence and Catherine Allen, cited in Allen, *Century to Celebrate*, 240.
26. Allen, *Century to Celebrate*, 238.
27. Allen, *Century to Celebrate*, 240.
28. Fannie Breedlove Davis, handwritten memoir, biographical file, Musick Alumni Center and Museum, University of Mary Hardin-Baylor, Belton, TX.
29. J. E. McCulloch to F. E. S. Heck, Mar. 3, 1913, Heck Papers, NCBHC.
30. A full report on the Southern Sociological Congress is included in *Royal Service*, May 1915, 26. See also *Royal Service*, Mar. 1916, 8–14.
31. The names of Personal Service committee members listed on Personal Service reports during Lulie Wharton's tenure included Mrs. F. T. Grady, Mrs. A. J. Clark, Kathleen Mallory, Mrs. George Stevens, Susan Bancroft Tyler [Mrs. James Pollard], Mrs. James W. Kirkman, Mrs. W. H. Baylor, Mrs. Oscar G. Levy, and Mrs. A. J. Fristoe. In 1924 Mrs. Peyton A. Eubank took over as chairman of the Personal Service committee. The women were listed by their married names in the literature, and I have not been able to ascertain the given names of all the women.
32. Allen, *Century to Celebrate*, 215.
33. *WMU Annual Report* (1915), 65.
34. *Minutes (1913)*, Corpus Christi Missionary Baptist Association, SBHLA; and *Minutes (1913)*, Portsmouth Baptist Association, SBHLA.
35. These included Arkansas, Alabama, Louisiana, Mississippi, North Carolina, South Carolina, Tennessee, Texas, and Virginia. See *WMU Annual Report* (1912), 52.

36. Allen, *Century to Celebrate*, 215; and Alma Hunt, *History of Woman's Missionary Union* (Nashville, TN: Broadman Press, 1976), 125.
37. *Royal Service* continued the emphases of personal service until 1962. In the 1940s "Personal Service" was reorganized as "community missions." See Allen, *Century to Celebrate*, 215.
38. *A Manual of Personal Service* (1911), WMUA.
39. *Handbook of Personal Service*, 4.
40. *Manual of Personal Service*, 4.
41. *WMU Annual Report* (1915), 60–61.
42. *WMU Annual Report* (1912), 51.
43. Eighmy, *Churches in Cultural Captivity*, 110.
44. *Handbook of Personal Service*.
45. *Our Mission Fields*, Oct.–Dec. 1913, 29.
46. *Royal Service*, Oct. 1914, 24.
47. *Royal Service*, Nov. 1921, 30.
48. *Handbook of Personal Service*.
49. *The Survey*, n.d., Personal Service Notebooks, WMUA.
50. Joyce E. Williams and Vicky M. McLean, *Settlement Sociology in the Progressive Years: Faith, Science, and Reform* (Boston, MA: Brill, 2015), 28.
51. *Royal Service*, Nov. 1921, 30. There are two different publications called *The Survey*. One was a publication of Baptist women designed to help local societies gather information about their communities. The other was the magazine of the Charity Organization Society movement, and the first social work publication in the United States, published from 1907 until 1952. I believe the writer is referring to the latter in this instance. Elizabeth A. Ferguson, *Social Work: An Introduction* (New York, NY: Lippincott, 1963), 67.
52. *Royal Service*, Nov. 1921, 30.
53. *Minutes (1917)*, Portsmouth Baptist Association, SBHLA .
54. *WMU Annual Report* (1915), 64.
55. *WMU Annual Report* (1915), 65.
56. *Manual of Personal Service*.
57. William Link, *The Paradox of Southern Progressivism*, 322–24; John Dittmer, *Black Georgia in the Progressive Era, 1900–1920* (Urbana: Univ. of Illinois Press, 1977); Edwin J. Cashin and Glenn T. Eskew, eds., *Paternalism in a Southern City: Race, Religion, and Gender in Augusta, Georgia* (Athens: Univ. of Georgia Press, 2001); and Morton Sosna, *In Search of the Silent South: Southern Liberals and the Race Issue* (New York, NY: Columbia Univ. Press, 1977).
58. Ronald C. White Jr., *Liberty and Justice for All: Racial Reform and the Social Gospel, 1877–1925* (San Francisco, CA: Harper and Row, 1990), 47.
59. Rev. Robert Ryland DD, "The Colored People" (1898), 7, WMUA.
60. *Our Mission Fields*, Oct.–Dec. 1910, 38. This article cited Josiah Strong and Shailer Mathews as experts on the "problems of the cities" but also stated that "individual salvation, and that alone," could solve the problems of the "negro" in the cities.

61. *Royal Service*, Aug. 1925, 33.
62. Fannie Heck to Lulie Wharton, ca. 1912, Heck Papers, WMUA.
63. *Royal Service*, Feb. 1915, 11.
64. *Royal Service*, Feb. 1915, 11.
65. *Royal Service*, Dec. 1922, 29.
66. *Royal Service*, Jan. 1923, editorial.
67. Edward Bagby Pollard and Mrs. H. M. (Lulie) Wharton, *Our Duty to the Community: A Course of Six Studies*, 1915, Personal Service Notebooks, WMUA. The content was provided by Lulie Pollard Wharton, chairman of the Personal Service committee, and a Dr. Edward Bagby Pollard. There is no definitive evidence that Edward Bagby Pollard was related to Lulie Pollard Wharton, although it is highly likely.
68. Pollard, "Fifth Study: Studying A Town—Essential Facts," *Our Duty to the Community*, n.p.
69. The bibliography included two books by Shailer Mathews, *The Social Gospel* and *The Individual and the Social Gospel*; one by Samuel Zane Batten, *The Social Task of Christianity*; and another by Charles Gardner, *The Ethics of Jesus and Social Progress*. It is worth noting that Mathews was not only an early leader and author in the Social Gospel movement but a liberal Northern Baptist theologian who became dean of the University of Chicago Divinity School. Samuel Zane Batten, also a Northern Baptist, helped establish a core organization in the Social Gospel movement, the Brotherhood of the Kingdom. Charles S. Gardner, a professor of sociology at the Southern Baptist Theological Seminary in Kentucky, would have been the most familiar name to Southern Baptists, but he also endorsed the Social Gospel.
70. Samuel Zane Batten, "Modern Miracles of the Church in Health Conservation," in *The New Chivalry—Health*, ed. James E. McCulloch (Nashville, TN: Southern Sociological Congress, 1915).
71. *Royal Service*, Mar. 1916, 13.
72. *Royal Service*, Mar. 1916, 13.
73. *Royal Service*, Mar. 1916, 13.
74. *WMU Annual Report* (1915), 59. The bibliography and recommended reading section of the Feb. 1914 *Royal Service* listed Graham Taylor's book *Religion in Social Action* in addition to recommending the reports of the 1913 and 1914 Southern Sociological Congresses.
75. *Royal Service*, Aug. 1917, 8–10.
76. *Our Mission Fields*, Oct.–Dec. 1913, 29.
77. For anti-Social Gospel sentiment among Southern Baptist leaders, see James J. Thompson Jr., *Tried as by Fire: Southern Baptists and the Religious Controversies of the 1920s* (Macon, GA: Mercer Univ. Press, 1982).
78. Minutes of the Woman's Missionary Societies, Auxiliary to Baptist State Convention of North Carolina (1898), NCBHC.

79. *Royal Service*, Oct. 1921, 28.
80. *Handbook of Personal Service*, 7.
81. "Some Questions Answered," Personal Service Notebooks, WMUA.
82. *WMU Annual Report* (1913), 41.
83. *Our Mission Fields*, July 1909, 6.
84. *Our Mission Fields*, July 1909, 8.
85. *WMU Annual Report* (1915), 59–60.
86. Again, Southern Baptist progressives, like the majority of Progressive Era reformers, were blind to the social injustice of segregation and the moral scandal of white supremacy.

Five

MAKING A HOME IN THE NEW "HOUSE BEAUTIFUL"

The Woman's Missionary Union Training School Negotiates Change and Decline, 1942–1963

T. Laine Scales

In 1942, Doris Devault walked quickly from her dormitory lobby "in a little huddle" of five students enrolled at the Woman's Missionary Union (WMU) Training School, affectionately known as "House Beautiful."[1] The young women were on their way to take a New Testament class at the neighboring Southern Baptist Theological Seminary (Southern) in Louisville, Kentucky. They were among the first women to enter the classrooms of the seminary in nearly sixteen years. While enrollment at Southern had been restricted to men since its 1859 founding in Greenville, South Carolina, after its 1878 relocation to Louisville, it allowed women from the nearby WMU Training School to sit in on classes with men. When Southern moved from its downtown location to the suburbs in 1926, the women's school stayed downtown, so women stopped attending seminary classes. By 1942, however, the women's school had purchased property adjacent to Southern, built a new building, and resumed the arrangement of women attending some classes with seminary men.

Devault and her peers, as well as Southern's male students and professors, had to grow accustomed, once again, to at least some "coed" classrooms. Thus, when the learned professor called from his class roll for "Brother Devault" to respond to his question, he was surprised to see a woman rise for recitation. Devault, however, was well-prepared for his question, and she promptly delivered the correct response. In her words, "It just happened that going down one hill and up the other that morning I had read the footnotes," she recalled. Meanwhile, the other four women from her huddle sat "in fear and trembling" through the rest of the class hoping they would not be called on to recite.[2]

At the time of this incident, the WMU officially had been operating its Training School, informally called House Beautiful, for nearly thirty-five years. While there were other Southern Baptist women's colleges and programs, House Beautiful had been the first and the only school officially sponsored by WMU. The nickname, first used by WMU President Fannie Heck, referenced John Bunyan's *Pilgrim's Progress* in which House Beautiful was the house of learning for the daughters.[3] The school had begun in 1904 as a collection of "Ladies Courses" at Southern Seminary for women called to serve as missionaries. In 1907, the Woman's Missionary Union Training School was chartered after controversy with Southern Baptists who worried that the school would prepare women to preach. Over the next three decades the school expanded its programs beyond missionary preparation to develop two growing professions: religious education and social work. House Beautiful had its own principal and WMU board of trustees. Approximately 4,200 students enrolled between 1908 and 1962, and the school had awarded 2,017 bachelor's and master's degrees and certificates.[4] Not surprisingly, the Training School was the pride of the WMU and undoubtedly the "Crown Jewel" of Southern Baptist women's education.

Devault's years of study at the Training School occurred in what seemed like a bright new era following nearly four decades of successful operation. Its new home in the suburbs was symbolic of the WMU's hopes and aspirations regarding the school. Built in 1941, it cost 350,000 dollars, a number astounding for the time and also because it came from the contributions of everyday WMU women. Nevertheless, in spite of what seemed a hopeful new beginning as World War II came to an end, the Training School instead entered a period of steep and steady decline, which ended with the SBC taking over its operation in 1957 and eventually closing the school in 1963. This downhill trajectory put the Training School at odds not only with expectations but also with the rest of the denomination, which experienced a period of growth and expansion in the years after World War II. Indeed, scholars have long regarded these as the golden years of Southern Baptist Convention (SBC).

After World War II, the South experienced a period of unprecedented economic prosperity, prompting the emergence of the new Sunbelt South.

The SBC and its funding mechanism, the Cooperative Program, another brainchild of WMU women, benefited greatly from many of its members' new middle-class wealth. Expanding access to theological education, the SBC added three new theological seminaries across the nation by establishing Golden Gate in California (1944), Southeastern in North Carolina (1951), and Midwestern in Missouri (1957).[5] Alongside traditional church and academic historians, then, Southern Baptists have celebrated this story of denominational success in terms of numbers, money, and bureaucratization, often presenting growth as a sign of God's blessing.

As I will demonstrate, however, this standard interpretation is incomplete. When we reimagine the denomination's history by including the often-invisible story of its women, the historical narrative grows more complex. While the SBC and its all-male seminaries flourished, its foremost postgraduate institution for women struggled for survival and was eventually closed by the denomination. In contrast to the accepted history of the SBC, the Training School's story is more a tale of loss and one that compelled Southern Baptist women to rethink, and reimagine, their roles and opportunities in the denomination. In this chapter, then, I complicate the prevailing narrative of Southern Baptists and the SBC in the postwar period by exploring the Training School from the perspective of its women students, faculty, and administrators. From their perspectives, the story is hardly seamless, as Southern Baptist women certainly were not monolithic and their records present competing narratives both in their interpretations of the past and their hopes for the future.

Especially in the immediate postwar era, the Training School often served, sometimes inadvertently, as a path to marriage for numerous students. The physical relocation near Southern in 1941 facilitated that trend, as did the greater freedom awarded to Training School students in this era. At the same time, an increasing number of students advocated for more direct access to Southern and even equal access to the denominational opportunities afforded to men, thereby foreshadowing the developments of the 1970s, when women started to enroll in MDiv programs at Southern. For these women, closing the Training School might not have represented the loss of independence it did for others. Both of these trends, whether the focus was on marriage or equality with male peers, were often at odds with the goals of traditional WMU women, who wanted to keep the Training School viable as a separate school to prepare women for existing careers in the denomination, even if that institutional independence meant a somewhat lower status for the school and its women.

The eventual closing of the Training School mirrors a national postwar story in which women's schools from earlier eras declined as women entered higher education in unprecedented numbers, including coeducational graduate studies and denominational seminaries. By the 1950s, the largest Protestant denominational bodies of Methodists and Presbyterians were training women as ministers alongside men and ordaining them as full clergy. While I show that Southern Baptists slowly followed these trends in opening their seminaries to women, the denomination also maintained narrow choices for women graduates as the majority of its congregations limited roles for women, forbidding them clergy positions and confining them to non-ordained service.

"Our Students Are Adults," or Marriage and Dating in the Postwar House Beautiful

In 1904, when Southern opened its classes to single women, its male faculty asked the women to "take no public part," or, in other words, to sit silently in the classroom.[6] None could take an official seminary degree. As the women students joined the all-male classes again in 1942, they experienced significant changes in classroom culture. Unlike previous periods, when women sat silently alongside men, they were now expected to participate vocally, with professors regularly calling on them, as the experience of Devault demonstrated.

Women's participation, however, was not the only change. Student life in the new location reflected wider opportunities for social activities, and without the chaperonage of earlier decades. While the earliest students attended almost all of their social events in one large group, the midcentury Training School student could now tailor her own social activities to her interests and opportunities. In addition to their coursework, women students at the Training School maintained a vibrant student life and an active Student Government Association, whose handbook from this era contained a description of numerous clubs, organizations, and regulations. The women students of this era advocated for and gained more freedoms such as staying out later at night (curfew 11 p.m.), and there was no "lights out" time at House Beautiful as there had been in the early years, prompting the handbook by 1954 to pronounce: "Dormitory regulations . . . are based on the assumption that our students are adults. Therefore, the specific 'do's' and 'don'ts' have been reduced to minimum essentials for an orderly routine for group living."[7]

It may seem ironic that despite changes leading to a greater sense of independence, an increasing number of Training School women found themselves drawn to marriage. But the proximity to Southern, along with a newfound freedom, made dating and thus "falling in love" more likely, at least for some. This also reflected the rise of marriage and the nuclear family ideal after World War II, when many young people in American culture were focused on finding a spouse and starting a family. Marriage rates peaked in 1946, with couples marrying early, leading to the baby boom of 1946 to 1964. Historians of women's higher education point to the postwar era as a time when college women prioritized marriage and family in addition to education, and certain Training School women followed suit.[8] While marriage proposals had often been a part of life for many Training School students, with Southern Baptist culture generally encouraging and blessing such Louisville engagements, they escalated during this period. Indeed, on page after page, WMU magazines from this period praised Christian wives and mothers, and this emphasis on marriage and domesticity certainly affected Training School culture.[9]

The Training School's move in 1941 to be adjacent to Southern increased contact between seminary men and training school women, which was enhanced by dating practices that moved from the more tightly controlled practice of "calling" to allow women students more freedom. Indeed, the House Beautiful parlors were increasingly used for dates in the afternoons or evenings up until 11 p.m.[10] One of the symbols of a larger emphasis on courtship and marriage in the 1950s was the nicknaming of the "Valley of Decision," a clearing among the beech trees between House Beautiful and the seminary campus in which many marriage proposals took place.[11]

Of course, women came to the Training School because of their own sense of God's "calling" or "call" to Christian service, which was usually missionary work. The WMU cultivated an ethos of "call" early on in the lives of Southern Baptist girls who were instructed to listen carefully to the Spirit. If men were called to preaching ministry, women could be called to missions. And while on the one hand marriage was celebrated in Southern Baptist life, WMU tradition still cultivated respect for the single woman leader who did not divide her time between career and family but focused exclusively on her work for the mission cause. Turn-of-the-century heroines, such as Charlotte "Lottie" Moon, provided historic models for the single woman servant, and contemporary midcentury models of single women leaders were also part of the daily life of the school. The Training School's principals of this era, Carrie Littlejohn (1931–1951) and Emily Lansdell (1951–1958), along with many of the women faculty, were single. Despite growing marital rates, then, many women had chosen the Training School as a means of educational preparation to follow particular callings and career paths. Falling in love with a man added complications to their commitments. And this often led to intense internal conflict.

Not atypical were the experiences of the sisters Pearl and Helen Holmes, daughters of a Baptist preacher in Georgia. They attended the Training School in the late 1940s and early 1950s to answer what they felt was God's call to missions. At this point, however, the concept of call in Southern Baptist life and culture was being extended to include responsibilities beyond church and denominational service. For women especially, one's calling could include marriage and motherhood. A young woman might not only be called to missions but could be called to marriage, to serving as a pastor's wife, or even to service as a missionary's wife, as the Foreign Mission Board appointed men officially as missionaries and women to serve (without compensation) as a partner and helper. Thus, as the Holmes sisters were being pursued by Southern men, with both sisters expressing ambivalence about choosing between a calling to missions and a life as a wife and mother, the Training School's principal, Emily Lansdell, insisted that "the Lord does not call in conflicting directions." In the end, both sisters married Southern graduates. Pearl married Wallace Duvall, and they served as missionaries in Nigeria for fifteen years while raising five children. Helen married W. C. "Dub" Ruchti, and the couple raised one daughter while serving as missionaries in Italy.[12]

While the Holmes sisters still graduated and followed their missionary callings, an increasing number of women chose marriage in place of attending or graduating from the Training School. The era's focus on marriage certainly contributed to the school's decline. Romantic love could be a distraction, and women might now follow "the Lord's call" in the direction of marriage and motherhood, indeed a temptation with the men of Southern pursuing godly wives. Moreover, as times were once again changing, women also found viable options and career paths elsewhere, and as many Training School students saw it, coeducational institutions were the wave of the future.

Seeking Seminary Admission as Southern Students

Despite the Training School's attempt to treat its women students more as adults, with their own choices and freedom, and thereby change with the times, an increasing number of its students expressed unhappiness, again brought on by the proximity to Southern. Their expressions of discontent mirrored the strivings of other postwar-era women who found their limited options to be overly restrictive. Such students perceived the House Beautiful curriculum, which had traditionally included subjects such as elocution, piano, domestic science, and nursing, to be out of date. While there had been certain changes to the curriculum such as the addition of courses in the emerging professions of social work and religious education, for some women, those changes were not extensive enough. According to Principal Carrie Littlejohn, students of 1950 "were interested in Bible, theology, and such courses, but had no interest in the 'little study courses at the Training School.'"[13]

Relatedly, some women students felt undervalued, expressing a desire for equality with seminary men and the few other women who had enrolled directly in Southern's music school. As early as 1943, women were allowed to enter Southern as students but in the music program only. Their entrance frustrated many Training School women. "We are looked down on here on the campus as Training School girls," one complained. "The Music School girls are part of the Seminary and we are not."[14] To be enrolled directly into the flagship seminary of the SBC would elevate their status. They had been proving that they could hold their own in Bible and theology classes with the men. In their eyes, it was a simple administrative change to allow their enrollment. For the SBC, however, admitting women into its seminaries was no small matter.

In a controversial move, a few of these women sidestepped their administration, particularly the Training School's principal, Carrie Littlejohn, to pursue a merger of the Training School with Southern, hoping they would be able to enroll directly in seminary courses. Rather than approach the WMU trustees or Littlejohn herself, in 1950 they went instead to those they viewed as having the power to make change: members of the Southern faculty.

Littlejohn understood the gravity of what the students were asking, and having been principal for nearly three decades, she was particularly incensed at the way they had handled the matter. She showed her fury in a letter to the Training School trustees, women of the WMU: "If that were not so pathetic (in its revelation of the spirit, the immaturity and utter lack of understanding of basic ethics in human relationships) it would be funny. . . . For a group of students to be so presumptuous as to think they could give away an institution with assets worth around three-quarters of a million dollars or to initiate plans to change its basic policies without so much as 'by-your-leave' from the owners, would raise the blood pressure of a calmer person than I am!"[15]

Perhaps most hurtful, Littlejohn felt that the students placed little value in the curriculum she had worked so hard to adapt and strengthen. From her perspective, the Training School was changing with the times. She immediately gathered the student body, firmly chastising the students for their actions, and reported to the WMU that she "tried to make them see that to accept all that the [Training] School is doing for them and to attempt at the same time to undermine its work is ingratitude of the worst type, and unethical from every point of view."[16]

Despite Littlejohn's efforts, the women's petitioning for direct and full enrollment signaled changing times. The WMU had created a separate school for women for the very reason that, in 1904, the coeducation idea had been rejected outright and by women as well as men. By 1948, Southern had reversed its previous decision, even moving beyond admitting women into its music program, when its trustees authorized the seminary "to admit qualified women who are wholly committed to an educational ministry and who have completed the Master of Religious Education at the Training School as candidates for the B.D. [Bachelor of Divinity] and Th.D. degrees."[17]

Two important clarifications, however, still reinforced women's limited roles. First, the statement specified that the women were to prepare for educational ministry rather than pastoral ministry. Second, it also stipulated women could earn a Southern degree only after receiving one from the Training School first. These qualifiers limited significantly the pool of eligible women while benefiting the Training School. So, in 1949, it was only after completing the MRE degree at the Training School that Helen Armstrong became the first woman to enroll in the Southern's School of Theology, and in 1950, she was the first to graduate with a BD, which later became the MDiv. Her comments recalling her motivations roughly twenty-eight years later are telling: "My two years at the Training School had opened some doors," she said, "but I wanted to know more." In addition, she made clear that she, or "Brother Armstrong" as "kiddingly called by some," was "not intending the degree for a pastorate but perhaps to teach or do counseling or both."[18]

In 1950, Littlejohn assured the WMU trustees that the problem was over and that "the 'movement' in its aggressive form seemed to disintegrate."[19] However, the writing was already on the wall. This action by the students, though curtailed in the moment, would foreshadow the changes that would take place within the next decade.

Carver School of Missions and Social Work

While Helen Armstrong (Wright) was the first woman to receive the BD in 1950, women taking music and religious education courses at Southern had been bypassing the Training School as a means to gain theological education since the 1940s. In fact, the Training School accelerated Southern's music program when, in 1943, it eliminated its own music courses and began contributing $15,000 each year to Southern for opening its music classes to Training School women. The largest gift to the seminary came in 1945 when, over the private objections of some key WMU leaders, the WMU gave Southern $50,000 for its new building program. Opponents within the WMU believed that the SBC's Cooperative Program, still largely funded by church women, should cover the cost of the building project.[20]

If the small group of Training School students who advocated a merger with Southern frustrated Littlejohn, their actions signaled the coming trend as women advocated for more choices about their preparation for church work. Littlejohn's retirement in 1951 and a growing concern over declining enrollment stirred a reexamination of the school's purpose and vision.[21] The Training School needed a visionary leader who could think broadly about the possibilities and consider new directions. In 1951, the WMU chose Emily K. Lansdell, a former Southern Baptist missionary and teacher in China. Lansdell's parents had been students at Southern at the turn of the twentieth century. In fact, her mother had been one of the seminary wives sitting in classes before the Training School officially began. After earning a BA at Coker College in her native state of Georgia, Emily Lansdell earned an MA degree in English from Duke University and another in Oriental languages from Yale University. Her strong educational credentials and Southern Baptist pedigree made her well-suited for serving at the helm of the Training School.[22]

Lansdell and the WMU's Training School trustees explored several options for redirection. The Training School and Southern Seminary faculties also gave their input. Training School faculty minutes reveal a great deal of effort to imagine what changes might result in increased enrollment, an important part of financial stability. Four courses of action were considered by the faculty on October 11, 1951, with a lengthy discussion of each: first, "to be absorbed into the Seminary"; second, "admit girls to a school of religious education [at the Seminary] and the Training School will go on as it is"; third, "a missions department of the Seminary"; and fourth, "to become a co-ed School of Missions and Social Work with greatly enlarged faculty and budget."[23] As the meeting came to a close, the Training School faculty decided to consult the two SBC mission boards to determine denominational needs. The Home Mission Board and the Foreign Mission Board, along with the WMU, had been the primary employers of Training School graduates and would likely have ideas about what type of curriculum would best prepare their future workers.[24] In addition, the WMU had been formed as an auxiliary to the SBC and its mission boards and still often deferred to their opinions.

After months of deliberation and consultation, the final recommendation of the trustees was announced at the WMU's annual meeting in 1952 in Miami, with the women voting to make three organizational changes. The curriculum would be altered to focus on social work as well as missions; the school would open its doors to male students and pursue racial integration; and finally, to denote the new emphasis and express gratitude for longtime supporter and Southern professor W. O. Carver, the school would take a new name: the Carver School of Missions and Social Work (Carver).[25] That was not all, though. When WMU approved the proposed changes during its annual meeting on May 12, 1952, it also approved a building expansion. The SBC had allocated $320,000 from the Cooperative Program for an additional wing for the ten-year-old building to provide more offices, classrooms, and library space.[26]

As the changes took effect in 1953, the newly named school worked to create its new image even as it assured past supporters that these developments would be gradual and continue the historic goals of the Training School. Its brochures indicated, for instance, that while men would be admitted, the preparation of Carver graduates would still remain "different from that of the pastor and the educational director of a local Baptist church." In addition, missionaries on furlough and newly appointed mission candidates could complete a curriculum for "advanced missionary training."[27] Most significantly, perhaps, a new word entered the vocabulary of Southern Baptists: *church social work*.

The word conveyed that sense of the new but as a means to promote traditional Southern Baptist values. Social work courses had been taught at the Training School for decades, but the qualifier "church" signaled a particular kind of social work that usually took place in a denominational agency and had evangelism as its central focus. After describing how church social workers might serve in a variety of roles in churches, schools, hospitals, children's homes, Good Will Centers, and even mission work overseas, one 1955 brochure, for instance, emphasized the primary theme of evangelism: "The motivating purpose of the school and its graduates is that all peoples may be introduced to Jesus Christ and made whole by Him."[28]

While the new plan did not reflect shifts in ownership or control, the discussion may have sparked side conversations about the WMU's role in Carver's future. In fact, in his recounting of the school's history, George A. Carver, faculty member at Carver and nephew of the school's namesake, suggested that at this time the WMU was already considering the possibility that Carver "would eventually become an agency of the SBC."[29] To maintain its focus and guard its finances, throughout the 1950s the WMU had divested from some of its more successful programs, as the SBC assumed direct control over initiatives that had long been under the purview of the WMU. This strategy also reflected the expanding reach of WMU programs and its women's increasing sense of partnership with other SBC entities. The mission boards, for example, took control of allocating the WMU's Annie Armstrong Easter and Lottie Moon Christmas offerings collected annually.[30] And the Home Mission Board gradually took over the WMU's Good Will Centers. Such transfers may have prompted some WMU women to reconsider the WMU's ownership of Carver, but at least for the moment, the WMU promised to keep the school under its wing.

Racial Integration at the Training School

Students at Carver were very similar demographically to those who attended the Training School in its earliest days: white women from Southern Baptist colleges and churches, steeped in WMU culture, and often recruited by WMU women they knew. Yet within the next few years, the first male student and the first two African American female students would appear.[31] While Louis Stone, citing the opportunity for graduate study in social work with a free tuition, entered Carver in 1953 as the first full-time white male student, very few men followed. This was largely because Southern opened its new School of Religious Education shortly afterwards. In 1955, two years after Stone, two African American women enrolled in Carver, integrating the school racially as well.

When Carver opened its doors to students of any race in 1952, its actions followed Southern, which integrated officially in 1951. Kentucky's Day Law, enacted in 1934, had made it illegal for African American and white students to attend school together, but the Day Law was amended in March of 1950 to exempt higher education institutions, thus making a way for both the Training School and Southern to integrate racially. As soon as the Day Law amendment allowed desegregation, Southern students were polled, with 94.7 percent in favor of integrating their classrooms. This strength of opinion contrasted with the negative attitudes most Southern Baptists had toward racial integration at the time.

While Southern's move to integrate in 1951 may have inspired Carver to admit African American students, it was not the only influence. WMU women were historically more progressive in terms of racial reconciliation than their

SBC brethren, as documented by their working relationship with the African American women of the National Baptist Convention.[32] Carver, along with Southern, would be among the first Southern Baptist schools to open their doors to African Americans. Other Southern Baptist schools moved more slowly, with some considered "white flight" destinations. For example, another decade would pass before Baylor University in Waco, Texas, the world's largest Baptist university, would vote to admit African American students.[33]

As both Southern and Carver moved toward integration, Dr. Guy Bellamy, the Home Mission Board secretary to the Department of Work with Negroes, began searching for African American women students whose education the board would support in a bid to hire them for the department afterward. Bellamy was part of an expanding outlook of the Home Mission Board as the agency broadened its focus from evangelism and church plants to address the important social issues of the day. In short, Bellamy needed African American employees to successfully expand the ministries of the Department of Work with Negroes. Two students from Oklahoma were willing to take on the venture, and Carver admitted Freddie Mae Bason and Verlene Farmer in the fall of 1955. Both women belonged to churches associated with the National Baptist Convention and were members of the National Baptist Woman's Auxiliary, a group that cooperated with WMU in joint mission projects.[34] Each felt called to church service. Their enrollment at Carver was a groundbreaking moment of racial integration in Southern Baptist history, and the stories of Bason and Farmer offer a glimpse into the experiences of African American women involved with Southern Baptists in this era.

When Freddie Mae Bason grew up in segregated Oklahoma City, she had longed to serve in a church. "I wanted to be in full time Christian service, but I knew that was only a dream," she recalled years later.[35] It was not simply that Bason was a woman; she had only seen white women fulfill this role. Bason's educational background was extensive. She had attended Langston University, a college serving African American students in Langston, Oklahoma; the Oklahoma School of Religion, a National Baptist Convention-supported institution that trained ministers, Christian workers, and laypersons; and the University of Tulsa. She met Bellamy through summer mission work. As she remembered, "they wanted students to integrate Carver School, and he [Bellamy] asked me to do that. That's about it. I had finished the Oklahoma School of Religion, and I was working in Tulsa, and then he [Bellamy] knew about it and asked my pastor to pray all about it."[36]

Bason was pragmatic, and, supported by her pastor, she wanted assurance that employment would follow her tenure at Carver. While only 5 percent of African American women attended college in this era, they still failed to locate employment equaling their educational qualifications. In fact, most working African American women remained employed as domestic servants until the 1960s.[37] Bason's pastor, T. O. Chappell, queried Guy Bellamy about her employment prospects, indicating that he had influence over her decision. According to Bason, "he talked with Guy Bellamy, and he says, 'Now, the only reason I'm gonna let her go depends on how you're gonna answer this question. Will you have a job for her when she gets out?'"[38] Bellamy assured Chappell that a job would be waiting at the Home Mission Board.

A fellow Oklahoman, Verlene Famer, also had become interested in missionary work as a child and had attended Langston University. While doing summer missionary work in the urban areas of several major American cities, Farmer met Bellamy, who promptly asked her to enroll in Carver, even before she had completed her senior year at Langston.[39] As the women prepared to go to Louisville together, the WMU of Oklahoma, led by Margaret Fairborne, raised scholarship funds. When the time came to go, both women had some concern about moving to attend the all-white Carver. Bason recalled: "Definitely, I was quite apprehensive, because this was a new . . . venture, and history at that point had not been very kind, and I just really didn't know what to expect . . . I was afraid . . . that Verlene and I would always be looked at and probably not treated very well, but we were willing to take the venture . . . we really wanted to be in full-time Christian service, and this was an avenue to which we could pursue."[40]

When they arrived, Bason and Farmer were greeted at the Louisville bus station by two of their white Carver classmates.[41] Carver integrated Bason and Farmer into dormitory life by assigning each a white roommate. Farmer found her roommate, Alice Carver, granddaughter of W. O. Carver, to be a good friend. As Farmer related nearly sixty years later, "Alice was not prejudiced, and Alice loved the Lord and loved people, and that's what helped me so much."[42] While Farmer's recollections generally contrast with the experiences of many African American women who encountered far more overt forms racism as they bravely integrated institutions of higher education across the South, the prejudices of Carver students may have been more subtle. And perhaps the long relationship between the white women of the WMU and the African American women of the National Baptist Convention, complicated as that relationship might have been, had prepared Carver for a culture of more thorough integration than in some other schools. Or perhaps they judged the school in relative terms; for in spite of their generally positive recollections of Carver, Bason and Farmer found the broader Louisville community unwelcoming. The women recalled numerous instances of being denied entry to movie theaters, restaurants, and even some churches.[43]

Verlene Farmer left Carver after only a year and returned to Langston University to complete her undergraduate education, which was put on hold when she matriculated at Carver. From there, she was called to the mission field of Liberia, Africa, where she served with Suehn Industrial Mission, a project supported by the National Baptist Convention. Freddie Mae Bason stayed on to graduate in 1957, and true to his word, Bellamy ensured that she found employment.[44] For the rest of her career she worked in Atlanta with the Home Mission Board serving urban community centers, local churches, and volunteering as editor of *The Worker*, a magazine published by the women of the NBC.[45] While Bason's graduation might have seemed a turning point, after both Farmer and Bason left Carver, no other African American students followed them for nearly a decade. Carver's efforts to recruit and support Bason and Farmer, as well as Stone, were noteworthy at the time, but the strategy of integration did not significantly alter the makeup or boost the numbers of Carver's student population.

Further Decline

As Carver trustees, faculty, students, and other supporters watched carefully, hoping that new strategies would bring the anticipated increase in enrollment, they were sorely disappointed. In the 1956–57 session, only 86 students enrolled compared to 112 in the previous session. The ever-declining numbers of students resulted in a financial crisis, and the school struggled to meet its payroll for five full-time and ten part-time faculty, its president, and several supporting staff members.[46]

A few years earlier, the WMU had boldly requested the SBC Executive Committee increase its funding for the women's school. In terms of allocations for theological education, the Cooperative Program supported six seminaries and Carver, with the latter receiving 1 percent of the funds. The request was to increase allocations by a half percent, equaling 1.5 percent of the Cooperative Program budget.[47] Ironically, WMU women had been among the most enthusiastic supporters of the Cooperative Program, which was the SBC's centralized funding entity, since its inception in 1924 and had shown their support by encouraging women to give to the Cooperative Program rather than the WMU directly. Time and time again, WMU women had salvaged the SBC and the Cooperative Program from financial disaster.[48] Now, when they needed more funding from the Cooperative Program, their request was denied based on the fact that Carver was not under SBC control. According to the WMU historian Catherine Allen, several male leaders already considered Carver an unnecessary drain on funds.[49] The SBC, after denying the request, created a committee to study the situation.

In the midst of Carver's financial crisis, Lansdell offered her resignation to its board of trustees, only three years after her appointment to replace Littlejohn. Her March 1954 letter to Olive Martin, the board's chair, indicated that she felt the need to make way for a new president who would be "a vigorous administrator and one who was qualified to direct a graduate program."[50] Martin notified trustees of the resignation letter in July, adding information not included in Lansdell's letter. "In resigning," Martin wrote, "Miss Lansdell expressed the feeling that perhaps the time had come when a man could better administrate the affairs of the school. She did not want to stand in the way of a change that might benefit the school."[51] Kay Bigham, a faculty member who knew Lansdell well, later stated: "I think she [Lansdell] was trying to be realistic. I think her foremost interest was to have the content that she felt essential for missionary service, no matter where. . . . And I think she was convinced that it could be more readily accepted by having a man in leadership."[52]

Although women had made strides within the SBC over its centennial history, many WMU women, even leaders like Lansdell, recognized that most Southern Baptists probably preferred male leadership. Lansdell's concern for missions apparently led her to place this preference above her own interests—in the self-sacrificial manner of many Southern women—in order to advance training for future missionaries. Lansdell did indicate in her letter a willingness to continue serving temporarily until a new president was hired, which would be another two years.

With no resurgence in enrollment, the SBC leadership expressed increasing impatience with the redesigned Carver School. An ultimatum was coming, as described in the Georgia Baptists' state newspaper: "The Southern Baptist Convention will be asked next month to either assume operation of the Carver School of Missions and Social Work at Louisville, Ky. or discontinue sharing in its financial support."[53] Frustrated that the SBC provided half the funding, apart from student fees, " but has had no voice in management," the Special Committee on Theological Education recommended that Carver operate as an institution of the SBC, which would elect half the trustees while the WMU elected the other half.[54] In 1956, in response to the Theological Education Committee's analysis, the SBC requested that the WMU turn over Carver to the denomination.

As the nation and the SBC experienced newfound wealth and success in this postwar period, and the denomination underwent a period of reorganization and bureaucratization, its male leadership expanded its oversight to the formerly independent women's school. And WMU women, now unable to support the school on their own, accepted this development. In 1957, following its celebration of the fiftieth anniversary of the Training School, the WMU voted for the transfer.[55] It was clearly a vote of desperation and came at a high cost, for the assets that the WMU simply transferred to the SBC were considerable: approximately $1 million, which included Carver's land, buildings, equipment, and funds.[56] Such assets had come from the early sacrifices of WMU women, mostly without their own incomes, sharing their pennies and dimes to support women's missionary education. That the women had launched an enterprise worth such a sum by the 1950s was remarkable, which makes their transferring it without remuneration all the more poignant. Perhaps, on one level, the women of the WMU really did believe their wealthier "big brother," the SBC, could now more adequately provide for the school's needs. But at the end of the day, with their funds waning and within their conservative context, WMU leaders had little choice.

"The Women Did Not Understand That the School Would Be Killed"

After fifty years of female leadership, Carver found itself at the close of the 1950s under the umbrella of the male-dominated SBC. A board of thirty male and female Carver School trustees appointed by the SBC (with fifteen of those names recommended by the WMU) would manage the school's affairs. Additionally, in 1958, Dr. Nathan C. Brooks, a Pensacola pastor and Carver trustee, was named as Lansdell's replacement.[57] Within the first year of his presidency, when the newly appointed trustees proceeded to discuss Carver's future, some immediately advocated for its closure. Brooks pleaded that they give the school, and himself as its leader, some time. In 1959, he reminded one trustee of the SBC's obligation to safeguard the school the WMU had given to it: "Let me point out again the moral obligation to Woman's Missionary Union that the Convention assumed in taking over the School. The women did not understand that the school would be killed. They did understand that if it did not prove itself that it might be closed. However, it was definitely understood that there would be an opportunity for the School to prove itself."[58]

However, in 1962, after Brooks and his faculty tried and failed to achieve accreditation from the Council on Social Work Education, the trustees voted to close Carver and merge its assets with Southern's School of Religious Education. Both Carver and the School of Religious Education were hesitant about this "shotgun wedding." Carver's alumni association predicted that the "ultimate result shall be the complete dissolution of Carver School programs and the purposes for which the institution was founded." Once it merged with Southern, they predicted, the SBC leadership would destroy the institution that many Southern Baptist women had worked sacrificially to create.[59]

The agreed upon merger was carried out in 1963 with no Carver faculty members, most of whom were women, hired on to teach at Southern, whose faculty remained all male. When Carver was absorbed into Southern at this time, the WMU's endowment was used to fund several scholarships, as well as the Woman's Missionary Union Chair of Social Work, which was, not surprisingly, filled by a male.

The merger with Southern did eventually provide a pathway to future success for social work as an area of study. The power and resources of the SBC's flagship seminary and its male faculty drew support from the Home Mission Board and other SBC agencies to grow the program under the umbrella of Religious Education. When Carver graduate Anne Davis was hired in 1970 to teach social work as one of Southern's first women faculty members, she was instrumental in developing a reimagined Carver School. And in 1984, Davis became Southern's first woman dean of the Carver School of Church Social Work as well as Southern's first woman dean in any school or unit.[60] The new Carver School was coeducational, focused on preparing denominational workers with master of social work degrees, and, in 1987, accredited by the Council on Social Work Education.

After initial success in its first decade, the story told in this chapter came to repeat itself but within the context of a public storm of media attention as the Southern Baptist Convention was splitting at the seams. In 1997, in the midst of intense battles over women's proper role in church leadership and social work's place in the denominational agenda, Southern closed the doors of the Carver School of Church Social Work. Thus ended the House Beautiful legacy of WMU that provided a place of leadership for Southern Baptist women in social work, religious education, and missions. As Southern's only woman dean and the women faculty from Carver and other areas of the seminary departed, Southern's faculty and administration returned to emphasize male presence and power, looking at the century's close very much as it did at its opening.

Notes

1. This chapter is an adaptation of chapter three in T. Laine Scales and Melody Maxwell, *"Doing the Word": Southern Baptists' Carver School of Church Social Work and its Predecessors, 1907–1997* (Knoxville: Univ. of Tennessee Press, 2019).
2. Carrie Littlejohn, interview by Doris DeVault, Apr. 16, 1979, Birmingham, AL, tape recording and transcript, WMU Archives (WMUA), WMU Training School/ Carver School Collection, National WMU Office, Birmingham, AL, 6.
3. Carrie Littlejohn, *History of Carver School of Missions and Social Work* (Nashville, TN: Broadman Press, 1958), 42. Isla May Mullins explains the naming of the school in her institutional history, *House Beautiful* (Nashville, TN: Sunday School Board of the Southern Baptist Convention, 1934), 49.
4. T. Laine Scales, *"All That Fits a Woman": Training Southern Baptist Women for Charity and Mission, 1907–1926* (Macon, GA: Mercer Univ. Press, 2000); George A. Carver, "Carver School of Missions and Social Work, 1907–1962," *The Quarterly Review* 23 (Spring) 1963: 42–43.
5. Charles D. Johnson, *Higher Education of Southern Baptists: An Institutional History, 1826–1954* (Waco, TX: Baylor Univ. Press, 1955).
6. Catalogue, Southern Baptist Theological Seminary, 1902–3 and 1903–4, Southern Baptist Theological Seminary Archives (SBTSA), Southern Baptist Theological Seminary, Louisville, KY.
7. *Student Handbook*, 1954–55, SBTSA, WMU Training School/ Carver School Collection, 16.
8. Linda Eisenmann, *Higher Education for Women in Postwar America, 1945–1965* (Baltimore, MD: Johns Hopkins Univ. Press, 2006), 28.
9. For a detailed analysis of WMU writings on wives and mothers in the 1950s and 1960s, see Melody Maxwell, *The Woman I Am: Southern Baptist Women's Writings 1906–1926* (Tuscaloosa: Univ. of Alabama Press, 2014).
10. *Student Handbook*, 1955–56, SBTSA, WMU Training School/ Carver School Collection, 19.
11. The phrase is a biblical reference to Joel 3:14.
12. "Pearl Holmes Duvall," Southern Baptist Biography Project, circa 1955, Southern Baptist Historical Library and Archives (SBHLA); Pearl Holmes Duvall and Helen Holmes Ruchti, interview by T. Laine Scales, Feb. 8, 2003, in Birmingham, AL, and located in Baylor University Institute of Oral History (BUIOH), Baylor University, Waco, TX, 16.
13. Carrie Littlejohn to Training School Trustees, May 1, 1950, WMUA, WMU Training School/ Carver School Collection.
14. Carrie Littlejohn to Training School Trustees, May 1, 1950.
15. Carrie Littlejohn to Training School Trustees, May 1, 1950.
16. Carrie Littlejohn to Training School Trustees, May 1, 1950.

17. Catalogue, Southern Baptist Theological Seminary, 1950, SBTSA, 20.
18. Helen D. [Armstrong] Wright to Marilyn Helton, Apr. 23, 1978, SBTSA, WMU Training School/ Carver School Collection.
19. Wright to Helton, Apr. 23, 1978.
20. Catherine B. Allen, *A Century to Celebrate: History of Woman's Missionary Union* (Birmingham, AL: Woman's Missionary Union, 1987), 275–76.
21. Allen, *Century to Celebrate*, 278.
22. Littlejohn, *History of Carver School*, 168–69.
23. WMU Training School, Faculty Minutes, Oct. 11, 1951, SBTSA, WMU Training School/ Carver School Collection.
24. WMU Training School, Faculty Minutes, Oct. 11, 1951.
25. WMU Report, *Annual of the Southern Baptist Convention, 1952* (Nashville, TN: Executive Committee of the Southern Baptist Convention, 1952), 47; Littlejohn, *History of Carver School*, 174; C. Anne Davis, "The Carver School of Church Social Work," 1987, Unpublished Manuscript, SBTSA, WMU Training School/ Carver School Collection, 8.
26. Allen, *Century to Celebrate*, 279.
27. Carver School of Social Work and Missions, *A Doorway to Larger Service* (brochure), 1953, SBTSA, WMU Training School/ Carver School Collection.
28. *Carver School of Missions and Social Work* (brochure), 1955, WMUA, WMU Training School/ Carver School Collection.
29. George A. Carver, "Carver School," 39.
30. Allen, *Century to Celebrate*, 224.
31. These stories were originally documented in Tonya S. Brice and T. Laine Scales, "The First and the Last: A Confluence of Factors Leading to the Integration of Carver School of Missions and Social Work, 1955," *Journal of Sociology and Social Welfare* 40, no. 1 (March): 83–100.
32. WMU women's more progressive stance on racial reconciliation is documented by Allen, *Century to Celebrate*, 234, 248; and Paul Harvey, *Freedom's Coming: Religious Culture and the Shaping of the South from the Civil War through the Civil Rights Era* (Chapel Hill: Univ. of North Carolina Press, 2005), 74–75. See, too, the chapters by Carol Crawford Holcomb and Melody Maxwell in this volume.
33. "Baylor Votes to Integrate," *Waco Times-Herald*, Waco, TX, Nov. 2, 1963; Meghan Merchant, "Prof Recalls Racial Integration at BU," *Baylor Lariat*, Feb. 1, 2005.
34. Freddie Mae Bason and Reid Maddox Coons, interview by T. Laine Scales, Feb. 22, 2003, in Atlanta, GA, BUIOH.
35. Bason and Coons, interview by Scales, 2.
36. Bason and Coons, interview by Scales, 3.
37. Eisenmann, *Higher Education for Women*, 27.
38. Freddie Mae Bason, Reid Maddox Coons, and Gloria Wright, interview by Tanya Brice and T. Laine Scales, Oct. 29, 2011, in Decatur, GA, BUIOH, 3.

39. Verlene Farmer Goatley, interview by Tanya Brice and T. Laine Scales, Dec. 10, 2010, in Oklahoma City, BUIOH.
40. Bason and Coons, interview by Scales, 7.
41. Bason and Coons, interview by Scales, 9. As of this writing, Bason and Coons have remained friends for many decades, with both retired to the Atlanta area.
42. Goatley, interview by Brice and Scales, 56.
43. Bason and Coons, interview by Scales, 14.
44. Farmer returned to Langston to complete her undergraduate degree and later served as a missionary to Liberia with the National Baptist Convention. Upon her return home, she directed the Baptist Student Union at Langston. More than fifty years after leaving Louisville, she returned to Kentucky to marry Rev. Wilbert H. Goatley, one of the first African American students to graduate from Southern Seminary. See interview with Goatley.
45. Bason worked first at the Magnolia Street Good Will Center, and when Magnolia closed, the Home Mission Board moved her to the nearby Memorial Drive Baptist Center, where she oversaw the afterschool and family support programs. Alongside her work with the Home Mission Board, Bason maintained ties with the African American women of the National Baptist Convention for the rest of her career. See interview with Bason, Coons, and Wright.
46. Booz, Allen and Hamilton, Report to John P. Sandidge, Apr. 25, 1958, SBTSA, WMU Training School/ Carver School Collection, 12.
47. Allen, *Century to Celebrate*, 279.
48. Allen, *Century to Celebrate*, 286.
49. Allen, *Century to Celebrate*, 279–80.
50. Emily Lansdell to Olive Martin, Mar. 27, 1954, WMUA, WMU Training School/ Carver School Collection.
51. Olive Martin to Trustees, July 1, 1954, WMUA, WMU Training School/ Carver School Collection.
52. Kathryn Bigham, video interview by Catherine Allen, Aug. 2, 1985, in Louisville, KY, SBTSA, WMU Training School/ Carver School Collection.
53. *The Christian Index*, Apr. 5, 1956, 3.
54. *The Christian Index*, Apr. 5, 1956, 3.
55. Allen, *Century to Celebrate*, 280; WMU Report, *Annual of the Southern Baptist Convention, 1958* (Nashville, TN: Executive Committee of the Southern Baptist Convention, 1958), 24.
56. Allen, *Century to Celebrate*, 280.
57. C. Anne Davis, "History of the Carver School of Church Social Work," *Review and Expositor* 85 (Spring 1988): 216.
58. Nathan C. Brooks Jr. to Dr. Douglas M. Branch, Feb. 10, 1959, SBTSA, WMU Training School/ Carver School Collection.
59. "A Resolution Presented to the Carver School Alumni from Six Recent Graduates," June 6, 1962, SBTSA, WMU Training School/ Carver School Collection.
60. C. Anne Davis, interview by T. Laine Scales, Mar. 15, 2005, in Waco, TX, BUIOH.

Six

"A CHRISTIAN ATTITUDE TOWARD OTHER RACES"

Southern Baptist Women and Race Relations, 1945–1965

Melody Maxwell

Southern Baptists were largely resistant to the civil rights movement of the 1950s and 1960s. In 1956, for example, the editor of the *Alabama Baptist*, Leon Macon, deemed desegregation a "grave problem" infringing on individual rights.[1] That same year, W. A. Criswell, pastor of First Baptist Church of Dallas—the SBC's largest church—condemned integrationists as "a bunch of infidels, dying from the neck up."[2] Many other local church leaders expressed disapproval of civil rights activism and prohibited African Americans from joining their congregations. As late as 1964, messengers to the SBC annual meeting rejected a recommendation supporting civil rights legislation.[3] Passionate opposition to racial equality was normative throughout the SBC.

Some Southern Baptist leaders, however, were contextually progressive in their racial attitudes.[4] After World War II, the denomination's Home Mission Board (HMB), Foreign Mission Board (FMB), and Social Service Commission (SSC)—renamed Christian Life Commission (CLC) in 1953—challenged prevalent attitudes toward race among Southern Baptists. The SBC's missions agencies, HMB and FMB, published occasional articles related to race in their magazines, such as "Southern Baptists and Race Relations" and "FMB Asks Race Trouble End."[5] Leaders of these organizations frequently related to people of color on the mission fields, whether through supporting African American Baptist colleges in the United States or urging the evangelization of the African continent. SSC/CLC leaders advocated ideas about racial progress that often raised the ire of SBC conservatives, although civil rights leaders might have considered them inadequate. For example, the organization presented to the SBC in 1947 a "Charter of Principles on Race Relations" and led the denomination to officially observe an annual Race Relations Sunday beginning in 1965.[6] Leaders of these institutions, along with a handful of Southern Baptist professors and other progressives of the era, advanced a new understanding of race within the SBC.

Yet the strongest and broadest promotion of racial equality within the denomination during these years came from Southern Baptist women, a fact that scholars have occasionally noted but infrequently analyzed.[7] Many Southern Baptists, for example, are familiar with T. B. Maston, an ethics professor at Southwestern Baptist Theological Seminary whose teachings and writings on racial justice were influential in the SBC in the mid-twentieth century. But few may be aware of Maston's 1966 assertion that "the Woman's Missionary Union has generally made . . . the most directly challenging approach [in the SBC] to the whole area of race."[8] During this period, the Woman's Missionary Union (WMU), the women's auxiliary to the SBC, published hundreds of articles urging Southern Baptists to reconsider their prejudices and seek the advancement of African Americans, among other actions.

Thus, while leaders at SBC annual meetings argued about race and issued occasional resolutions on the topic, many more Southern Baptists spent month after month in their women's missionary societies studying WMU magazines full of exhortations about the "genuine acceptance" of African Americans.[9] The former were largely male pastors approving one-time statements with which many church members disagreed; the latter were active female laypeople with informal influence both at church and at home. WMU literature had a significant impact on Southern Baptist women as they contemplated article after article on race. Yet this transformation and its effects on the women, their churches, and their families have been underrepresented in the historiography of Southern Baptists. As Alan Scot Willis maintains, "The influence of Baptist literature for women and youth [in shaping attitudes about race] has been underestimated."[10]

Historians have often focused on male-dominated convention institutions and leaders. In his institutional history of the SBC (1994), for example, Jesse Fletcher includes only one sentence about the WMU and race relations—and that related to the WMU's study of Maston's book.[11] Chapter-length studies of the SBC and civil rights by Edward Queen (1991), David Stricklin (1999), and William Tillman (2008) focus almost exclusively on Southern Baptist men.[12] But as my chapter here makes evident, by neglecting women's writings and actions, scholars have overlooked the gradual but powerful efforts of Southern Baptist women toward changing attitudes about race and thus have failed to adequately understand the history of Southern Baptists and race relations.

Indeed, through the WMU—the largest Protestant organization for women in this period—hundreds of thousands of Southern Baptists were encouraged to adopt "a Christian attitude toward other races," as one writer put it in 1952.[13] While WMU leaders sometimes also used their speaking engagements and events to urge racial reconciliation, their monthly magazines for women reached a much larger audience. As many as five hundred thousand Southern Baptists subscribed to the WMU's magazines for women in the mid-twentieth century.[14] These magazines included *Royal Service*, the WMU's flagship magazine for women ages twenty-five and above, and *The Window of YWA* (hereafter *The Window*), for young women sixteen to twenty-four. More Southern Baptists subscribed to these publications than to those of Southern Baptists' predominantly male-controlled FMB, HMB, or CLC—and used them not simply for leisure reading but as part of the regular meetings of their churches' Women's Missionary Societies and Young Women's Auxiliaries.[15]

In addition to having more subscribers, during this period WMU magazines also discussed race more frequently than other Southern Baptist publications.[16] Both *Royal Service* and *The Window* included frank discussions of Southern Baptists' relationships with African Americans. While editors and writers did not directly advocate participation in the civil rights movement, from 1945 to 1965 they repeatedly urged women to probe their racial prejudices and seek to "bring . . . about racial harmony and justice."[17]

Why did Southern Baptist women have more to say about race relations than their male counterparts, even though the primary purpose of their organization was missions? How were WMU leaders able to embrace contextually progressive attitudes at a time when most Southern Baptists were wary of advancement for African Americans? And what effects did these women's emphasis on equality have on Southern Baptists' views of race? Examining questions such as these helps reshape historical understanding of Southern Baptists and race from 1945 to 1965. Based on their sheer numbers of subscribers—not to mention the quantity of articles related to race—an investigation of articles in *Royal Service* and *The Window* during this period is essential to any serious study of Southern Baptists' attitudes about race.

In this chapter, I first analyze the content of these publications and argue for the contextually progressive attitudes that developed among WMU members during this period. I then probe the motivations and progressive leadership that helped advance the organization's advocacy of racial reconciliation, thereby demonstrating that WMU writers consistently defended racial equality, becoming the strongest advocates of this concept within the SBC. Exploring this development, along with WMU members' strategies for navigating their conservative denomination, provides scholars with a more complex and complete understanding of Southern Baptists'—and more broadly, white Southern evangelicals'—attitudes toward African Americans during this tumultuous period.

Developing Attitudes

In the years following World War II, both of the WMU's magazines, *Royal Service* and *The Window*, frequently included articles about race, which a 1946 writer declared "the most acute world problem of today."[18] In an effort to influence readers' views of this contemporary issue, the magazines' programs of study began to regularly feature topics such as "The Sin of Racial Discrimination" and "What Do You Know about the Negro?"[19] These programs constituted the primary study material for WMU groups as they met on a weekly or monthly basis in Women's Missionary Societies for older women and Young Women's Auxiliaries for younger women. Most printed program material included discussion questions and other teaching aids, such as this 1949 suggestion: "Close the program by asking each girl to formulate a question in her own mind relative to what she can do about race tension."[20] Such curriculum plans intensified the impact of the magazines' articles through the women's guided conversation, study, and reflection. Participants likely learned more from interacting with their peers through these WMU-led programs they did from listening to a sermon or reading a column in their state Baptist newspaper.

The idea that racial discrimination was a problem to be addressed, as advanced in *Royal Service* and *The Window* during these years, caused dissent among WMU members, the vast majority of whom were white women living in the racially divided South. Implicitly acknowledging this reality, a large banner at the top of one article on race in *The Window* read, "WARNING: If you are afraid to be disturbed, to make fearless decisions, to think clearly and independently, then don't read this article."[21] Editors obviously intended to challenge readers' thinking; the inclusion of such features in magazines that primarily focused on missions demonstrated the priority these leaders placed on addressing racial prejudices. From the early years of this period, WMU magazines mentioned race more frequently than other SBC publications did. In 1947, for example, *Royal Service* and *The Window* each discussed race about twice as often as did FMB's *Commission* magazine.[22] Among other topics, post-war WMU writers described the achievements of notable African Americans, denounced the Ku Klux Klan, and explained that "in the heart of God, black is as beautiful and dear as white."[23]

Before the landmark 1954 *Brown v. Board of Education* decision, however, *Royal Service* writers were not nearly as likely to criticize segregation as they were after the civil rights movement became an unavoidable reality. Occasional articles that denounced prejudice also mentioned that "each race may have its individual life and yet live in peace and harmony,"[24] displaying an attitude that was common among even "progressive" Southern Baptist leaders of the day. In the midst of paragraphs describing the equality of all people, a few writers briefly defended segregation. A 1946 article proclaimed that "there is nothing unfair to the Negro in our southern policy of segregation" before going on to condemn discrimination and mistreatment on the basis of race.[25] The writers of such features were unwilling to fully acknowledge the injustices inherent in contemporary Southern society.

Such sentiments were not present in *The Window*, however, whose younger audience editors likely felt were more open to new ideas. Instead, multiple articles in that magazine positively portrayed integrated facilities, including a school system in Massachusetts, "many . . . large corporations," and a teacher's college in Washington, DC.[26] Whenever readers had "an opportunity of not being segregated," a 1945 writer counseled, they should "take it quietly."[27] Another proclaimed that segregation was against both "Christian philosophy and the Constitution of the United States."[28] This advice, while not advocating disruption, was unusual for Southern Baptists of the day. Writers joined what Mark Newman calls "a minority of progressive [Southern] Baptists" in criticizing segregation.[29] Although Northern and especially African American Baptists of the day would likely have gone further, the repeated support of integration in *The Window* in the years immediately following World War II was subtlety subversive within its conservative context. Thousands of young Southern Baptist women likely thought twice about their own views after reading such content.

Even in these early years, both *Royal Service* and *The Window* were more likely than other Southern Baptist publications to include articles challenging both segregation and negative attitudes toward other races. In *Royal Service*, for example, a 1952 "attitude test" asked women, "Do you favor people of all races using public places and common carriers without segregation? . . . Theater, banks, hotel, restaurants, buses, trains, streetcars[?]"[30] If not, the feature implied, a reader should reconsider her attitude. Such promotion of integration would likely have offended many of the magazine's subscribers, whose defense of segregation only strengthened as opposition mounted. When the segregation of public schools was ruled unconstitutional, *Royal Service* editors made a point to encourage "Baptist leaders [to] take a stand against segregation," urging hesitant readers that "Baptist schools must move as fast or faster than public schools [in integrating]."[31] These editors' attitudes toward segregation were more progressive than most Southern Baptists, and with increasing regularity they published opinions with which the majority of their readers disagreed, in the hopes of changing their minds.

The Window likewise leaned in to its promotion of racial equality even more strongly after the *Brown* decision. A July 1954 article declared that, for a Christian, segregation was a "jarring clash of his creed."[32] These were strong words for segregationist readers who were still tending fresh wounds from what they considered to be the Supreme Court's attack on their position, but writers did not stop there. Playing on a common anxiety of postwar Americans, multiple writers for *The Window* warned that Russian communists portrayed American democracy negatively because the country's citizens were not truly equal. "We must do all within our power to prove the truth of democracy as opposed to the lie of communism," one writer urged.[33] In this view, espousing segregation was not simply a personal decision; it was a serious concession to Cold War foes. Furthermore, writers asserted that segregation was a "Nazi idea" of lower treatment for a lesser race—a shocking comparison after a fierce world war against Hitler's forces.[34] By equating segregation with ideologies that their readers most despised, writers for *The Window* attempted to provoke them into reconsidering their views on the topic. After all, they explained to their young readers, "to be grownup is to think for yourself."[35]

By 1960, both *The Window* and *Royal Service* regularly and persuasively counseled readers to adopt a posture of racial equality, heeding what one writer described as "the new urgency in these days."[36] WMU members, like other Southerners, could not avoid the escalating civil rights movement, with its sit-ins, school integration, and protests—some not far from the WMU's offices in Birmingham. As these civil rights debates intensified, *Royal Service* editors unhesitatingly urged WMU members "to turn aside from all racial discrimination and injustice—to take a strong stand for people of all nations and all colors."[37] More pages of *Royal Service* than ever before were dedicated to discussing race. Article after article in the magazine encouraged readers to make friends across racial lines, view those of other races through "God's eyes," and observe Race Relations Sunday, among other efforts.[38] However, writers did not usually dictate particular actions urged by civil rights activists. Instead of specifically advising women to participate in marches or sit-ins, for example, writers more generically encouraged readers to "help solve the race problem."[39] Such exhortations echoed the general spirit of the emerging civil rights movement without embracing the movement's calls to organized action against racial injustice.

While broadly reform-minded, these features reflected editors' awareness of the restrictions of their Southern Baptist context. Although WMU leaders were generally educated, urban white progressives, *Royal Service*'s typical reader was a conservative, middle-aged white homemaker living in the rural South, where racial equality was generally less favored.[40] The content that editors did publish in the magazine proved controversial enough to stir debate among these readers in the magazine's "We Get Letters" column and surely in local meetings as well. Women wrote in with passionate and varied responses to *Royal Service*'s features on race. "God had a purpose in making people of different races and to live in different parts of the world," an anonymous reader avowed.[41] One of the magazine's minority of African American readers, though, maintained that a "child of God" should be able to "worship in God's house wherever he may be."[42] Hundreds of canceled subscriptions demonstrated that a number of readers agreed with Dorothy Robinson of Florida: "I see no signs of *Royal Service* being willing to look at the 'other' side of the racial question."[43] However, others sympathized with Mrs. S. A. Williams of Arkansas, who explained that after much Bible study and prayer "I no longer feel that I can be a real Christian and hold on to race prejudices."[44] Although they were not participating in marches or sit-ins, many Southern Baptist women like Williams were experiencing a gradual shift in their attitudes toward African Americans, in no small part due to the content they frequently encountered in *Royal Service*. As SBC leaders debated integration in their official meetings and statements, hundreds of thousands of Southern Baptist women participated in their own conversations—and often transformations—facilitated by the pages of WMU magazines.

Not surprisingly, with its younger audience *The Window* went further than *Royal Service* did in its support of the civil rights movement. While not explicitly urging readers to participate in protests and other activism, at least one of the magazine's articles praised the son of SBC missionaries who had participated in a sit-in and spent two days in jail.[45] This feature was written by the associate secretary of the CLC and originally published by that organization, demonstrating the WMU's affiliation with other Southern Baptist progressives. Yet the WMU consistently published more about civil rights than did any other SBC organization. Additional articles in *The Window* urged young women to "learn about the freedom fight in our own land" and "take action"; in fact, the magazine's entire September 1964 issue challenged readers to "involve themselves positively . . . in this modern revolution."[46] Writers disparaged churches that feared "kneel-ins" and explained that public demonstrations were legal, although without instructing readers to participate in such actions.[47] They did remind the women, however, that "it is the duty of Christians to protest error and injustice" while avoiding violence.[48] With such words, *The Window* implicitly sanctioned civil rights activism, encouraging readers to stand up for racial justice without directing them to the exact actions they should take or naming the leaders they should follow. This stance, though not as strong as it potentially could have been, was remarkable within a context in which most individuals still opposed integration.[49] As they met together regularly in their YWA groups, thousands of young women from conservative Southern Baptist churches were repeatedly challenged to reconsider their perspectives on race and take action. More than the SBC's Sunday School, Training Union, or BSU curriculum of the day, *The Window* brought racial activism to the forefront.

Although it did not advocate specific forms of civil rights activism, throughout this period *The Window* urged its readers to take more specific race-related actions than *Royal Service* did. Suggestions were plentiful: Stop telling "nigger jokes," participate in pulpit and choir exchanges with African American churches, study booklets from groups like the Anti-Defamation League, donate library books to African American colleges, invite friends to visit an integrated school, and even join the NAACP.[50] Some articles invited readers to take more public actions. For example, in 1956 Lillian Smith suggested that women convene a round-table discussion about race on their local radio or television station.[51] Likewise, more than one writer urged young women to write the editors of their local newspapers, either praising or criticizing the papers' coverage of racial issues. Perhaps the most common recommendation was to use "courtesy titles" of Mr., Mrs., or Miss when addressing African Americans, contrary to the practice of many white Southerners at the time.

Very few articles, however, gave their readers advice from an African American perspective; writers were typically white WMU members, not people of color. Although WMU leaders had assisted African American

Baptist women with their missions publications for years, evidence suggests this relationship was often more paternalistic than reciprocal. In their own magazines, WMU editors defaulted to articles written by WMU members, who were largely white Southerners. The suggestions that these women included in their magazines did not approach the "highly politicized, left-wing ideology" that United Methodist leaders felt characterized their young people's magazine, *motive*, but they did challenge young Southern Baptists to take more specific actions toward racial reconciliation than most had previously considered.[52] While these sentiments were far from radical, they were progressive within their Southern Baptist context.

During these years, then, both *The Window* and *Royal Service* prioritized changing Southern Baptist women's attitudes about African Americans. Although it is impossible to gauge the reactions of all the magazines' readers, subscription rates and letters suggest that many gave serious consideration to this topic, which almost no Southerner could avoid during these years. Many readers apparently experienced a gradual transformation of their attitudes about race. A Southern Baptist seminary student, for example, joined her YWA group in leading a weekly Bible study for African American children as the WMU suggested—and reflected, "Is it strange to find it no loss at all to have become color blind?"[53] In North Carolina, Woman's Missionary Society members met together with African American women and "the eyes of the white women were opened to our mutual kinship."[54] Many other Southern Baptist women exhibited changed attitudes and actions as, prompted by *Royal Service* and *The Window*, they sought "earnestly to take out of our hearts the prejudice against the Negro race which may be planted there."[55] While Southern Baptist men carried out the official work of the church and denomination, the women were doing important business of their own. Sitting in Sunday school rooms and fellowship halls, WMU members did not simply learn about missionaries; they also discovered the personal and communal implications of the most progressive statements about race within the SBC at the time.

Contributing Influences

Why was race at the forefront of WMU leaders' thoughts when their organization consisted of white Southern women in positions of implicit if not explicit privilege? The WMU's missionary purpose provided one significant rationale. While Southern Baptist men enjoyed a wide range of positions within the denomination, women found most formal avenues of service closed to them because of their sex. Missions was a notable exception and a cause that thousands of Southern Baptist women wholeheartedly embraced as their own. Since the WMU's founding in 1888, the organization's members had labored "to distribute missionary information and . . . collect and rais[e] money for missions."[56] These women had grown accustomed to learning about and supporting bold efforts to spread the gospel among peoples around the world. Unlike many of their neighbors, WMU members and leaders regularly read about the importance of "presenting the Saviour to the Negro in Africa and in America."[57] They encountered firsthand accounts from missionaries who had come to "love the Negro people . . . better" after serving in places like Nigeria and Ghana.[58] They also heard reports of African converts and on occasion even hosted these men and women in their own towns. Such experiences often gave WMU members a more sympathetic understanding of other races than most white Southerners held. As one writer explained, "the command of Jesus to win all men leaves no room for race prejudice."[59]

Many WMU leaders also believed that the future of missions was at stake in the American debate over racial equality. Both *Royal Service* and *The Window* published alarming statements by FMB leaders, who asserted that foreign missions efforts were "gravely imperiled by the racial problem in our country."[60] Individuals in other nations, these leaders explained, were reluctant to accept a gospel propagated by those who news reports told them were prejudiced against people of color. According to a missionary in Nigeria, "Our African friends . . . burn with indignation over the way certain people are treated in America."[61] Missions leaders warned that such responses, provoked by America's racial crisis, "threaten[ed] our entire missionary program."[62] Instead of counseling readers to end prejudice simply because of the Christian morality of this action, then, WMU and FMB writers additionally appealed to foreign missions concerns to increase the urgency of this issue. According to one missionary author, "We must be Christian in this matter or else we must pull down our missionary banners and admit that we do not mean business in winning our world."[63] In this view, the cause of Christ around the world depended on Southern Baptists' actions towards those of other races.

As important a motivation as this provided for *Royal Service*'s criticism of racial prejudice, just as influential on writers' views was their own involvement with interracial work in the South. The WMU had participated in ministry efforts among and with African Americans since the early twentieth century, although this work was often paternalistic. In the postwar period, the WMU's program of Community Missions encouraged Southern Baptist women to "witness to . . . minority and racial groups in [their] community," among others.[64] Home missions work, this emphasis avowed, was just as important as evangelistic efforts overseas—and in the women's view large numbers of African Americans in the South were in need of their help. Numerous articles in *Royal Service* and *The Window* described the ways that WMU members led "Negro" vacation Bible schools, nursery schools, training institutes, and similar programs.[65] In 1958 alone, around nine hundred SBC churches "provided leadership for Negro [Vacation Bible] schools"—largely planned by women.[66] Some of these interracial ministries were at least nominally conducted in conjunction with African American Baptist leaders, such as the establishment of the Carver Baptist Center in New Orleans.[67] Others were guided primarily by WMU leaders. While these efforts did not represent true partnership, they did familiarize WMU leaders and members with local African American individuals and communities. "We found those women had the same interests we had," a North Carolina leader testified.[68] Such encounters encouraged WMU leaders to continue to promote interracial understanding within their conservative context.

Nannie Helen Burroughs, a prominent women's leader in the National Baptist Convention (NBC), played no small part in these interracial efforts. Active in Baptist life from 1898 through her death in 1961, Burroughs served as corresponding secretary and later president of the NBC's Woman's Convention, guiding that group's missions and ministry efforts much as WMU leaders did for their organization. WMU leaders provided financial, editorial, and training support for the Woman's Convention, and that organization's leaders sometimes spoke at WMU events among other endeavors.[69] In this turbulent postwar period, WMU leaders' ongoing relationship with Burroughs evolved and reflected their developing understanding of race relations.[70] The June 1947 cover of *Royal Service* featured a large photo of "Miss Nannie H. Burroughs"—a remarkable editorial decision at a time when most Southern Baptists supported racial segregation.[71] In this issue editor Kathleen Mallory, a native of the Deep South, demonstrated a respectful attitude toward this prominent African American leader as she praised Burroughs's "faithful . . . serv[ice] through the many years in Southern Baptist bi-racial relationships."[72] Unsurprisingly, the WMU office received "one or two" letters from upset readers in response.[73] Despite this opposition, the close relationships that WMU leaders like Mallory developed with Burroughs shaped their views of African Americans and their leadership abilities. Indeed, multiple magazine features throughout this period especially praised the work of

Burroughs, calling her the "doorkeeper" to work with African American women and discussing her own missions and publication work through the NBC.[74] Although WMU leaders' relationships with women such as Burroughs was at times still patronizing, these WMU editors and writers after World War II were more likely to consider their work with African Americans as a mutual, interracial friendship than in previous generations and encouraged their readers to adopt more respectful approaches to race relations.

Specific WMU leaders were particularly important in influencing the content that *Royal Service* published about race. According to Alma Hunt, WMU executive secretary from 1948 through 1974, WMU employees Mildred McMurry and Juliette Mather were especially "fearless" in expressing their opinions about racial equality.[75] Mather, the editor of *The Window* from 1929 to 1957 and of *Royal Service* from 1948 to 1957, clearly carried out this emphasis in the magazines' pages, explaining how God "called [believers] from all races."[76] Unlike most WMU employees, Mather's family came from the North; her parents were raised in Michigan, and Mather herself lived in Chicago until her midteens.[77] This doubtless gave her a different perspective on race relations than that of her Southern peers. Indeed, more than once Mather remarked that she came "from a home and background which loved all people, regardless of race or creed."[78] Her father, a railroad agent, had once invited an African American woman to live with the family for a short time while she earned funds to purchase a ticket—a radical action by the standards of white Southerners.[79]

Mather also recalled with delight stories of antebellum Southern Baptist women who taught African American women to read, even though this was illegal. "I'm proud of women with this spirit," she affirmed.[80] Throughout her career with the WMU, Mather exhibited a similar attitude. She participated alongside WMU leaders in what she called the "great step forward" of interracial institutes—meals and training meetings with African American leaders—throughout the 1940s.[81] In addition, she apparently helped select diverse speakers for YWA conferences, including "a black girl who had been sweeping the hall," Nannie Helen Burroughs, and Clarence Jordan, who explained that "he'd gotten his idea of racial equality as a Sunbeam"—a member of the WMU's organization for young children.[82] In her actions as well as her words, Mather expressed that serving among African Americans was "rooted in the work of Woman's Missionary Union."[83]

In addition to Mather, Mildred McMurry served in a variety of leadership roles on the WMU staff from 1951 to 1962.[84] McMurry worked in turn as mission study director, department of missionary fundamentals secretary, and promotion division director. Even as she promoted the study of missions material, she explained that learning about mission efforts around the world helped Southern women "to develop an appreciation for the cultures of races and nations different from our own."[85] Although McMurry did not edit any of the WMU's magazines, she wrote numerous articles for multiple publications about the WMU and race, and thereby influenced many others.

"God is not class or color conscious," McMurry repeatedly affirmed.[86] Though a daughter of the South, she had completed graduate work at the University of Chicago, which surely influenced her understanding of race. According to a colleague, McMurry "hung on every word that Martin Luther King [Jr.] said." Indeed, McMurry was described by one admirer as "a firm, though non-violent, believer in civil rights"; she carefully compiled articles about Mahatma Gandhi and his nonviolent efforts for justice in India.[87] One newspaper headline unequivocally declared McMurry a "civil rightist."[88]

Unsurprisingly, McMurry refused to ignore the racial crisis happening just outside the doors of the WMU. Despite jeers, threats, and obscenities used against her, she boldly participated in the controversial Public Education Peacefully committee, which began in 1963 to urge peaceful integration of Birmingham schools.[89] She calmly departed these meetings despite a "spray of hate," which even the *Christian Century* reported.[90] Realizing the great need for racial reconciliation in the city, McMurry began an informal interracial prayer group that met monthly in Birmingham. She also reported on racial progress that was occurring in the city, such as in her 1964 *Baptist Press* release about Birmingham's integrated Billy Graham crusade.[91]

In speeches she gave across North America, McMurry repeatedly emphasized racial justice. She explained in 1964, as she had previously, that "the treatment of minority groups in the United States, and particularly of the Negro, has not only been a hindrance to our foreign policy but has proved to be a stumbling block to the work of the missionary overseas." Yet information was not enough; McMurry advocated action: "What are you and I doing in this crisis?" Few occasions for speaking or writing passed without McMurry mentioning the needs of the diverse groups of individuals in the United States. Her articles in *Royal Service* and *The Window*, for example, included "Our Freedoms," "Attitude Test," "Where You Are" (on community race relations), and "The Atlanta Minister's Manifesto" (on a progressive statement about race).[92] McMurry's voice on racial reconciliation was unwaveringly strong.

When T. B. Maston published his influential work *The Bible and Race* in 1959, it only strengthened the racial reflection that was already well underway in the WMU. McMurry reviewed Maston's book in the July 1959 issue of

Royal Service, which built on her own body of work to change the attitudes of Southern Baptists regarding race relations.[93] As Southern Baptist men published increasingly progressive materials about race, WMU women incorporated this work into their own messaging. WMU writers throughout this period quoted Maston numerous times, advancing his arguments for the "elimination of all distinctions and discriminations based on color or class."[94] Maston's ideas clearly influenced their own. *Royal Service* and *The Window* also occasionally referenced other progressive leaders and programs of the FMB, HMB, and SSC/CLC. One writer for *The Window*, for example, highlighted HMB's "training of more Negro ministers."[95] *Royal Service* reprinted the SSC's Charter of Race Relations and praised other Southern Baptist examples of "vital Christianity at work."[96] Multiple SSC/CLC leaders wrote for WMU magazines, while other articles urged readers to obtain copies of CLC pamphlets on race. Although women were not allowed the same leadership roles as men within the SBC, during this period WMU leaders worked cooperatively with progressive male denominational leaders in order to spread more broadly the message of equal rights for African Americans. WMU editors and writers were not content to simply disseminate other entities' content to an audience of Southern Baptist women though. As demonstrated above, these women authored numerous unique articles that gave their magazines one of the most consistent and progressive publication records on race within the SBC.

Conclusion

The voluminous content about race published in the WMU's *Royal Service* and *The Window* magazines from 1945 to 1965 was clearly shaped by their own women's missions experiences overseas and at home, as well as their relationships with African American leaders and Southern Baptist progressives. These influences led WMU leaders to challenge their members to consider the "change in [their] concept of race" that they believed was "long overdue."[97] Writers' contextually progressive ideas, although often not explicitly championing the civil rights movement, provided the strongest challenges found in Southern Baptist publications in this period for whites to reexamine their attitudes about race. While twenty-first-century interpreters will surely wish that WMU leaders had taken their ideas further, the recommendations that the women did make confirmed Juliette Mather's statement that within the SBC "we [the WMU] did the most for the racial [issue]."[98]

At times, though, even WMU leaders themselves downplayed their role in racial reconciliation. Mather, for example, refused an interview with *Ladies' Home Journal* about the WMU's interracial work, a move that would have resulted in tremendous publicity for the women's efforts. She explained to the disappointed reporter that such an interview would "undo more than we are doing" by making Southern Baptist husbands aware of—and unhappy with—the broad scope of their wives' reading materials and ministries.[99] As Mather put it, "the men . . . would get all excited and the churches would get excited and everybody would be agitated . . . [and] that would have closed the door."[100] Not simply out of humility but out of what seemed to them necessity, then, the women went quietly about their efforts without provoking too much scrutiny—or asking permission from their husbands or pastors. In this way, the women demonstrated their agency amidst limitations faced due to their gender, ably negotiating their denominational context in order to continue learning about and working for a cause they saw as just. WMU leaders' understanding that they had progressed further than most Southern Baptist men in their views of race compelled them at times to refrain from publicizing their attitudes and efforts beyond their own constituency. While it is certainly possible that decisions to keep a relatively low profile during the civil rights era were ultimately for the benefit of Southern Baptist women's own comfort and privilege, it is also conceivable that, if they had rocked the boat too much, WMU leaders would have lost their ability to challenge the status quo to the extent they did.

This occasional strategy of silence along with the male-dominated perspectives of some historians of the SBC have muted the words and influence of WMU leaders regarding racial equality. In several historical accounts of race and Southern religion, male leaders and convention proceedings have taken precedence over the perspectives of Southern Baptist women. However, including these women's words and actions helps recover a more complete history of Southern Baptists and civil rights. Hundreds of thousands of Southern Baptists repeatedly confronted questions of race and justice not from the words of their pastors, their families, or their Sunday School lessons, but from reading and discussing WMU magazines. These conversations led many women to examine and incrementally change their attitudes and actions related to race—and to convey these new convictions to their fellow WMU members, their children, and at times their churches and communities as well. In this sense *Royal Service* and *The Window* were much more widely influential than SBC resolutions, CLC conferences, or occasional sermons on race. Analyzing these publications is essential to reimagining Southern

Baptist history as it unfolded among some of the most racially attentive members of the denomination. The women who challenged the deeply entrenched racism of Southern Baptists were part of the denomination's long and slow journey of grappling with its legacy of white supremacy, a journey that continues today, drawing both criticism and praise.

Notes

1. Leon Macon, "The Segregation Problem," *Alabama Baptist*, Mar. 8, 1956.
2. W. A. Criswell, *Baptist Message*, Mar. 1, 1956; quoted in Andrew M. Manis, "'Dying from the Neck Up': Southern Baptist Resistance to the Civil Rights Movement," *Baptist History and Heritage* 34, no. 1 (Summer/Fall 1999): 33. See also Andrew M. Manis, *Southern Civil Religions in Conflict: Civil Rights and the Culture Wars* (Macon, GA: Mercer Univ. Press, 2002).
3. *Annual of the Southern Baptist Convention, 1964* (Nashville, TN: Executive Committee of the Southern Baptist Convention, 1964), 73.
4. Mark Newman characterizes this group as a "progressive minority" in *Getting Right with God: Southern Baptists and Desegregation, 1945–1995* (Tuscaloosa: Univ. of Alabama Press, 2001), 20–22, 65–86. See also Paul Harvey, *Freedom's Coming: Religious Culture and the Shaping of the South from the Civil War through the Civil Rights Era* (Chapel Hill: Univ. of North Carolina Press, 2005), 213–15.
5. W. T. Moore, "Southern Baptists and Race Relations," *Home Missions*, Jan. 1965, 14–15; "FMB Asks Race Trouble End," *Commission*, July 1963, 28–29.
6. "Praise, Criticism Greet Race Relations Sunday," *Baptist Press*, Feb. 24, 1965.
7. See, for example, Alan Scot Willis, *All According to God's Plan: Southern Baptist Missions and Race, 1945–1970* (Lexington: Univ. Press of Kentucky, 2004); and Betsy Flowers, "Southern Baptist Evangelicals or Social Gospel Liberals? The Woman's Missionary Union and Social Reform, 1888 to 1928," *American Baptist Quarterly* 19, no. 2 (June 2000): 119. For similar sentiments from African American SBC leader Emmanuel McCall, see "Bridge Builder," *Baptists Today*, June 2014, 9; and Emmanuel McCall, *When All God's Children Get Together: A Memoir of Race and Baptists* (Macon, GA: Mercer Univ. Press, 2007).
8. T. B. Maston, "Southern Baptists and Race Relations," *Home Missions*, Sept. 1966, 38.
9. Laurella Owens, "Viewpoint," *The Window of YWA*, May 1964, 11.
10. Willis, *All According to God's Plan*, 8.
11. Jesse C. Fletcher, *The Southern Baptist Convention: A Sesquicentennial History* (Nashville, TN: Broadman and Holman, 1994), 200.
12. See Edward L. Queen, "Race and Southern Baptists," in *In the South the Baptists Are the Center of Gravity: Southern Baptists and Social Change*, 1930–1980 (New York, NY: Carlson, 1991), 75–96; David Stricklin, "'Who Is Their God? Where Were Their Voices?': Southern Baptist Dissenters and Civil Rights," in *A Gene-*

alogy of Dissent: Southern Baptist Protest in the Twentieth Century (Lexington: Univ. Press of Kentucky, 1999), 48–81; and William M. Tillman Jr., "Baptists and the Turn toward Racial Inclusion: 1955," in *Turning Points in Baptist History* (Macon, GA: Mercer Univ. Press, 2008), 261–74. John Lee Eighmy makes a similar omission in *Churches in Cultural Captivity: A History of the Social Attitudes of Southern Baptists*, rev. ed. (Knoxville: Univ. of Tennessee Press, 1987). Willis, *All According to God's Plan*, and Newman, *Getting Right with God*, do a better job of incorporating women into the history of the SBC's race relations.

13. "Hints to Committee Chairmen," *Royal Service*, Mar. 1952, 15.
14. This number estimates the subscriber base in 1965 and does not account for the total number of women who subscribed to the magazines at some point throughout this period—perhaps more than a million. See Catherine Allen, *A Century to Celebrate: History of Woman's Missionary Union* (Birmingham, AL: Woman's Missionary Union, 1987), 507.
15. See Willis, *All According to God's Plan*, 6; and Allen, *Century to Celebrate*, 507. At least a few Southern Baptist men probably perused the magazines from time to time too!
16. See Newman, *Getting Right with God*, 131; and Allen, *Century to Celebrate*, 254.
17. Mildred McMurry, "Our Freedoms," *Royal Service*, June 1963, 13.
18. "The World Significance of Justice and Cooperation among the Races of the South," Program, *Royal Service*, May 1946, 22.
19. "The Sin of Racial Discrimination," Circle Program, *Royal Service*, Nov. 1947, 15; Pen Lile Pittard, "What Do You Know about the Negro?" Program, *The Window of YWA*, June 1947, 28.
20. Hilda Hall Drake, "Christ for All Mankind," Program, *The Window of YWA*, Mar. 1949, 19.
21. Jane Marsh, "Thinking? Or Rearranging Prejudices?" *The Window of YWA*, Sept. 1948, 4.
22. See "Periodicals Database," IMB Archives and Records Services, accessed Nov. 26, 2019, https://solomon.imb.org/public/ws/perdl/www2/documentp/SearchForm.
23. Myrtle Creasman, "Meet the American Negroes," Program Material, *Royal Service*, June 1947, 9–14; Pearl D. Longley, "The Ku Klux Klan," *The Window of YWA*, June 1947, 14; and Mrs. Edgar Godbold, "An Experiment in Race Relations in Raleigh," *Royal Service*, Mar. 1947, 9.
24. Mary R. McCormick, "One Saviour for the Negro in Africa and in America," Program, *Royal Service*, Sept. 1948, 30, quoting an unnamed source.
25. Mrs. C. D. Creasman, "The World Significance of Justice and Cooperation among the Races of the South," Program, *Royal Service*, May 1946, 23.
26. Pen Lile Pittard, "A Laboratory of Democracy," *The Window of YWA*, May 1946, 2; Pen Lile Pittard, "What Do You Know about the Negro?" Program, *The Window of YWA*, June 1947, 29; and Mildred Dunn, "News," *The Window of YWA*, July 1952, 13.

27. Margaret Bronson, "Workshop Reports—America's Minorities," *The Window of YWA*, Jan. 1945, 14.
28. H. Henlee Barnette, "Racial Segregation and Higher Education," *The Window of YWA*, Mar. 1950, 6.
29. Newman, *Getting Right with God*, 71.
30. Mildred McMurry, "Hints to Committee Chairmen: Attitude Test," *Royal Service,* Feb. 1952, 19.
31. John E. Mills, "Are You Helping?" *Royal Service,* June 1956, 15, quoting the FMB's *Commission* magazine.
32. Ralph McGill, "Segregation by Law No Longer Fits," *The Window of YWA*, July 1954, 3. This article was reprinted from the *Atlanta Constitution.*
33. Hugh A. Brimm, "What's Wrong with Racial Segregation?" *The Window of YWA*, Sept. 1955, 4.
34. Jane Marsh, "Thinking? Or Rearranging Prejudices?" *The Window of YWA*, Sept. 1948, 5.
35. Lois Marshall, "San Andres Island to USA," *The Window of YWA*, Aug. 1952, 8.
36. Mildred McMurry, "When Your Circle Studies *The Bible and Race* by T. B. Maston," *Royal Service,* Apr. 1962, 17.
37. Marie Mathis, "Tomorrow Beckons," *Royal Service,* May 1963, 11.
38. Mathis, "Tomorrow Beckons," 37–39; Mary Allred, "Using God's Eyes," *Royal Service,* Mar. 1964, 37; and "Race Relations Sunday," *Royal Service,* Feb. 1965, back cover.
39. John E. Mills, "Are You Helping?" *Royal Service,* June 1956, 15, quoting the FMB's *Commission* magazine.
40. A 1965 survey indicated that 80 percent of *Royal Service* subscribers were "housewives" between the ages of thirty-five and sixty-four. Elaine Dickson, "Here's How Royal Service Subscribers Look in Statistics," *Royal Service,* June 1965, 10.
41. "Content to Ponder," We Get Letters, *Royal Service,* Apr. 1964, 12.
42. Gladys M. McClain, "Another Reply to Mrs. Robinson," We Get Letters, *Royal Service,* Dec. 1965, 12.
43. Dorothy B. Robinson, "Persistent Question," We Get Letters, *Royal Service,* Oct. 1964, 15. See too Alma Hunt, *Reflections from Alma Hunt* (Birmingham, AL: Woman's Missionary Union, 1987), 75.
44. Mrs. S. A. Williams, "Reply to Mrs. Robinson's Letter in Oct. *Royal Service,*" We Get Letters, *Royal Service,* Dec. 1964, 15.
45. Ross Coggins, "Missions and Race," *The Window of YWA*, Sept. 1964, 38.
46. Marjorie Penney, "A Time to Love," *The Window of YWA*, Sept. 1964, 18; Laurella Owens, "Viewpoint," *The Window of YWA*, Sept. 1963, 7.
47. See Laurella Owens, "Viewpoint," *The Window of YWA*, Sept. 1963, 7; and "Let's Face It," *The Window of YWA*, Feb. 1964, 8.
48. "Let's Face It," *The Window of YWA*, Feb. 1964, 8.
49. See Newman, *Getting Right with God*, 20.

50. See Margaret Bronson, "Workshop Reports—America's Minorities," *The Window of YWA*, Jan. 1945, 14; Hugh A. Brimm, "Honestly Now, What about You?" *The Window of YWA*, Feb. 1950, 8; Dorothy Green Napier, "Saving Health among All Nations," Program, *The Window of YWA*, Mar. 1960, 45; R. Orin Cornett, "Who Cares?" *The Window of YWA*, Apr. 1956, 6; and Lillian Smith, "Simple Things We All Can Do," *The Window of YWA*, Feb. 1956, 42.
51. Lillian Smith, "Simple Things We All Can Do," *The Window of YWA*, Feb. 1956, 42.
52. Quote from "Central Alabama Conference," Collections of the North Alabama Conference, United Methodist Church, accessed June 13, 2015, http://library.bsc.edu/special%20collections/Collections%20of%20the%20NAC.pdf. The UMC magazine *motive* is spelled with a lowercase *m*.
53. Beverly Goss, "All Yours—Seminary YWA Spreads 'JOY,'" *The Window of YWA*, Sept. 1964, 11.
54. Mrs. Edgar Godbold, "An Experiment in Race Relations in Raleigh," *Royal Service*, Mar. 1947, 9. Not surprisingly, the perspective of the African American women is not included in this article.
55. Elsie Renfroe, "It Can Be Done," *The Window of YWA*, Aug. 1945, 8.
56. "Sketch and Constitution of the Woman's Missionary Societies (Auxiliary to S. B. C.)," Report of the Annual Meeting of the Woman's Missionary Union, Auxiliary to Southern Baptist Convention, 1888, 5.
57. Mary R. McCormick, "One Saviour for the Negro in Africa and in America," Program, *Royal Service*, Sept. 1948, 25.
58. Leigh Whittington, "Just Because They Are Negroes," *The Window of YWA*, June 1947, 6.
59. Ross Coggins, "The Ins and Outs of Race Prejudice," *Royal Service*, Sept. 1964, 6.
60. Baker James Cauthen, "Comments: On Race," *Royal Service*, Dec. 1963, 8.
61. Leigh Whittington, "Just Because They Are Negroes," *The Window of YWA*, June 1947, 6.
62. Mary R. McCormick, "One Saviour for the Negro in Africa and in America," Program, *Royal Service*, Sept. 1948, 25.
63. John E. Mills, "Are You Helping?" *Royal Service*, June 1956, 15, quoting the FMB's *Commission* magazine.
64. Hermione Jackson, "You—A World Baptist," Program, *Royal Service*, Sept. 1960, 34.
65. See, for example, Mrs. C. D. O'Neill, "Starched Shirts and Eager Faces," *Royal Service*, June 1952, 10–11; Hilda Hall Drake, "Christ for All Mankind," Program, *The Window of YWA*, Mar. 1949, 17; Eva Berry, "Together in Missouri," *Royal Service*, Mar. 1950, 8–9; and Elsie Renfroe, "It Can Be Done," *The Window of YWA*, Aug. 1945, 8.
66. Hermione Jackson, "Negro Work of the Home Mission Board," Program, *Royal Service*, Sept. 1961, 39.
67. "It's Just for Them!" *Royal Service*, Feb. 1952, 12.
68. Mrs. Edgar Godbold, "An Experiment in Race Relations in Raleigh," *Royal Service*, Mar. 1947, 9.

69. Allen, *Century to Celebrate*, 248–54.
70. For more on this relationship, see Bill Sumners, "Bridge Builders: Baptist Women and Race Relations at the Turn of the Century," *Journal of African American Southern Baptist History* 2 (2004); T. Laine Scales, "Women's Ways of Reconciliation: Fifty Years of Cooperation between the Woman's Missionary Union of the SBC and the Woman's Convention of the National Baptist Convention, 1904–1954" (paper presented at the Baptist History and Heritage Society Conference, Nashville, TN, Apr. 21, 2015); and Nicholas Pruitt, "Working Towards Baptist Interracial Fellowship: The Friendships Southern Baptist Women Cultivated and the Limits They Faced in Improving Race Relations during the 1930s and 1940s" (paper presented at the Baptist History and Heritage Society Conference, Nashville, TN, Apr. 21, 2015).
71. *Royal Service*, June 1947, front cover.
72. Kathleen Mallory, "For Everything . . . A Season," Editorial, *Royal Service*, June 1947, 3.
73. Juliette Mather, interview by Catherine Allen, Jan. 26–28, 1976, transcript, 101, WMU History Research, Biographical Files (6A5A4), WMU Archives (WMUA), Birmingham, AL.
74. "Doorkeeper: Dr. Nannie Burroughs," *Royal Service*, Aug. 1958, 20; and Marjorie Moore Armstrong, "What's Happening Now!" *Royal Service*, Oct. 1956, 31.
75. Hunt, *Reflections*, 71.
76. Juliette Mather, "For God So Loved . . . That He Called from All Races," *Royal Service*, Dec. 1957, 67. Mather also influenced Ethalee Hamric, a longtime WMU employee who was promoted from Mather's assistant to editor of *Royal Service* and *The Window of YWA* after Mather stepped down from these positions.
77. Mather interview transcript, n.p., WMUA; and "Mather, Juliette Edla," Biographical Sketches (8A2), WMUA.
78. Gail Linum, "Before Response, There Must Be Exposure," *Contempo*, Feb. 1975, 37.
79. Juliette Mather to Gail Linum, Feb. 4, 1974, WMU History Research, Biographical Files (6A5A4), WMUA.
80. Debbie Baird Buie, "WMU Celebrates 90th Year, Hears 82-Year-Old Missions Pioneer," *California Southern Baptist*, June 8, 1978.
81. Mather interview transcript, 128, WMUA.
82. Mather interview transcript, 98–99, WMUA.
83. "Miss Juliette Mather's Address to WMU upon Its 90th Birthday," WMU History Research, Biographical Files (6A5A4), WMUA.
84. Helen Fling, interview by Catherine Allen, Feb. 14, 1985, transcript, 12, WMU History Research, Biographical Files (6A5A4), WMUA.
85. "Miss Juliette Mather's Address," WMUA.
86. Mildred McMurry, "All Men Are Created Equal!" *Western Recorder*, Jan. 16, 1964.
87. Mrs. Edgar Bates, "Tribute to Mrs. William McMurry," *Together* 4, no. 2 (Spring 1963): 2; "Gandhi File," McMurry Files (5A4.1), WMUA.

88. Billie McMurry Emmons, *Letters from Mother* (Nashville, TN: Broadman Press, 1967), 86.
89. Emmons, *Letters*, 86.
90. Samuel Southard, "The Southern 'Establishment,'" *Christian Century*, Dec. 30, 1964, 1621.
91. Mildred McMurry, "38,000 Prove It Can Happen in Birmingham," *Baptist Press*, Apr. 4, 1964.
92. Mildred McMurry, "Our Freedoms," *Royal Service*, June 1963, 11; Mildred McMurry, "Hints to Committee Chairmen: Attitude Test," *Royal Service*, Feb. 1952, 19; Mildred McMurry, "Where You Are," Program, *The Window of YWA*, Apr. 1962, 31; Mildred McMurry, "Did You Read It?" *Royal Service*, Mar. 1959, 50.
93. Mildred McMurry, "Did You Read It?" *Royal Service*, July 1959, 25.
94. Mary R. McCormick, "One Saviour for the Negro in Africa and in America," Program, *Royal Service*, Sept. 1948, 25.
95. Hilda Hall Drake, "Christ for All Mankind," Program, *The Window of YWA*, Mar. 1949, 19.
96. Kate Bullock Helms, "How Christian Is America?" Your Program, *Royal Service*, Feb. 1950, 29.
97. "Christ the Answer to Racial Tension," Program Plans, *Royal Service*, Mar. 1949, 22.
98. Mather interview transcript, 98, WMUA.
99. "Miss Juliette Mather's Address," WMUA.
100. Mather interview transcript, 70, WMUA.

Seven

"I'M FOR ERA"

Faith, Feminism, and the "Southern Strategy" of a Southern Baptist First Lady

Elizabeth H. Flowers

In January 1974, the Georgia State House of Representatives prepared to vote on the Equal Rights Amendment (ERA). At this point, two years after passing the US Congress, the amendment had sailed through thirty of the thirty-eight states needed for constitutional ratification. But the Catholic lawyer and self-described Midwestern mother, homemaker, and wife, Phyllis Schlafly, had recently founded STOP ERA, with Georgia now experiencing some of the first major protests over ratification. After walking through the posters and placards emblazoned with red stop signs on his way to the capital each morning, then governor Jimmy Carter invited the demonstrators into his office. Climbing up on his desk to be seen and heard amidst the clamor, he loudly announced, "I am for [the amendment] but my wife is against it."

If the crowd was surprised to hear that its governor, often praised as a devout, church-going Southern Baptist, favored the ERA, few would have questioned his comment regarding Georgia's first lady, Rosalynn Carter, who, on the surface, appeared and sounded as traditionally Southern and Southern Baptist as her husband. Southern Baptists were the very people Schlafly was most successfully recruiting for her cause. Perhaps Jimmy offered the caveat regarding Rosalynn as a politically savvy form of reassurance.[1] If so, his strategy failed. The following day an infuriated Rosalynn marched past the protestors into Jimmy's office wearing a big "I'M FOR ERA" button. "How could you?" she later recollected asking him. The two have joked that he "never lived that one down." Jimmy by no means confused Rosalynn's opinion on the issue again. Neither did Georgia's growing number of anti-ERA constituents, who booed Rosalynn on her way out of the capital building.[2]

This story, somewhat humorous in the Carters' recollection, is indicative of Rosalynn in that she, similar to Jimmy, often defied expectations. In fact, the "Steel Magnolia," as she was later nicknamed for her soft-edged toughness, became one of the most vocal champions of the amendment during the later 1970s, securing both the ire of the emerging Christian right and the Alice Paul Award in 1980 for her efforts. Despite her prominence then, political and religious historians have since focused almost exclusively on the paradox of Jimmy Carter as the first evangelical president whose politics around women, gender, and other social issues prompted the rise of the Christian right in his own denomination. And both moderate Southern Baptists and left-leaning evangelicals have long celebrated him as their hero. Thus, in narrating the history of the Christian right within the context of the Carter presidency, scholars and denominationalists alike have largely neglected the first lady.[3] While the tales of "great men" have often sidestepped their personal intimacies and relegated their wives and children to secondary status, Rosalynn's absence seems particularly conspicuous when considering that she, a dedicated Southern Baptist, served as the most public symbol of womanhood at a moment when the roles of women and understandings of womanhood were undergoing radical changes. In fact, her activism led to some of the most bitter name-calling in the history of the office of the first lady since Eleanor Roosevelt.

In this chapter, I reexamine the Carter presidency and its significance to Southern Baptist history during the rise of the Christian right by starting with the first lady. My thesis is threefold. First, after chronicling how a small-town Southern girl became a national spokesperson for the ERA, I argue that the nature of the criticism Rosalynn received as first lady was strikingly gendered when compared to that initially received by Jimmy and was largely based on the public's perception of her as a Southern Baptist wife and mother. Because of this stinging attack, she more immediately felt the threat of the new Christian right that would soon sweep through the Southern Baptist Convention (SBC), transform the South, and in the eyes of some, cost Jimmy a second-term presidency. I next show that the vitriol against her, along with her own religious convictions, compelled her to downplay the more revolutionary elements of the feminist movement behind the ERA. She hoped this would assuage conservative Americans in Southern states, including rank-and-file Southern Baptists, and would make them more likely vote for the ERA. Finally, I conclude that the rise of the Christian right as it involved Southern Baptists began earlier than the 1979 date many historians assume. This later date is connected to both the founding of Jerry Falwell's Moral Majority and the election of Adrian Rogers to the SBC's presidency. But by starting with Rosalynn rather than Jimmy, or Schlafly rather than Falwell, we find that the anti-feminist groups of the mid-1970s mobilized Southern Baptists and conservative evangelicals on the ground much earlier. And it was conflicts over gender, even more so than theological matters, that led to this early mobilization.[4]

Rosalynn's approach to the ERA backfired, earning her the wrath of both the political left and the Christian right. For this reason, she has often been written out of the history of the feminist movement. Still, although her advocacy has been downplayed in almost every scholarly venue, she is noteworthy.[5] In terms of denominational history, as the first lady, and thus one of the most visible and influential women in American culture during the 1970s, she signaled that Southern Baptist women could be "FOR ERA." While she did not change the course of the denomination, per se, she represented Southern Baptist womanhood, serving as a cultural symbol in the most public forum. Relatedly, she was forced to negotiate private matters (motherhood, marriage, and piety) publicly—at a moment when the American family and gendered understandings of women were experiencing dramatic redefinition, indeed changes that further threatened the conservative white South. Rosalynn, therefore, embodied the internal and everyday struggles of many Southern Baptist women who did not immediately find themselves in step with emerging politics of the day. While her struggle has been largely forgotten, her legacy can still be seen and felt in the development of an evangelical feminism that inspired Southern Baptist women over the 1980s and 1990s to lobby for greater authority in the denomination, including ministerial and ordination rights. This evangelical feminism has continued to inform progressive Baptist circles, pointing to an underestimated potential in the beleaguered yet ongoing struggle for the amendment.

No Shrinking Violet

On the surface, Rosalynn did not seem a natural ally to feminism and the ERA. Born Eleanor Rosalynn Smith in the small town of Plains, Georgia, in 1927, Rosalynn left college at eighteen to marry Jimmy.[6] She was so quiet and shy in personality that the feisty Lillian Carter feared her eldest son had wed a shrinking violet. Indeed, when compared to the outspoken Lillian and the unruly and unconventional Carter clan, Rosalynn was extraordinarily "well-behaved," staying within boundaries of conventional dictates. Her mother, Allie Smith, described Rosalynn as a "very feminine little girl" who liked dolls, cooking, and sewing and could put on a white frock in the morning with it still clean by late afternoon.[7] Indeed, the only backstory about Rosalynn during her early years, more of a humorous misstep really, was that she arrived, with Jimmy, late to her own wedding and missed the first playing of "Here Comes the Bride."

Jimmy's father, James Earl Carter Sr., did not think much of his eldest son's choice either, though more because of position than personality. In a small Southern town like Plains, social hierarchies were well established. And Jimmy's family had greater clout than Rosalynn's, whom she remembered as poor. Indeed, James Earl Carter, with his 360-acre peanut farm, hired help, and sharecropping labor, was far higher on the ladder than Rosalynn's father, Edgar Smith, who had held various odd jobs from bus driver to auto mechanic before his sudden death in 1944. Perhaps the Carters' wealth enabled a bit of unconventional behavior. To be sure, the senior Carter had higher hopes for his namesake, who was also a recent Annapolis graduate.

Within six years of marriage, Rosalynn and Jimmy had three sons: Jack was born in 1947, Chip in 1950, and Jeff in 1952. By all accounts, Rosalynn settled into the rather typical role of stay-at-home military wife, mother, and homemaker. "I was living the totally conventional life," she recalled of those early married years. "As the total wife and mother, I washed and ironed, I cooked and cleaned, mopped floors . . . I bought women's magazines and clipped recipes and household tips. I bought how-to books and learned how to crochet and knit and make curtains."[8] While it has been pointed out that the Carters did not regularly attend church during this period, this was largely because of Jimmy's traveling. Raised Methodist, Rosalynn did join the Carters' Baptist church.

While Rosalynn may not have seemed a ready-made feminist, there were hints, if one looked closely enough under the surface, of a hidden narrative. Perhaps, for instance, both Rosalynn's keen sense of propriety and her early marriage were the results of a girl forced to mature rather quickly. Rosalynn often stated that her "childhood really ended" at age thirteen, on the night that her father died. There was little time for frivolity after that. Allie Smith later acknowledged depending heavily on Rosalynn, who was the eldest of four siblings, in running the family and making many of the major financial and household decisions while she, Smith, worked long hours to make ends meet, initially as a seamstress and later as the town's postmistress. Besides giving Rosalynn a heightened awareness of responsibility, forcing her to become "very strong," she said, this arrangement also meant that Rosalynn was no stranger to women's paid labor and the gendered inequities therein.[9]

Rosalynn was smart too, graduating valedictorian of Plains High School and thus trumping Jimmy who, three years earlier, had been merely the class salutatorian. Despite a promise to her father to complete her education, she could only afford two years at the local community college before marrying Jimmy. And while she did wed young, marriage to a naval officer became her route out of Plains, taking her to the Northeast, the West Coast, and Hawaii. Like Jimmy, she began questioning Southern ways, particularly those around Jim Crow. Moreover, because Jimmy often toured at sea, Rosalynn found that a military marriage offered a higher degree of independence than the ordinary middle-class housewife of the 1950s. And she rather enjoyed making her own decisions.

The story of her begrudging return to Plains in 1953 so that Jimmy could take over the family farm at the early death of his own father has been often told. "I argued. I cried. I screamed at him," she later wrote. Not only did Plains lack amenities she had grown to enjoy, from restaurants to swimming pools, but she had changed, she said, and feared losing that level of independence she had come to love.[10] In fact, she refused to speak to Jimmy for the entire car trip from upstate New York, where they were located, to southwest Georgia, informing Jack when she needed his father to stop for the restroom. She felt so angry upon her arrival that she secluded herself from family and friends.

Only upon her mother's chiding that the people of Plains were finding her aloof did Rosalynn decide to make the best of it. And make the best of it, she did. Within a couple of years, she had plunged into peanuts. As Jimmy studied agriculture and handled the crops, she increasingly assumed control of the business side of farm and warehouse, even earning a certificate in accounting through a correspondence course. Soon, she was explaining the books to Jimmy and making major operational decisions. Despite her protestations over the move, Rosalynn came into her own during these days, developing an inner strength and confidence. Sometimes described by outsiders as cool and aloof, she nevertheless proved hard working and eager to learn. Those friends closest to her found her warm and caring, and they often referenced her self-improvement efforts, which led to her mastering art history, Southern literature, classical music, the violin, Spanish, and, in this case, farm life.[11]

Lillian soon left the farm to become house mother for the Kappa Alpha fraternity at Auburn University and then, from 1966 to 1968, served in the

Peace Corps in India. As friends and family commented, there was little space or room for both Lillian and Rosalynn. That said, Lillian's outspokenness in the one controversial area they agreed upon most, civil rights, pushed Rosalynn further in her own advocacy. Lillian had even run the county's reelection headquarters for Lyndon Johnson when almost every white Democrat in southwest Georgia abandoned him for his support and signing of the Civil Rights Act of 1964. Around that time, Rosalynn, Jimmy, and their sons joined Lillian to provide the only affirmative votes for integrating worship in Plains Baptist Church.[12] The Carters' commitment to civil rights, though sometimes wavering in Jimmy's gubernatorial campaigns, eventually led to his being heralded as one of a handful of New South governors wresting the Democratic Party from the throes of Jim Crow segregation and George Wallace. And Rosalynn began to push the boundaries limiting women as well.

Peanuts and Politics

On his thirty-eighth birthday, Jimmy shocked Rosalynn by waking up, donning a suit, and announcing that he was running for state senate. Rosalynn backed his decision although she would rather he had consulted with her first. It was a tight and contested race, and Jimmy secured the seat only after it was settled in court. Gaining a reputation as a moderately progressive Democrat, Jimmy did not make the same mistake regarding consulting Rosalynn four years later, in 1966, when he decided to run for governor.

Although he lost the Democratic primary in another bitter campaign, Rosalynn, much to her surprise, found that she loved campaigning, and she was good at it. Her fourth and last child, daughter Amy, was born in 1967, but Rosalynn maintained a focus on campaigning for the 1970 election. From the start, Jimmy, Rosalynn, their immediate and extended family, and eventually the entire Peanut Brigade of Plains supporters took a divide-and-conquer approach. Battling her fear of public speaking and poring over the issues, Rosalynn traveled the state, engaged constituents, and addressed audiences, mostly without Jimmy. To Jimmy's delight, and perhaps everyone else's amazement, she proved a savvy strategist, both during his first gubernatorial race, in 1966, and then another four years later, in 1970, when he ran a second time victoriously.

Ideologically, Rosalynn viewed campaigning, and politics in general, as possessing the potential to generate change. While her religiosity was less experiential than Jimmy's, she nevertheless connected her faith to social action and community awareness, or what she eventually referred to as her commitment to creating a more "caring society." Rosalynn began to actively develop this sensibility while on the campaign trail and then as first lady of Georgia. While she had run the farm and warehouse during the years Jimmy served as state senator and their three sons were in school, when he became governor in 1971, she made clear that she wanted to be his political partner rather than his political wife. In her own words, "I hadn't planned to spend all my time pouring tea!"[13] Or, as her good friend Edna Langford put it, it was "fun to have teas and coffees and cut ribbons," but Rosalynn, she added, found it "rewarding to instigate and further programs."[14] Seen from a certain wry angle, it was payback for returning to Plains. Moreover, if some historians have dismissed their partnership as simply being more Southern agrarian than anything politically or culturally progressive, others have indicated that the equality of their partnership developed over time. While not wanting to push tradition too far in terms of Southern gender conventions, Rosalynn did see herself in contrast to her predecessors, attributing her trajectory to both changing times and personal preferences.

As first lady of Georgia from 1971 to 1975, Rosalynn found her voice by devoting herself to several issues, but the primary one over these four years was mental health. Her commitment was largely, she explained, because of the people she met on the campaign trail, whose struggles with caring for mentally ill relatives moved her to action. An example she often referenced was that of a mother forced to work night jobs to pay the necessary expenses for her mentally ill son. Although she could not technically head the newly formed Governor's Commission to Improve Services to the Mentally and Emotionally Handicapped, Rosalynn was clearly the reason for its existence and drove its agenda. During this period, she also became an effective advisor to Jimmy, possessing the more real-world or applied political mind of the two, which he soon realized and valued.

At this point, Rosalynn underwent a shift in her practice, and perhaps her sense, of motherhood as it involved daughter Amy, who was only three when the Carters entered the governor's mansion in 1971. In contrast, the Carter boys were now young men. While she hated leaving Amy at home when campaigning or pursuing her first lady projects, Rosalynn often spoke of herself as having a God-given chance to better the world—one very few experienced, at least on such a grand scale. In other words, she felt not only an opportunity but a responsibility. It also seemed inevitable to her that Amy would simply grow up surrounded by the press, crowds, and security. It helped, she later commented, that Amy was so young, often reminding those who "had a tendency to feel sorry for Amy" that "ever since she had been born, she's been in the public eye" and "knows what it is to have microphones pushed toward her." The long hours and trips away from Amy also led to a greater sympathy for working mothers, she said.[15]

There seems little criticism of Rosalynn as mother during the Carters' gubernatorial years. Georgians clearly enjoyed seeing a toddler in the mansion. Moreover, the practice of extended family caring for Amy, as grandmothers "Miss Lillian" and "Miss Allie" often stepped in, was traditionally Southern. So, too, was their use of a full-time, live-in black nanny. Here, the Carters employed a trusty, or prison laborer, Mary Fitzpatrick, who remained with the family, caring for Amy, through the White House years.[16] The intense criticism Rosalynn received as wife and mother when she moved from Georgia to the national stage, then, came as something of a surprise. This was due not only to her being on a larger media platform but also because of Schlafly's efforts to defeat the ERA.

Encountering the ERA

When the Carters set their sights on the White House in 1974, the ERA seemed to be moving at breakneck speed toward ratification, with both Republicans and Democrats nationally behind the amendment. Introduced in 1923 by famed suffragist and first-wave feminist Alice Paul, the amendment found little support in members of Congress until the beginning of the 1970s. In 1966, inspired by the success of her book *The Feminine Mystique*, Betty Friedan helped feminists overcome several decades of crippling division to form the National Organization of Women (NOW), thus birthing the second-wave movement. In 1971, emerging feminist leaders and political activists such as Gloria Steinem, Bella Abzug, Shirley Chisholm, Liz Carpenter, and Elly Peterson, along with a host of others, organized the National Women's Political Caucus (NWPC). Over the next few years, NOW and the NWPC witnessed a spate of legislative victories, including Title IX. While divisions between feminists remained, and new cracks and fissures appeared, passage of the ERA served as their ultimate and unifying goal.

Introduced in the House by Representative Martha Griffiths in 1971, it passed by a vote of 354 to 243, and in 1972, by the Senate, with the vote 85 to 8. To become part of the Constitution, three-fourths of the fifty states, or thirty-eight, needed to ratify the amendment. Fourteen states ratified it within one month, and twenty-two states followed suit within its first year. Even Richard

Nixon, no friend to feminists, offered the Oval Office's endorsement. By the time of his resignation in 1974, the ERA needed only eight more states. Sensing a national enthusiasm for women's rights overall and strongly encouraged by First Lady Betty Ford, Gerald Ford established a National Commission on Women, naming well-recognized feminists and distinguished women's rights advocates as its key players. In a highly publicized Rose Garden ceremony, he signed into action its suggested agenda, which included a review of all federal laws that might discriminate against women. Under Ford, Congress voted to mandate and fund the National Women's Conference to be held in Houston in 1977.

Then the ERA began to lose to steam, stalling in the more conservative Midwest and especially in the deeply Democratic South, including Georgia. On the one hand, this did not mean that the South was solidly against the ERA. As early as 1968, when running for president, Alabama governor George Wallace sent an affirmative telegram to Alice Paul. The populace of Texas, Tennessee, and Kentucky voted for passage in 1972, and one-house ratifications included South Carolina, North Carolina, and Florida. Moreover, Southern Baptists, who have often been seen to function as the Catholic Church of the white South, held a Christian Life Commission conference, with the title "Christian Liberation for Women," which was overwhelmingly supportive of the ERA. The commission presented a report at the 1974 convention that called on Southern Baptists to "bear witness to the rest of society by rejecting sexual discrimination against women," "providing equal pay for equal work," and "electing women to positions of leadership."[17] Texas pastor Jimmy Allen, who also served as president of the Baptist General Convention of Texas in 1972, voted for ratification in Texas that same year, with Texas being one of the first states to affirm the amendment. As president of the Southern Baptist Convention six years later, he acknowledged his support.

On the other hand, few Southerners and Southern Baptists were enthusiasts. Most were disinterested and disinclined to give the ERA much thought, dismissing it as a Northern movement designed to benefit highly educated career women. Admittedly, much of the leadership of NOW and the NWPC was exactly that. When Southern Baptists were asked to adopt the Christian Life Commission's report at the 1974 convention, they declined (while passing a resolution on abortion that proved decidedly pro-choice). Rosalynn herself even admitted being concerned about the ERA until she read the twenty-four words: "Equality of rights under the law shall not be denied or abridged by the United States or by any state on account of sex." And as indicated, she and Jimmy had never even discussed it with much depth before it hit the Georgia legislature. In retrospect, the ERA's failure to pass in Georgia in 1974 marked a dramatic reversal, with only two more states in the next three years voting for ratification. But even at the time of the presidential election in November 1976, few suspected that any such slowdown would end in the amendment's defeat.

One might naturally ask what happened and why the Carter presidency served as such a decisive turning point in the history of the ERA. First, Schlafly picked up on the South's hesitancy, transforming and organizing it into a powerful force for STOP ERA. While she initially had been presenting the ERA as an assault against traditional womanhood and the nuclear family, after the National Women's Conference, she tied the ERA more tightly to abortion and homosexuality.[18] Up to this point, the antiabortion movement had been mostly, in terms of religion, a Catholic one and politically more Democratic than Republican.[19] In addition, feminists had been divided on homosexuality and the inclusion of what some referred to as "our lesbian sisters," with Betty Friedan arguing vociferously against taking up their cause. In 1977, siding with Schlafly, the popular Southern Baptist beauty queen, pop singer, and "Florida Oranges" commercial star Anita Bryant forced the issue of homosexuality on feminists by launching her Save Our Children Campaign, which meant saving children from the "pedophilic dangers" of homosexuals. A growing number of feminists responded by strengthening their support of the burgeoning gay and lesbian rights movement. As a result, the Carters entered the White House just as conservative evangelicals were connecting the ERA to the demise of the heteronormative nuclear family and an assault on traditional womanhood. Moreover, even if the nuclear family was a more contemporary development, presenting it as a part of traditional womanhood, as Schlafly and Bryant did, appealed to the gendered hierarchy of the South, with the two soon conflated.

Second, and more subtly, the anti-ERA movement gave Southerners a way to articulate what they increasingly referred to as conservative or traditional values without tying them to race at the very time segregation was more likely to be seen as a blot on Southern history.[20] By 1976, for instance, George Wallace had switched positions not only on civil rights (now for) but also on the ERA (against). So, the anti-ERA movement offered a new history of the traditional South and sanctioned it with a religious sensibility both Carters rejected.

As a Southern Baptist first lady "FOR ERA," Rosalynn posed a danger to Schlafly, Bryant, and their followers, as she had the potential to take control of the narrative around ERA and make the case that a seemingly traditional

Southern Baptist wife, mother, and grandmother could support gender equality as represented by the amendment. Soon she became a prime target and one who rallied the troops both for and against the amendment. The catch here was her religion and gender, or being a Southern Baptist woman. In the end, though, Rosalynn was a potential danger whom Schlafly and her followers turned into an opportunity.

Baptist but Not (Fully) Born Again

Like Jimmy, Rosalynn supported the ERA as an extension of civil rights and thus an avowal of her religious convictions. But there were certain differences in their rhetoric and expressions of faith. Much has been written about Jimmy's religiosity. Having been brought up as a Southern Baptist, he deeply admired the spirituality of his faith-healing Pentecostal sister, Ruth Carter Stapleton, who ran her own ministry out of North Carolina. She was connected to his famous born-again experience in 1966, though the extent of this is debatable. Visiting Jimmy in Plains shortly after he lost his first gubernatorial race, Ruth took a walk with him through the woods, asking him pointedly about his personal relationship with Jesus. While Ruth later talked about this particular walk more vividly than Jimmy, remembering it as a moment filled with tears and emotions, he did call it a "deeply profound religious experience that changed my life dramatically."[21] The walk coincided with his hearing a particularly jarring sermon: "If You Were Arrested for Being a Christian, Would There Be Enough Evidence to Convict You?"

These two events precipitated a year of intense spiritual reflection, during which Jimmy read the theological works of Paul Tillich and Reinhold Niebuhr and studied the Bible.[22] He also went on Baptist Brotherhood mission trips to Pennsylvania and Missouri, where he knocked on doors to share his personal testimony and helped with Spanish-speaking revival meetings, having learned the language in the navy. It was during this period, Jimmy stated, that he formed "a very close personal intimate relationship with God through Christ."[23] Campaigning for the presidency nearly a decade later, Jimmy discussed being "evangelical," "born-again," and "saved" so often and openly that, according to the historian Randall Balmer, he had reporters scrambling to define terms that were second nature to most Southerners Baptists. Such rhetoric, along with a squeaky-clean image and a church-going piety that had the Carters in the pew every Sunday, led *Newsweek* to name 1976 the "Year of the Evangelical."

Rosalynn, who became a Southern Baptist upon marrying Jimmy, was as active as he in church. And indeed, strict church attendance was a part of her own religious heritage. She often commented on the ecumenism of her small Southern hometown in which she found herself attending the Lutheran and Baptist churches almost as much as the Methodist church of which she was a member. Rosalynn's mother had been raised Baptist but converted to the Methodist faith of her husband and Rosalynn's father, Edgar Smith. While her maternal grandfather stood firm in his Primitive Baptist ways, her maternal grandmother remained a lifelong Lutheran. "I went to all three churches" Rosalynn recalled, "almost every time the doors opened, it seemed."[24] But when asked by interviewers about her identity as an evangelical or being born-again, Rosalynn would often hesitate or give a somewhat more perfunctory answer. Generally, in her rhetoric, she veered more mainstream Protestant than evangelical and was never at ease with the more pietistic language or experiential character of much of evangelical life. On at least one occasion, she stated that, because of the stresses of being governor, Jimmy relied on "a more personal sort of relationship [with Jesus] than I did."[25] The closest she came to articulating any sort of evangelical, born-again understanding was in acknowledging a profound sense of God's presence in moments when she might have felt lonely or burdened with a problem, especially in the first months of becoming first lady of Georgia.[26]

Rosalynn also expressed some ambivalence over Jimmy's walk in the woods with Ruth. There were "no flashing lights," she said, "no weeping, no trauma, no emotional scene." She felt that the experience had been "blown out of proportion by the news media, most of whom," she concluded, were "not sure what 'born again' actually meant." Rosalynn preferred to think of the walk as having precipitated a reaffirmation of faith or rededication and indicated that it was Ruth—not Jimmy—who mentioned any emotional shedding of tears.[27]

The historian Stanley Godbold has claimed Rosalynn was more informed by her Methodist childhood than her later Baptist identity largely because the heritage of the Methodist denomination "was rooted in concrete historical events," "was rational and private," and "did not require that its adherents express their commitments in terms of being born again."[28] And yet, such a conclusion seems to downplay Methodism's evangelical character, particularly in the South. The Methodist Church was born of the Great Awakening, camp meetings, and "hearts strangely warmed," and in her 1984 autobiography, Rosalynn vividly recalled the revivals of her childhood and youth. It seems, rather, that Rosalynn rejected this particularly intense evangelical aspect of Southern faith, as her religious sensibility held much more in common with those Protestant women's mission societies emphasizing active service over traditional evangelism. Rosalynn grew up in the heyday of Southern Methodist and Baptist women missions. She spoke specifically, again in her autobiography, of having attended the Southern Baptist Girl's Auxiliary of the Woman's Missionary Union. Overall, then, she gravitated toward a more service-oriented understanding of the Christian faith, and she was certainly most comfortable talking about her own religiosity as it informed her first-lady projects, which were endeavors to create a more "caring society."

There were also differences between Jimmy and Rosalynn in how their faith and feminism coalesced. While both Rosalynn and Jimmy connected their support of the ERA to their religious convictions, Rosalynn faced her endorsement not simply as a Southern Baptist but as a Southern Baptist woman—and as a Southern Baptist woman increasingly at odds with certain notions of womanhood taking hold of the denomination. This discrepancy grew more apparent in the White House and invited criticism for the ways she functioned as first lady.

An Activist First Lady

Historically, a first lady's popularity has reflected the extent to which she embodied American ideals of womanhood at a particular moment in time. While the position of first lady began somewhat ambiguously, it evolved over the nineteenth century, reflecting notions of Victorian domesticity. By the twentieth century, the public had come to view the primary responsibility of the first lady as serving as a hostess of sorts for the nation, as she was to oversee the domestic agenda and social functions of the White House and welcome guests to the United States. It was a distinctly feminine role, not unlike that of a pastor's wife. Beyond campaigning during election season, the first lady was expected to remain fairly apolitical. There were notable exceptions, Eleanor Roosevelt being the most obvious for her outspoken stances regarding civil rights and other matters. But as admired as Roosevelt is today, she courted controversy during her time.[29]

Not surprisingly, a string of either more cautious or disinterested types followed, at least when it came to politics. Bess Truman, for instance, famously said that she believed a woman in public life should "sit beside her husband, be silent and make sure her hat is on straight." Both Mamie Eisenhower and Pat Nixon seem to have performed this best, with

Richard Nixon's aids joking that they did not know the sound of Pat's voice. Jacqueline Kennedy had a distinct distaste for politics and, while highly visible, was nevertheless celebrated for the glamour of her hats, high fashion, and expertise in interior design, all decidedly feminine virtues.[30] Lyndon Johnson's advisors cautioned that Lady Bird should present her "pet project" around environmentalism and conservation as "beautification," which made it fittingly female and within the boundaries of a first lady's duties. From Bess Truman to Pat Nixon, then, few first ladies stepped out of their place.

Rosalynn's immediate predecessor had been more daring. A divorcee before marrying Gerald, Betty Ford sometimes disagreed publicly with her husband, lobbied politically for legislation like the ERA, supported abortion personally as well as legally, and went on record making controversial comments, noting, for example, that she would not be surprised if her children had smoked marijuana or if her eighteen-year-old daughter Susan should one day have an affair. Such comments cost the president some of his more conservative followers. Indeed, his advisors had worried over Betty from the start. His abbreviated presidency, however, curtailed any ongoing critique. And much of her two years were spent battling breast cancer.

Unlike the Fords, who were longtime Washington insiders, the Carters were new to the national scene. Americans welcomed the Southern Baptist couple as a repudiation of the corruption of Washington and its growing elitism. Catholic theologian Michael Novak noted at the time that, in Carter, "millions of Protestant Americans experience a smack of recognition," only that, this time, "he's them in their idealized self."[31] Expectations ran high and, given the post-Nixon moment, higher than usual for an incoming president. These expectations then carried over to Rosalynn and the first family.

Presidential historians have often commented on the political misfortune of Jimmy, who faced crisis after crisis at home and abroad. In the words of Balmer: "Carter was dealt a bad hand as president—the reverberations of the Arab Oil embargo, runaway inflation, the Soviet's imperial ambitions, and the Iranian Revolution—and it was a hand that, in many ways, he played badly." Balmer tempered this judgment by adding that "with the benefit of hindsight, however, many of his policies seem prescient."[32] But if the honeymoon for Jimmy proved brief, it was briefer still for Rosalynn. And in her case, the criticism invoked gender.[33]

Surveying the negative media surrounding Rosalynn as first lady is telling, especially when compared to that experienced by Jimmy. One of the first issues involved the Carters' renowned frugality. Jimmy's financial prudence in the White House, extreme in comparison to his predecessors, was initially heralded by his supporters as fiscal responsibility. Jimmy, for example, required invited guests to pay their own way at Camp David. To save energy and decrease the bills, Jimmy set the White House thermostats at draconian temperatures. Rosalynn begged for more heat in the winter for the sake of her staff, who would show up in long underwear, while Walter Mondale recalled summer cabinet meetings that were "hotter than a bug and muggier than hell."[34] Still, when poking fun and perhaps resentful of Jimmy's penny-pinching ways, his critics did not use it to question his manliness until much later.[35]

Rosalynn's thriftiness, though, was evaluated through a gendered lens. Trying to save money and time, for instance, she cut her own hair, had friends purchase practical department store dresses for her, shared a wardrobe with her daughters-in-law, and used furniture from the executive storeroom to decorate the family residence and other rooms of the White House. She even wore a chiffon gown to the inaugural balls that she had worn before, including to Jimmy's inauguration as governor of Georgia. In terms of entertaining, she failed to purchase White House china, served wine rather than hard liquor, hosted parties rather than balls, and favored casual buffets, lawn picnics, and dessert and finger-food receptions to formal dinners. If planning an elaborate event, she often arranged something the following day to recycle the flowers and table decorations.

Detractors immediately questioned her femininity and fit as first lady. Whether they be Washington insiders or popular news outlets, cultural elites or women's magazine editors, they disparaged her parsimony and preferences as an unsophisticated neglect of her womanly role rather than highlighting any fiscal responsibility. It did not help such criticism that Rosalynn also went on record saying that, as first lady, she intended to "entertain less and work more." Historians of first ladies have pointed out that in her autobiography the chapter on entertaining is one of the shortest.

That Rosalynn was a well-read patron of the arts seemed to escape notice. Perhaps this oversight was because she had, for the most part, been self-taught. Along with a deep Southern accent, she lacked the formal credentials of her immediate predecessors and avoided the Washington social scene. Thus, while Jimmy played up his small-town Southern image, his toothy grin being a feature that got him to the White House, Rosalynn was questioned for it, often having to prove herself as capable of serving as first lady. Her pronunciation of Jimmy as "Jimmeh" received so much ridicule that she referred to him as the "president" in public. Jimmy admitted that the caricatures of the two of them as country bumpkins were more about her. "We had a lot to overcome when we moved up to Washington," he told one *New York Times* reporter. "You probably saw the cartoons and so forth of us coming up here barefooted, in ragged overalls, with ignorant expressions on our faces . . . like we'd come to destroy the beautiful image of the Presidency. Rosalynn was probably affected by that criticism more than I was because it was really a reflection on her. It was serious for her."[36] When asked by interviewers about the relentless jokes, even when their source was revealed to be Joan Kennedy or someone prominent from the Democratic party, Rosalynn shrugged them off, saying that it did not matter. But it did, and she took the disparagements personally.

Even more scathing criticism of Rosalynn was aimed at her political interests and involvements. In her attempt to "work more," she reorganized the "office of the first lady," as she named it, added employees, and hired the first chief of staff for the East Wing. Interestingly, Rosalynn's own projects were varied, dispersed, and, with the exception of the ERA, failed to garner public attention. In terms of priorities, she emphasized community volunteerism and care for the aging as well as continued lobbying for those suffering from mental illness. But it was the extent of her political partnership with Jimmy that perturbed her faultfinders. At home, many interpreted her attendance at cabinet meetings, note-taking presence at Camp David summits, and so-called power lunches with the president an inappropriate will to insert herself into presidential politics, with headlines reading "Who Elected Her?" In foreign affairs, she often traveled alone, serving more as Jimmy's diplomatic representative than his wife, explaining policy, and even, in the case of her 1977 visit to Latin America, negotiating it. Despite initial praise, the trip raised enough eyebrows to avoid repetition. Some White House insiders expressed frustration over what they experienced as her undue power and influence. In fact, Jimmy's West Wing advisors recognized that the president often heeded the first lady's advice when it came to appointments, and that meant firings as well as hirings. According to aides, during the infamous 1979 cabinet shakeup, it was Rosalynn who wanted those "beheadings." In the press, Rosalynn was referred to as Jimmy's "equal partner," "co-president," and "second president" in running the country. Some presented her as a "Lady Macbeth" figure.[37] One tabloid even predicted Rosalynn as secretary of state, should Carter be reelected in 1980, with a run for the presidency in 1984.[38] Amidst what they viewed as an inappropriate will to power, conservatives accused her of neglecting, if not exploiting, Amy.

Relatedly, then, most damning were the accusations around her advocacy for the ERA. Unlike Betty Ford's efforts, Rosalynn's came as something of a surprise. According to her harshest critics on the right, her endorsement signaled a betrayal to her denomination, her faith, and her family.

"FOR ERA"

Feminists have often viewed Rosalynn's initial support as too much "behind the scenes" and hesitant, but this interpretation is contrary to the evidence, particularly in light of her context.[39] After all, as noted, at the time of the election, the ERA needed just four more state ratifications over the next two years for final passage. Despite the amendment having slowed down, most Americans, and undoubtedly the Carters with them, considered victory inevitable. When the Indiana Senate passed the ERA by two votes in January 1977 after the incoming first lady made a last-minute phone call to persuade a wavering Democratic senator toward a positive vote, ERA supporters and opponents alike credited Rosalynn for the win.

If both Carters endorsed the ERA, Rosalynn often took the lead in lobbying for the amendment. And she made sure that her projects secretary, Kathy Cade, worked closely with the West Wing on all ERA matters, including establishing the White House ERA Task Force. When it became apparent that the ERA was faltering and phone calls to other states did little, Rosalynn visited those soon to vote on ratification, even raffling herself off for dances at an ERA fundraiser in Florida in 1978. Rosalynn Carter's archived files are crammed with notes regarding a range of meetings, briefings, and strategy sessions over the ERA. One memo demanded that any memos on the ERA be sent to the first lady as well as the president.[40] Another memo from the president stipulated that all White House personnel, which would include the East Wing, mention the ERA at every public appearance and occasion.[41] White House records show that Rosalynn hosted nearly twenty major White House events promoting the ERA within her first eighteen months. In fact, soon into her tenure, she stopped announcing many of her scheduled ERA activities because of the escalation in anti-ERA picketing in front of the White House.

Overall, Rosalynn's ERA activities varied. Some were the more typical political meetings and briefings. Others involved consultations with and speeches to religious groups.[42] Additionally, she had her office sponsor ERA days at the White House, participate in ERA mail outs and marches, celebrate Women's Equality Day, and set aside national days of prayer for the amendment. In July 1979, Rosalynn held an extensive strategy session that brought together state consultants, legislators, and ERA advocates to chart a path toward ratification. That fall, she and the president hosted a gala salute to the ERA, inviting more than eight hundred ERA supporters to the White House for dinner, followed by a day of intensive ERA meetings. Most notably, in 1980, she co-chaired with Betty Ford a "National ERA Evening," which raised close to $100,000 for the cause. Phyllis Schlafly accused the president of "using his wife" for the ERA.[43] Interestingly, some feminists agreed, holding that Jimmy relied too heavily on the first lady when it came to the amendment's passage.

Historians have tended to see Jerry Falwell's founding of the Moral Majority in 1979 as marking the rise of the Christian right, with most activity occurring in the 1980s. Scholars of the Southern Baptist controversy have consistently reinforced this timetable, pointing to the victory of the ultraconservative or fundamentalist Adrian Rogers in winning the denominational presidency that same year. However, the historian Marjorie Spruill has more recently explored the National Women's Conference in Houston in 1977 as the turning point in the direction of feminism and the debate over the ERA. Commissioned by Gerald Ford, the National Women's Conference was the culmination of a series of state and regional conferences, during which delegates were elected for the Houston event. It was largely organized and promoted by feminists such as Betty Friedan, Gloria Steinem, Liz Carpenter, and Ellie Smeal, who were also the movers and shakers of the NWPC (National Women's Political Caucus), NOW, and ERAmerica. Jimmy Carter appointed the outspoken former New York congresswoman Bella Abzug, who had organized the NWPC, as presiding officer. When Schlafly could not sway the delegate elections, STOP ERA hosted the alternative Pro-Life, Pro-Family Rally across town in the Astrodome. Each event attracted thousands to its venue: approximately twenty thousand attended the National Women's Conference with fifteen thousand appearing at the Astrodome.[44]

Rosalynn was not as involved in the planning of the National Women's Conference. Launched by Ford, it occurred rather soon in her tenure; moreover, she found Abzug, whom she viewed as another one of those "bra-burning feminists," somewhat off-putting. Still, she helped open the ceremonies and lent it her vocal support. And her photograph with former first ladies Betty Ford and Lady Bird Johnson, the three holding hands and raising their arms together, proved iconic.

The conference lasted four days, as did its counterpart rally, and touched upon a range of needs and issues, from domestic abuse and inadequate childcare to workplace discrimination and welfare reform. The most controversial planks in its final Plan of Action called for greater reproductive freedoms for women, including access to government-funded abortions and civil rights for lesbians. These two items proved divisive because not all ERA advocates wanted them associated with the amendment. But with mounting attacks from anti-feminist groups such as STOP ERA and Save the Children as well as pressures from those more far-reaching feminists, the majority of delegates at the National Women's Conference were persuaded that abortion and homosexuality were integral to a comprehensive program regarding women's rights.

Not surprisingly, anti-feminists had a heyday. One pamphlet from the Pro-Family, Pro-Life Rally was typical in rallying the opposition with its boldfaced header: "Federal Festival for Female Radicals Financed with Your Money. DO WOMEN'S LIBBERS, HOMOSEXUALS, AND ABORTIONISTS SPEAK FOR YOU? This is what they intend to do."[45] After Houston, the ERA, abortion, and homosexuality became inseparable, forming what some might call the "holy triumvirate" of feminist thought and which opponents of the ERA fully exploited to their advantage.[46]

Thus, when starting with Phyllis Schlafly and Anita Bryant rather than Jerry Falwell and Adrian Rogers (or STOP ERA rather than the Moral Majority), the timeline for the Christian right and its family value agenda shifts, with far more activity occurring earlier in the 1970s. Even Beverly LaHaye's Concerned Women of America, which she organized in 1978, predates Falwell. So, too, do a host of smaller regional anti-feminist women's networks, Bible study groups, and meetings.[47] There are likewise hints that Rosalynn recognized the threat of the Christian right prior to Jimmy. The nature of the criticism she received when in office undoubtedly contributed to her greater awareness.

To be sure, a disproportionate number of letters addressed to the first lady focused on her ERA politicking, with most being quite hostile.[48] "Shame on you," wrote Mrs. R. R. Wyncoop from Colorado, for "trying to influence voters on that phony obnoxious ERA. One only has to look at Steiman (?spelling) [*sic*] to vote against anything she is for. I should think it would be beneath the dignity of the First Lady to influence voters."[49] Another insisted that ERA proponents were "a radical militant minority group interested in the legalization of homosexuality and lesbianism and radical social changes that effect our entire American tradition system and family units."[50] Echoing the furor over racially integrated bathrooms, Mrs. R. L. Nowlin of California expressed her horror that, upon stopping for gasoline, she and her husband found a "single Men and Women [rest]room." "Stop pressing the legislators to ratify this fraud called ERA less this become the norm," she protested.[51] Mrs. Lora Likens was typical in asking, "If you and your husband claim to be a born again Christians How in heavens name can you be for that ERA."[52] The "Ladies of Henderson United Methodist Church" in Mabelvale, Arkansas, reminded Mrs. Carter that "He [God] said that the man was to be the head of the house."[53] Another "Christian Baptist" admonished Mrs. Carter that the ERA "goes against everything you have been taught as a Baptist."[54] Ann Bowker of Oklahoma agreed. Citing North Carolina's vote against the amendment, she proclaimed that "the Power of the Lord is mightier than all the power of the Executive Branch, tax funds, and social feminist women's libbers in the matter of the ERA."[55]

The letters offered remedies and suggestions. "Get back to the church," wrote one to the first lady whose church attendance exceeded all other first ladies. Many admonished her to read her Bible and pray, seemingly ignorant that she did so nightly. A "concerned housewife and mother" from Birmingham, Alabama, encouraged a call to Phyllis Schlafly "to listen to her very sound arguments against ERA."[56] Overall, largely because of her position on the ERA, hundreds of Southern Baptist and evangelical women rebuked Rosalynn, claiming that she had failed to be the godly woman they expected of one of their own.

"FOR ERA" as a Southern Baptist Woman

Rosalynn understood many of these complaints. Perhaps because of the gendered nature of the criticisms directed toward her, she sought to temper what she viewed as feminism's most radical aspects in ways that might secure ERA support among her fellow Southerners and Southern Baptists back home. Her approach was threefold.

First, fighting against the Gloria Steinems on the one side and the Phyllis Schlaflys on the other, she addressed the ERA as separate from abortion and homosexuality. Rosalynn had struggled with the latter two issues on religious grounds. In terms of abortion, she said that it had taken her four to five years to come to any agreement with Jimmy as to how they both felt.[57] For the most part, she, like Jimmy, echoed moderate Southern Baptists who, over the 1970s, passed a series of denominational resolutions that sought a middle ground between "no abortion legislation" and "no legal abortion," or the polarized positions of "abortion on demand" and "abortion as murder." Because the 1970s SBC resolutions reflect the Carters' understanding, they are worth noting. A 1971 resolution, for instance, which was reaffirmed several times over the decade, advocated for the legal "possibility of abortion" under such conditions as "rape, incest, severe fetal deformity," and "damage" to maternal health. The resolution did, though, assert the need to protect the "sanctity of life, including fetal life." A 1976 resolution denounced and warned against using abortion as "a means to birth control," while insisting on the "right of expectant mothers to the full range of medical services and personal counseling."[58]

In interviews, Rosalynn always began her answer to the topic of abortion by emphasizing her personal opposition on religious and ethical grounds and admitted that it had taken her even longer than Jimmy to come to support *Roe v. Wade* as the law of the land. She also called herself old-fashioned in holding that she was against premarital sex, which was, in her opinion, a cause of the rising number of abortions.[59] When letters complained of her position or asked for clarification, she and her staff crafted a careful response that reinforced her affirmation of the ERA along with her personal opposition to abortion (though sometimes acknowledging that she did not advocate a constitutional amendment overturning the Supreme Court ruling).

Somewhat more privately, it appears, Rosalynn resented the ERA's growing association with the abortion debate and she made little, if any, comment on homosexuality. Thus, rather than argue for abortion as a constitutional right, Rosalynn focused on the need to improve the conditions into which many children were born. In interviews, she frequently encouraged alternatives to abortion and argued for expanding family planning clinics, making the adoption process easier, better promoting birth control and sex education, and even funding teenage pregnancy centers. In her arguments, she often depended on evidence and statistics used by pro-life forces and questioned by pro-choice feminists, maintaining in one interview, after being asked about the lack of funding for poor women, "But do you know how many abortions are repeat ones? A large number. A very large number. I think we should stress the prevention of pregnancy rather than say, 'Go ahead and get pregnant and you can have an abortion.'"[60] It is revealing that her White House files marked "ERA," "women's rights," "women's issues," or, less frequently, "feminism" were crammed with articles addressing how issues like poverty, unemployment, divorce, lack of state-funded childcare, and inadequate healthcare devastated a range of women. In contrast, only a few were marked, or even addressed, "abortion," and fewer still "homosexuality."

Several East Wing notes and memos discussing Rosalynn's speech at the National Women's Conference reflected the increasing difficulty of her position. Staff members agreed that she "choose a theme far from the more radical and emotional topics of the ERA, something that that shows ERA is good for the Family." Citing an example, they proposed that Rosalynn address the ways the ERA would provide economic assistance to women forced into the workplace, adding that she include "some Mother, Flag and Apple Pie to it, which is," they explained, "the dominant morality in the country and it is this morality that does not understand or fights against the ERA."[61] When letters to Rosalynn after the conference queried her acceptance of "lesbianism," her staff was quick to point out that "Mrs. Carter has made no statement on homosexuality" and that her attendance at the Women's Conference indicated her support of the ERA rather than those more controversial issues.[62]

Second, as the amendment faltered, she not only became more vocal but partnered with her daughter-in-law, Judy Langford Carter, to court homemakers and housewives, those white, middle-class, and Southern Baptist women Schlafly was winning. This was also the demographic Rosalynn and Judy knew best. A Georgia native and Southern Baptist, Judy had married Jack when working for Jimmy's first gubernatorial bid in 1966. When the rest of the Carter family moved into the White House in 1977, they stayed behind, living in Calhoun, Georgia, with their toddler Jason. To be sure, Judy appeared the typical Southern housewife, harkening back to the newly married Rosalynn.

Rosalynn and Judy agreed that the stereotypical image of the ERA posed "a serious problem." "Attention," Rosalynn later wrote in her autobiography, "had centered on those [feminist ERA advocates] who have appeared demanding strident man haters and mostly urban professional women." "Nice women," as Judy commented and Rosalynn echoed, not without criticism from feminists, "have been reluctant to be identified with such a group."[63] With Judy's help, Rosalynn attempted to counter this image. One East Wing memo suggested a new "Southern strategy" that "gets away from its rather liberal East Coast flavor and appeals to housewives and women in the South and Midwest." It even suggested "the help of new kinds of personality to speak out—e.g. country and western singers like Tammy Wynette."[64] While not quite reaching out to Wynette, Rosalynn and Judy did work diligently to recruit popular personalities like humorist Erma Bombeck and *All in the Family's* Jean Stapleton to the cause. And they pushed beyond the usual feminist and political circles to address more traditional women's organizations. On at least one occasion, Rosalynn met with a pro-life women's group, inviting its officers to the White House.[65] She hosted the wives of numerous religious leaders, consulted with moderate Christian evangelicals, and addressed the

ERA in popular women's home magazines such as the *Ladies Home Journal, Family Circle*, and *McCalls*. For her part, Judy organized Housewives for ERA, which sponsored luncheons and teas throughout Georgia. She, too, gave frequent interviews in traditional women's magazines and even penned a regular column for *Redbook*. In addition, she sometimes took Rosalynn's place in giving speeches and attending fundraisers, visiting eleven of the unratified states in a fifteen-month period.

In most every venue, Rosalynn and Judy pointed to themselves as women who were outside the liberal feminist framework and for the ERA. As Rosalynn put it, "I feel it is extremely important to explain that women like me support the ERA. I am a relatively traditional person, I enjoy my roles as wife, mother, partner and business woman. I care about how I look—and what I think."[66] In her *Redbook* column, Judy signed her name as "Judy, a rural housewife and homemaker from Georgia." The "movement for the ERA," they emphasized, was just as much for "women who chose to remain at home and care for a family." Someday, Rosalynn warned, they might find themselves on hard times—either divorced or widowed and supporting a family, perhaps becoming, in the words of Judy, "a little old lady in the trailer parks" or one of "the ladies in the laundromat."[67] Rosalynn even pointed to her own mother's struggle to make ends meet after her husband's early death. Homemakers and housewives, they insisted, were those most vulnerable in terms of property rights, inheritance, credit, insurance, and alimony.[68] Over and over, the two maintained that the problem with the ERA was that everyday women "simply do not know what it means" and that the opposition's "distorted stories frighten people," citing fears about mandatory military service for women and homosexual marriage.[69] It seemed almost impossible, Rosalynn admitted, to convince women "that ERA will not require changes for those who do not want changes."[70] But Rosalynn and Judy made it their goal to do so, thereby creating their own "Southern strategy."

Finally, it was no secret that Rosalynn opposed Jimmy's appointment of Midge Costanza as assistant to the president for public liaison and Bella Abzug as chair of the National Advisory Committee on Women, largely because she perceived the two as embodying, once again, that radical image of Northern feminism at odds with conservative Americans such as Southern Baptists. Both had been active in New York politics and the Democratic party. Costanza had run Carter's New York campaign and nominated him at the convention while Abzug represented a congressional district in Manhattan in the US House. True to Rosalynn's warnings, there were difficulties from the start. Costanza made Rosalynn uncomfortable, referring to herself as "that loud-mouth pushy little broad" who was as passionate about gay rights as women's rights, believing the two were conjoined. Likewise, "Battling Bella" began pushing the National Women's Conference's Plan of Action, some of which Rosalynn as well as Jimmy found problematic. Perhaps Rosalynn blamed her for Schlafly's rally across town, which siphoned those "nice" women she felt might accept the ERA if it were not so closely associated with Costanza's and Abzug's agendas.

In the fall of 1978, having been demoted and reprimanded for inviting the National Gay Task Force to the White House, Costanza, clearly under duress, resigned. Carter then fired Abzug a few months later. Their departures cost Jimmy the endorsement of the NWPC, NOW, ERAmerica, and most prominent feminists, all of whom blamed Rosalynn as much as Jimmy for betraying their cause. Interestingly, if conservative Southern Baptist and other women accused Rosalynn of being too assertive and even exploiting Amy, feminists blamed Rosalynn for doggedly following Jimmy. A *MS Magazine* editorial, for instance, rated her a five on a ten-point scale, noting "it's difficult to imagine her stating any serious view separate from the President's."[71]

Costanza's and Abzug's replacements were undoubtedly approved by Rosalynn. Sarah Weddington had already become assistant to the president and largely assumed those women's issues handled by Constanza. While the young lawyer who argued *Roe v. Wade* might appear a controversial choice, her Texas accent, Southern demeanor, and feminine appearance were perceived as nonthreatening, and her role in *Roe v. Wade* was downplayed. In fact, when she was introduced in certain circles, her official biography simply noted that "she was on the winning side in an important Supreme Court case."[72] The daughter of a Methodist minister, she understood the evangelical South. Replacing Abzug was the popular Lynda Johnson Robb, a friend of the Carters who appealed to mainstream Americans, many of whom remembered her as the Johnson daughter who married in the White House. All in all, the leadership of the National Advisory Committee on Women increasingly seemed more of a ceremonial position.

By late 1979, energies in the White House were shifting. Despite the looming reelection, Jimmy was forced to devote himself to the Iranian hostage crisis. Rosalynn took to the campaign trail, traveling in his stead, with Weddington assuming responsibility for the ERA. As she traversed the country once again, Rosalynn remarked that the failure of the ERA to pass within Carter's first term was her greatest White House disappointment to date, a sentiment she has rehearsed many times since.[73]

Final Days

The extent to which Rosalynn considered her activism around the ERA as a form of feminist advocacy remains unclear. She certainly perceived the feminism of Costanza and Abzug to be as threatening to the ERA's passage as she did the appearance of Steinem in Georgia years earlier. In addition, as she assumed responsibility for much of the reelection campaign, she became more keenly aware of the power, and dangers, of the new Christian right as it extended beyond Schlafly and STOP ERA to include the newly formed Moral Majority and to penetrate Carter's evangelical and Southern Baptist base. One example proved telling: "Making my way through the crowd after a speech in a Texas shopping center, I realized how organized the Moral Majority had become," she wrote, "when all along the path that the police had cleared were women holding their hands out with cards reading, 'You don't love Jesus.'" When Rosalynn exclaimed that she did love Jesus, several protesters explained, "If you loved Jesus, you wouldn't be supporting the ERA."[74]

In 1979, Rosalynn helped secure the appointment of the Southern Baptist minister and preacher Robert L. Maddox as the president's religious liaison, hoping he might curb the growing Christian conservative movement. Maddox served as the minister of Jack and Judy Carter's church in Calhoun, Georgia. With a seminary degree from Southwestern Baptist, a doctorate from Emory, and a taste for politics, Maddox had written the president several times, offering his services as a religious liaison. While he received only curt replies of "no thanks" from the West Wing, Rosalynn had responded more favorably and even suggested his name to assist in writing Carter's speeches. Upon his arrival at the White House that May, Maddox, by his account, interacted frequently with and had regular contact with the first lady.[75]

At first, the West Wing did not quite understand the new role or how to use Maddox. Admittedly, the president's attentions concentrated on the hostage crisis. And as for his reelection, Carter felt more threatened by the left and Ted Kennedy's internal bid for the Democratic nomination. Some might say the White House Conference on Families reflected his attempt to cater to the liberals in the party. Thus, despite others' mounting concerns, it appears that Jimmy still felt assured of the evangelical vote.

While much ink has been spilt over the White House Conference on Families, its significance has perhaps been exaggerated as indicating a turn in the election or evangelical sentiment towards Jimmy. It was merely one in a number of events that inspired the religious opposition. By the time the president opened the conference on June 6, 1980, the wheels of the Christian right were well in motion, carrying a multitude of conservative Christian groups and organizations, with thousands of followers. These groups had motivated Maddox to write the Oval Office in 1978, offering his services as he realized, along with Rosalynn, the urgency of the situation.[76]

Both Maddox and Rosalynn worked diligently to pull in evangelicals and Southern Baptists. According to Maddox, however, "by the time I got here [the White House], he [Jimmy] was in such deep trouble with the more conservative groups that I spent most of my time trying to put out the fires—unsuccessfully most of the time—among the conservatives who were, by then, really deeply set against Jimmy Carter."[77] Maddox's papers from the period are filled with "suggestions for relating to conservative evangelicals," lists of the names of figures who could assist (mostly Southern Baptists who proved moderates), and correspondence and notes from meetings with religious leaders, many of which included Rosalynn.[78] While somewhat successful with moderate Southern Baptists, the Carters' gatherings with extreme conservative types like D. James Kennedy, Tim LaHaye, Charles Stanley, and especially Jerry Falwell proved disastrous. By 1980, Maddox was questioning whether conservative evangelicals had actually voted for Jimmy in 1976, including those Southern Baptists who claimed to have endorsed him then. In his exit interview, Maddox pointed to a different kind of "born-again evangelical" from that of his traditional Southern Baptist upbringing. In his words, "for born-agains in the independent group and to born-agains in Ohio and Illinois and California, born again translates not only into a personal relationship but in a very definite moral code. And these days, it's abortion and ERA and anti-gay and stuff like that."[79]

By all accounts, including her own, Rosalynn harbored more anger over Jimmy's defeat in 1980 than he did. "I am bitter enough for both of us," she commented at the time. Most scholars and pundits have recognized that a host of issues and parties brought down the Carter presidency, with Jimmy himself accepting this interpretation. Rosalynn blamed the Christian right more directly. When asked about Rosalynn's irritation in the days after the election and whether she was "hacked at any particular forces," Maddox was candid: "Well, she puts them all in the Moral Majority crowd."[80] Jimmy might have underestimated the power of the Christian right, stating that it was only in 1979, with the election of Adrian Rogers to the SBC's presidency, that he recognized a problem. Rosalynn's struggle, however, reached back much further, with her early efforts to ratify the ERA. Her ongoing frustration had clearly morphed into a stronger, more acerbic resentment for this one particular force.

Conclusion

As "equality between the sexes" struggled to replace the prevailing "hierarchy of the sexes" during the 1970s, the private residence of the White House became a new public battleground, the lives of its occupants scrutinized around gender and its first lady judged accordingly. Rosalynn's was a nearly impossible task. But despite the insults hurled at her from all directions, questioning both her femininity and her feminism as she tried to develop her own "Southern strategy," the first lady did show Southern Baptists that they that could be for the ERA. Perhaps even more significantly, the public nature of her struggle inspired other Southern Baptist and evangelical women who were grappling over who they were and who they should be in light of their faith and the tumultuous changes introduced by feminism. Amidst the overwhelming criticism of Rosalynn, Ms. Patt Casey wrote: "I am a transplanted Southerner who has been transported to California . . . so I feel a special sense of sisterhood based on a mutual background and a mutual dedication to women's rights. I just want to help join the many women I know who are so grateful to you for the effort you have made to help pass the E.R.A. and to encourage you to keep the faith and keep the good works. I am especially pleased to see you teaching Southern women to think for ourselves and have the courage of our convictions for the first time in our history. You are an inspiration and model for us all."[81]

While it took women like Patt Casey some time to organize, there were those in the SBC who eventually formed networks. Groups like Southern Baptists for the Family and Equal Rights as well as Southern Baptist Women in Ministry published their ideas in newsletters and a journal *(FOLIO)* and hosted conferences (Theology Is a Verb and Women in Church Related-Vocations). They forged an evangelical feminism that pushed at least some Southern Baptists to advocate for the ERA, women's rights, and women's leadership in ecclesial matters, while often remaining tentative about abortion and striving to distinguish themselves from those Rosalynn viewed as "strident man-haters." In 2000, Rosalynn and Jimmy Carter left the Southern Baptist Convention for moderate Baptist life, largely because of the denomination's public stance against women's ordination. In a column written in

2009, Jimmy claimed he was willing to "lose my religion for equality." In 2015, he published *A Call to Action: Women, Religion, Violence and Power* and claimed that, "urged by Rosalynn," he was "making women's rights the fight of my life." While the sentiment of the Christian right against Jimmy persisted, the feminist animus against him seemingly vanished. Jimmy Carter has come to symbolize a "new kind of Baptist" regarding the cultural issues of women and gender. Rosalynn Carter, however, embodied that reality nearly forty years prior and suffered vitriolic criticism for her increasingly marginal stance among Southern Baptists, women as well as men.

Notes

1. Note that I will often use the first names of the Carters to avoid any confusion.
2. This story and its related quotes appear in multiple sources. For Rosalynn Carter's own account, see *First Lady from Plains* (Fayetteville: Univ. of Arkansas Press, 1982), 99–100. See, too, Rosalynn Carter, interview by Gail Sheehy, Records of the First Lady's Office, Press Office, First Lady's Audio Visual Files, Container 4, Jimmy Carter Presidential Library, Atlanta, GA. Jimmy wrongly assumed Rosalynn's position because she had responded negatively to a local news report that Gloria Steinem planned to lead an ERA march in Atlanta, mentioning to Jimmy that "it was the worst possible thing to do to get the ERA passed." Jimmy took Rosalynn's remark to indicate that she was against the ERA. She was not. Rosalynn later clarified that she had meant that Northern feminists like Steinem would prove ineffective in the traditional South, which proved to be a harbinger of things to come.
3. See Randall Balmer, *Redeemer: The Life of Jimmy Carter* (New York, NY: Basic Books, 2014); and J. Brooks Flippen, *Jimmy Carter: The Politics of Family and the Rise of the Religious Right* (Athens: Univ. of Georgia Press, 2011).
4. While early historians of the Christian right acknowledged women such as Schlafly, Bryant, and LaHaye, they usually cast them as secondary characters in minor plots to the major story. See, for instance, Michael Lienesch, *Redeeming American Piety and Politics in the New Christian Right* (Chapel Hill: Univ. of North Carolina Press, 1993); and William Martin, *With God on Our Side: The Rise of the Christian Right in America* (New York, NY: Broadway Books, 1996). Moreover, an ongoing debate over the origins of the Christian right, pitting race and civil rights legislation over and against abortion and *Roe v. Wade*, has focused almost exclusively on the rhetoric and machinations of key male figures like Jerry Falwell, Ed McAteer, Francis Schaeffer, and Paul Weyrich. In *Thy Kingdom Come, How the Religious Right Distorts the Faith and Ruins America* (New York, NY: Basic Books, 2006), Randall Balmer argued for civil rights as the "real origins" of the Christian right, assigning what he called the "abortion

myth" to Falwell, arguing that it was a calculated attempt on the part of the right to avoid charges of racism. More recent studies, however, have incorporated the networks and groups of women like Bryant, LaHaye, and Schlafly more fully into their analysis, thereby questioning Balmer. See, for example, Seth Dowland, *Family Values: Gender, Authority, and the Rise of the Christian Right* (Philadelphia: Univ. of Pennsylvania Press, 2015); and Daniel K. Williams, *God's Own Party: The Making of the Christian Right* (New York, NY: Oxford Univ. Press, 2010). In terms of the Southern Baptist controversy, the focus has been almost exclusively on the "fundamentalists takeover" or "conservative resurgence" that began when Paige Patterson and Paul Pressler successfully orchestrated a plan to have Adrian Rogers secure the presidency of the SBC in 1979. Most of these studies have been "insider" accounts, which considered male denominationalists in a theological and institutional battle somewhat removed from the culture wars of the Christian right. From a moderate perspective, see Grady C. Cothen, *What Happened to the Southern Baptist Convention* (Macon, GA: Smith and Helwys, 1993); his sequel *The New SBC: Fundamentalism's Impact on the Southern Baptist Convention* (Macon, GA: Smith and Helwys, 1995); and Walter B. Shurden, ed., *The Struggle for the Soul of the SBC: Moderate Responses to the Fundamentalist Movement* (Macon, GA: Mercer Univ. Press, 1993). Conservatives included James C. Hefley, *The Truth in Crisis: The Controversy in the Southern Baptist Convention*, 5 vols. (Hannibal, MI: Hannibal Books, 1989–1990); and Jerry Sutton, *The Baptist Reformation: The Conservative Resurgence in the Southern Baptist Convention* (Nashville, TN: Broadman and Holman, 2000). Bill J. Leonard, *God's Last and Only Hope: The Fragmentation of the Southern Baptist Convention* (Grand Rapids, MI: William B. Eerdman, 1990) and David T. Morgan, *The New Crusades, the New Holy Land: Conflict in the Southern Baptist Convention, 1969–1991* (Tuscaloosa: Univ. of Alabama Press, 1996) offered analysis that explored cultural matters, though the dates and characters remained the same. For considerations that accounted for gender, see Nancy Tatom Ammerman, *Baptist Battles: Social Change and Religious Conflict in the Southern Baptist Convention* (New Brunswick, NJ: Rutgers Univ. Press, 1990); Barry Hankins, *Uneasy in Babylon: Southern Baptist Conservatives and American Culture* (Tuscaloosa: Univ. of Alabama Press, 2002); as well as my own work, *Into the Pulpit: Southern Baptist Women and Power since World War II* (Chapel Hill: Univ. of North Carolina Press, 2012); and Eileen Campbell-Reed, *Anatomy of a Schism: How Clergywomen's Narratives Reinterpret the Fracturing of the Southern Baptist Convention* (Knoxville: Univ. of Tennessee Press, 2016).

5. To date, there is only one scholarly biography devoted to Rosalynn Carter: Scott Kaufman, *Rosalynn Carter: Equal Partner in the White House* (Lawrence: Univ. Press of Kansas, 2007).
6. Over 2015, I made several week-long archival trips to the Jimmy Carter Presidential Library in Atlanta. Unless otherwise indicated, early biographical information on Rosalynn Carter comes from the many interviews of Rosalynn Carter and her

family, most of which were conducted during her years in the White House and are now archived in the Carter Library. I depended heavily on the Carter Smith Oral History Project here. I also consulted Rosalynn Carter's autobiography, *First Lady from Plains;* Kaufman, *Rosalynn Carter: Equal Partner in the White House;* and E. Stanly Godbold Jr., *Jimmy and Rosalynn Carter: The Georgia Years, 1924–1974* (New York, NY: Oxford Univ. Press, 2010).

7. Allie Smith, interview by Marie B. Allen, Dec. 19, 1979, Carter Smith Family Oral History Project, Jimmy Carter Presidential Library.
8. Carter, *First Lady from Plains*, 22.
9. See Allie Smith, interview.
10. Carter, *First Lady from Plains*, 29.
11. See, for instance, the interview of Edna Langford and Linda Maddox conducted by Larry King, Aug. 29, 1980, *The Larry King Show*, Records of the First Lady's Office, Press Office, First Lady's Audio Visual Files, Container 5.
12. See Carter, *First Lady from Plains*, 49–52; and interview of Lillian Carter, Carter Smith Family Oral History Project.
13. Carter, *First Lady from Plains*, 93.
14. Edna Langford and Linda Maddox, interview by Larry King.
15. Memo to Mary Hoyt, "on RSC's role as mother for Lisa Myers piece," n.d.; and "Q's and A's for Barbara Walters Interview," Dec. 13, 1978, Records of the First Lady's Office, Press Office, Mary Hoyt's Press Clippings Files, Amy Carter file, Box 37. While Rosalynn Carter wrote about Amy in *First Lady from Plains*, questions from interviewers actually elicited more immediate responses. I also watched numerous videos and listened to many audio recordings from the First Lady's Audio Visual Files, during which interviewers and callers consistently peppered Rosalynn Carter with questions about Amy. See, too, the many articles, interviews, and clippings on Amy in Mary Hoyt's Press Clippings Files, Amy Carter and First Family files, Box 37.
16. Mary Fitzgerald was convicted and imprisoned for the murder of a man she did not know that occurred in a street fight. The Carters held she did not commit the crime and that her verdict was indicative of the injustices of the judicial system because she did not have access to a lawyer. Few Georgians seemed bothered that Fitzpatrick was a prison laborer, though the issue was raised when the Carters entered the White House. Interestingly, Jimmy Carter served as Fitzgerald's probation officer so she could continue as Amy's nanny and live in the White House.
17. Flowers, *Into the Pulpit*, 59.
18. See both Dowland, *Family Values*; and Marjorie Spruill, *Divided We Stand: The Battle Over Women's Rights and Family Values That Polarized American Politics* (New York, NY: Bloomsbury, 2017).
19. For a history of abortion and its changing politics, see Karissa Haugeberg, *Women against Abortion: Inside the Largest Reform Movement of the Twentieth Century*

(Urbana: Univ. of Illinois Press, 2017); and Daniel Williams, *Defenders of the Unborn: The Pro-Life Movement before Roe v. Wade* (New York, NY: Oxford Univ. Press, 2016).

20. I made this argument in *Into the Pulpit* as well.
21. As quoted in Balmer, *Redeemer*, 26.
22. See Balmer, *Redeemer*, 24–28, for an in-depth analysis of Jimmy Carter's born-again experience. Carter did not mention the walk with his sister, Ruth, in his campaign autobiography, *Why Not the Best* (Nashville, TN: Broadman Press, 1975), although in Bill Moyers's 1976 interview with Carter, he spoke of the sermon as leading to both a transformation and deepening of his faith. See Don Richardson, *Conversations with Carter* (Boulder, CO: Lynne Rienner), 14–15.
23. Balmer, *Redeemer*, 26.
24. Carter, *First Lady from Plains*, 2. See, too, Allie Smith, interview.
25. Interview conducted by Jan Jarboe, Nov. 29, 1978, Records of the First Lady's Office, Press Office, First Lady's Audio Visual Files, Container 2.
26. See, for example, the interview of Rosalynn Carter conducted by Clarence Davidson, Nov. 28, 1978, Records of the First Lady's Office, Press Office, First Lady's Audio Visual Files, Container 2; and the interview conducted by Jan Jarboe. When Rosalynn's two friends Edna Langford and Linda Maddox were interviewed and asked by Larry King, "We hear a lot about Jimmy Carter being religious and born again; is she?" they answered affirmatively, explaining that she had a close experience with God, read her Bible nightly, and that "God is her strength" and "Jesus Christ her savior." See interview of Langford and Maddox.
27. Carter, *First Lady from Plains*, 62–63.
28. Godbold, *Jimmy and Rosalynn*, 34.
29. For a history of the role of the first lady, I consulted: Betty Boyd Caroli, *First Ladies: From Martha Washington to Michelle Obama* (New York, NY: Oxford Univ. Press, 2010); Katherine A. S. Sibley, "Introduction," in *A Companion to First Ladies*, ed. Sibley (Oxford: Wiley Blackwell, 2016); Gilford Toy, *Mr. and Mrs. President: The Trumans to the Clintons* (Lawrence: Univ. Press of Kansas, 2000); and Robert Watson, *The Presidents' Wives: Reassessing the Office of the First Lady* (Boulder, CO: Lynne Rienner, 2000).
30. In promoting the idea of the first lady project, Lady Bird Johnson might be seen as something of an activist. But the description of "pet," which was often added to "project," was telling.
31. Quoted in Balmer, *Redeemer*, 61.
32. Balmer, *Redeemer*, xxvi.
33. The memos from Rosalynn Carter's press secretary, Mary Finch Hoyt, to Rosalynn pointed to these criticisms and indicated ways to address them to her advantage in interviews. See Records of the First Lady's Office, Press Office, Mary Hoyt's Subject Files, Memos to Rosalynn Carter from Mary Hoyt, Briefing Papers files, East Wing files, Press Interviews files, Box 31. See, too, her memoir of these years:

East Wing: Politics, the Press, and a First Lady (Philadelphia, PA: Xlibris, 2001). For a good overview of the criticism balanced with affirmation, see B. Drummond Ayres Jr., "The Importance of Being Rosalynn," *New York Times*, June 3, 1979; and Howard Norton, "She Argues with Carter," *The Atlanta Constitution*, Oct. 13, 1979. Mary Hoyt offers an in-depth view of the criticisms.

34. Walter Mondale, *The Good Fight: A Life in Liberal Politics* (New York, NY: Scribner, 2010), 229.
35. Despite his military service and avid outdoorsmanship, Jimmy Carter's detractors did question and attack his masculinity later in the term, which became a key tactic of the Reagan campaign.
36. Ayres, "The Importance of Being Rosalynn."
37. See Henry Fairlie, "First Ladies Should Be Nominated, Not Married," *The Washington Post*, Aug. 10, 1980; and Sara Wideman, "Portrait of a Lady," *The New Republic*, Aug. 20, 2001. Fairlie indicates differing opinions as to the extent of Rosalynn's power in relation to Jimmy.
38. Norma Langley and Mary Ann Norbom, "Rosalynn Carter Proves She's Not Just the Power behind the Throne—She's All Set to Take Over," *The Star*, Aug. 7, 1977.
39. This interpretation was largely the result of NOW's refusal to endorse Jimmy Carter for reelection. In terms of evidence, I consulted numerous collections and files from the Records of the First Lady's Office at the Carter Presidential Library. Unless indicated otherwise, my analysis of Rosalynn Carter's ERA activities is based primarily on this archival research. The Records of the First Lady's Office is subdivided into Rosalynn Carter's six offices. I spent most of my time reading files from the Correspondence Office, the Press Office, and the Projects Office. From the First Lady's Correspondence Office, I drew from Rhonda Bush's Correspondence Files: Abortion file, Box 1; Equal Rights Amendment files, Box 4; Families, White House Conference on, files, Box 4; International Woman's Year file, Box 5; and Women files, Box 10. From the First Lady's Press Office, I consulted Mary Hoyt's Subject Files, ERA Issues files, Box 31; and the many interviews in the First Lady's Audio Visual Files. The First Lady's Projects Office proved a goldmine, and I consulted the many files related to ERA and women in Kathy Cade's Projects Files, which filled Boxes 16–19, 46–49. From the Scheduling Office, the Secretary's Office, and the Social Office, I considered any file with an event, letter, note, or memo linked to the ERA, women's issues and groups, religion, and the first family.
40. Memo from Kathy Cade, no date, Records of the First Lady's Office, Projects Office, Kathy Cade's Subject Files, ERA-Memos and Correspondence file, Box 17.
41. Memo from the White House to the heads of departments and agencies, July 20, 1978, Records of the First Lady's Office, Projects Office, Kathy Cade's Subject Files, ERA file, Box 16.
42. These included, among others, the Women's Division of the United Methodist Church, the SBC's Christian Life Commission, the American Baptist Churches, and the Religious Committee for the ERA.

43. "ERA," UP press release, n.d., Records of the First Lady's Office, Projects Office, Kathy Cade's Subject Files, ERA-Memos and Correspondence file, Box 17.
44. For a history of the conference, see Spruill, *Divided We Stand,* 1–14, 205–61.
45. Pamphlet, Records of the First Lady's Office, Projects Office, Kathy Cade's Subject Files, ERA-International Woman's Year Conference files, Box 16.
46. See Dowland, "'Family Values' and the Formation of a Christian Right Agenda," *Church History* 78, no. 3 (Sept. 2009): 607.
47. Flowers, *Into the Pulpit*, 76–86.
48. All of these letters come from Records of the First Lady's Office, Social Office, White House Social Office Files, Human Rights-Women files, Boxes 35 and 36.
49. Mrs. R. R. Wyncoop to Ms. Carter, n.d. Mrs. R. R. Wyncoop actually questioned her own spelling with the parenthetical, though it is unclear whether she was intentional or not.
50. Mrs. J. Freeman to Mrs. Jimmy Carter, Mar. 1, 1977.
51. Mrs. R. L. Nowlin to Ms. Carter, Mar. 14, 1977.
52. Mrs. Lora Likens to First Lady Rosalynn Carter, n.d.
53. Ladies of Henderson United Methodist Church to Mrs. Carter, n.d.
54. Mrs. Doyle Dillahunty, Mar. 1, 1977.
55. Anne Bowker to Mrs. (Ms?) [*sic*] Carter, Mar. 2, 1977.
56. Anne (Mrs. W. Price Jr.) Hightower to Mrs. Carter, Mar. 22, 1977.
57. Rosalynn Carter, interview by Gail Sheehy.
58. The SBC passed and reaffirmed resolutions on abortion that advocated this middle ground in 1971, 1974, 1976, 1977, 1978, and 1979. In 1980, the denomination sent a different message with a resolution calling for a "constitutional amendment prohibiting abortion except to save the life of the mother." Subsequent resolutions followed this more conservative turn. For texts of SBC resolutions on abortion, see: http://www.sbc.net/resolutions/search/results.asp?query=abortion.
59. See, for example, "Rosalynn Carter Face-Off," *Ladies Home Journal*, Sept. 1980; and Rosalynn Carter, interview by Clifford Edwards, RKO General Broadcasting, Records of the First Lady's Office, Press Office, Mary Hoyt's Subject Files, Memos to Rosalynn Carter from Mary Hoyt-Press Interviews files, verbal transcript, Box 31.
60. Ann Blackman, "Abortion," AP press release, n.d., Records of the First Lady's Office, Correspondence Office, Rhonda Bush's Correspondence Files, ERA file, Box 4.
61. Memo from Coates Redmon to Mary Hoyt, "On Rosalynn Carter's ERA Speech in Houston," Nov. 7, 1977, Records of the First Lady's Office, Projects Office, Kathy Cade's Subject Files, ERA-International Woman's Year Conference files, Box 16.
62. See the series of memos and notes between Rhonda Busch, Kathy Cade, and Mary Hoyt on representing Rosalynn Carter's position after the National Women's Conference, Jan. 25 to Feb. 28, 1978, Records of the First Lady's Office, Correspondence Office, Rhonda Bush Correspondence Files, ERA file, Box 4. Other letters referencing Rosalynn's participation emphasized the conference's affirmation of

ERA and its addressing more noncontroversial issues, such as women's leadership in the arts, education, and fighting domestic abuse, leaving out abortion and homosexuality.

63. Carter, *First Lady from Plains*, 309; and Judy Carter, "Why Nice Women Should Speak Out for ERA," *Redbook Magazine*, Oct. 1977.
64. Memo from Kathy Cade for the files, "Summary of Meeting with Pat Schroeder and Barbara Mikulski," July 17, 1978, Records of the First Lady's Office, Press Office, Mary Hoyt's Subject Files, ERA Issues file, Box 31. For the proposed Southern strategy, see the attached Agenda, Meeting with the First Lady, n.d., Records of the First Lady's Office, Press Office, Mary Hoyt's Subject Files, ERA Issues file, Box 31. While the agenda does not have a date, it appears to accompany a group of memos and notes from July 1978.
65. "Houston Life Advocates Visit White House," *Life Advocate*, Feb. 1979, Records of the First Lady's Office, Press Office, Mary Hoyt's Press Clippings Files, Women's Issues files, Box 59. See, too, the clippings in the second file here for shifts in strategies and increasing feminist criticism of the Carters.
66. Rosalynn Carter, "Women and America Speech," Records of the First Lady's Office, Correspondence Office, Rhonda Bush's Correspondence Files, ERA file, Box 4.
67. Judy Carter as quoted by Anne Corwin in "ERA, Housewives . . . and Judy Carter," *The Atlanta Journal*, May 8, 1979.
68. See, for instance, Judy Carter, "The ERA—Misunderstood and Feared: Housewives Stand to Gain Most, Yet Are Most Vocal in Their Opposition," *Los Angeles Times*, Jan. 26, 1978.
69. Judy Carter, "The ERA—Misunderstood and Feared." See also her interview with Edward P. Morgan, Records of the First Lady's Office, Press Office, First Lady's Audio Visual Files.
70. Judy Carter, "The ERA—Misunderstood and Feared."
71. "Spousal Politics . . . Or, 'Betty Ford, Where Are You Now We Need You,'" *MS Magazine*, Jan. 1978, 46. Interestingly, the characterization of Rosalynn as being too assertive led conservatives to portray Jimmy as lacking in masculinity.
72. Susan Wood, "The Weddington Way," *The Washington Post*, Feb. 17, 1979.
73. Rosalynn has claimed the failure of the ERA as her greatest White House disappointment in numerous interviews and venues. See, too, the interview of Rosalynn Carter conducted by Barbara Walters, Dec. 15, 1978, Records of the First Lady's Office, Press Office, First Lady's Audio Visual Files, Container 2; and Carter, *First Lady from Plains*, 307.
74. Carter, *First Lady from Plains*, 361.
75. Maddox wrote a memoir of his White House experience: *Preacher at the White House* (Nashville, TN: Broadman Press, 1984). See, in addition, the rather extensive exit interview of Maddox conducted by Marie Allen, Dec. 8, 1980, Exit Interview Project, Carter Library.

76. Interestingly, with Jimmy's focus elsewhere, the burden of the White House Conference on Families fell to his White House staff, who viewed it rather simply as a matter of keeping a campaign promise.
77. Maddox, interview by Marie Allen.
78. See, for example, Records of the President's Office, Office of the Assistance for Public Outreach, Anne Wexler Collection, Robert Lee Maddox Religious Liasion Files, Memo file, Box 107.
79. Maddox, interview by Marie Allen.
80. Maddox, interview by Marie Allen.
81. Patt Casey (Ms.) to Mrs. Carter, Records of the First Lady's Office, Social Office, White House Social Office Files, Human Rights-Women files, Box 35.

Eight

CAMELOT REVISITED

Women Doctoral Graduates of the Southern Baptist Theological Seminary, 1982–1992, Talk about the Seminary and Their Lives since SBTS . . . Again

Susan M. Shaw, Kryn Freehling-Burton,
O'Dessa Monnier, and Tisa Lewis

An unprecedented number of women enrolled in the Southern Baptist Theological Seminary (Southern) in the 1970s and 1980s. They had come to the denomination's flagship seminary in Louisville, Kentucky, as a result of a "call" or "calling," as Southern Baptists often describe a believer's divinely sanctioned vocational pursuit.[1] They were buoyed by a women's movement opening doors to women in professions and a Baptist missions education that had told girls and young women that they could be anything God called them to be. Most of them arrived at Southern thinking their calling was missions, education, or local church work. Some already understood their call to be that of the ordained pastorate. Since the nineteenth century, Southern had been a bastion of male presence, power, and privilege, preparing men for ministry and leadership in the church and denomination. In 1970, women accounted for only 10.6 percent of student enrollment across all six Southern Baptist seminaries, but, by the 1981–82 academic year, women made up nearly 30 percent of the entering class.[2] This growing presence of women generated a rethinking of gender roles as well as the nature of ministry and leadership itself.

At that same historical moment, fundamentalists within the Southern Baptist Convention (SBC)—in response to the civil rights movement, feminism, and the prevalence of biblical historical criticism in Southern Baptist seminaries—launched a campaign to wrest control of the denomination from its more moderate leaders.[3] Caught in the crossfires of this conflict were Southern Baptist women pursuing seminary degrees, especially those who were beginning to demand an equal place in SBC seminaries en route to its pulpits. Two of us chapter authors (Tisa Lewis and Susan Shaw) were among these numbers at Southern in the 1980s. Tisa earned an MA in 1983 and a PhD in 1988, and Susan earned an MA in 1984 and a PhD in 1987. Thus, we have been intimately connected with and are a part of this story.

In the late 1990s, we (Lewis and Shaw) interviewed twenty-nine of the thirty-six women who had graduated from Southern with PhDs in theology, biblical studies, ethics, pastoral care, church history, or religious education from 1982 to 1992, during the height of the battles between fundamentalists and moderates that ultimately purged the denomination of most moderates. The women we interviewed were some of the first to enroll in PhD programs at Southern, particularly in the biblical and theological disciplines. Many were our peers and our friends. Our study, published in 1998 in *Review and Expositor* as "'Once There Was a Camelot': Women Doctoral Graduates of the Southern Baptist Theological Seminary, 1982–1992, Talk about the Seminary and Their Lives since SBTS," explored the conflicting and contradictory experiences of our participants when they were at Southern while the SBC was grappling with, among other things, the roles of women in church, home, and society.[4]

The Camelot metaphor came from a commencement address by former Southern seminary president Duke McCall in December of 1984. Some of the participants in our original interviews quoted that sermon in reflecting back on their time at Southern. McCall was issuing an early warning about the "fundamentalist takeover," as moderates referred to the conflict, or "battles," and its final outcome, and he urged students in chapel that day to go out and tell the world, "Once there was a Camelot."[5] He was referencing Jacqueline Kennedy's artful description of a longed-for era that was gone forever, which, for McCall, was the brief window in Southern Baptist life when moderates' values prevailed in the denomination.[6] For many of the moderate men who attended Southern in this era, the seminary was indeed a sort of Camelot, a mythical place out of time where callings were affirmed and knowledge and skills developed in an ivory tower. For women, however, the experience was more complicated.

In the first round of interviews conducted in 1997, we found that when the women in our study entered Southern during the late 1970s and early 1980s, they hoped that they could claim an equal place in ordained ministry.

Perhaps naively, they believed that changing social mores around gender and the greater presence of women in leadership in the secular world might mean parity in theological education and, eventually, ministry. In this way, Southern held the promise of Camelot for these women. And during their time at Southern, many held onto the vision that perhaps the seminary could become the Camelot for women that it had been for men. Nevertheless, despite faculty members' theoretical commitments to women in ministry, Southern was still fraught with overt and subtle sexism, and the controversy among Southern Baptists regarding women's roles cast a deepening shadow over any possibility of equality.

By 1997, the year of our study, our participants had recognized that their Camelot—a Southern Baptist seminary fully embracing their feminist ideals—was never to be. Equally revealing, the experience of being women PhD students at Southern had consistently pushed them further to the left on issues related to theology, gender, race, and sexuality. Spurred by their experiences of sexism on campus from ostensibly moderate male faculty members and fellow students, most of our participants began to embrace feminism well before the height of the moderate-fundamentalist controversy. The ultimate ascendancy of anti-feminist fundamentalists in both the seminary and the denomination led the women in our study to become even more convinced of the importance of their advocacy for feminist ideals. And while fundamentalists saw this ascendency as a "conservative resurgence," their term for the Baptist battles, the women in our study agreed with moderates in their understanding and experience of a "fundamentalist takeover."

This chapter picks up and continues our earlier work as nearly twenty years later, in 2016, we returned to the women we had interviewed to gauge their social locations and ministerial status and examine how they now reflected on their years at Southern. Kryn Freehling-Burton and O'Dessa Monnier joined us for this new research project. In all, we located and interviewed seventeen of the thirty-six women who had earned PhDs at Southern from 1982 to 1992.[7] In terms of religious affiliation, none of them were Southern Baptist anymore, although about a third of them had affiliated with the more moderate-leaning Cooperative Baptist Fellowship at some point after its founding in 1991. The next-largest group (three) had joined the UCC. The rest were scattered among a variety of other Protestant denominations. Most of the seventeen participants still described their work as "ministry," with the majority (twelve) serving as professors or administrators in higher education (which they viewed as a continuation of their calling to ministry), while others were pastors (two), a chaplain (one), and a counselor (one). One worked in the business world. A few, of course, had retired. But despite any differences, all of them had followed remarkably similar paths into more progressive theologies.

Unlike the other chapters in this volume, this one is not a reimagining of Southern Baptist history. Rather, read alongside our earlier work, it considers how these women reimagined their own lives, drawing on their Southern Baptist heritage and its history of call to move in a different direction than many, including other moderate Southern Baptist women. With seventeen participants, it is primarily a qualitative study and told, as closely as possible, from the women's perspectives, using their language and terms.

As we interviewed these seventeen women, three distinct themes emerged. First, years after their time at Southern, a dream of Camelot still lingered, in that women expressed a loyalty and appreciation for the historic seminary, or Southern as it was before the rise of fundamentalism. In fact, all but one of them would still have gone there when they did, were they given the choice again. A second major theme involved their feminist identity. Each and every one of these women identified as a feminist, and their feminism shaped their everyday lives and vocational careers. In fact, as we discovered, they proved more progressive in their feminist leanings in 2016 than in 1997. All seventeen women, for instance, articulated a broad spectrum of feminist goals: access to accurate sex education, contraception, and abortion; LGBTQ+ rights, including marriage equality and antidiscrimination protections; and safety from domestic violence, sexual harassment, and sexual assault. And they expressed an intersectional consciousness, paying close attention to the ways race, sexuality, social class, and other forms of difference shape and interact with gender. A third and closely related theme was the important role that their feminism played in their sense of resilience and purpose; in other words, their feminism became fused with the calling their Southern Baptist heritage had instilled in them. The SBC controversy that played out at Southern did not derail them, these women claimed, and in fact prepared them to resist and confront sexism across their careers. Their formative experiences with sexism forced them to recognize and embrace their own strength; thus, a common refrain was that "Southern made me tough." They now view their own social justice activism, no matter how challenging, to be a central component of their calling and identity.

Although small in number, these women and their experiences are significant at numerous levels and for a variety of audiences. Only a handful of studies have explored the educational and career experiences of Protestant women who have attended seminary.[8] Of these, none has offered longitudinal data across the careers of a group of seminary-educated women. And few have considered Baptist women in ministry in this larger context. Turning to Southern Seminary and Southern Baptists, it is worth noting that Gregory A. Wills's detailed 547-page history of the seminary, published in 2009, while remarkable in numerous ways, largely neglects the experiences and voices of the first women to attend Southern as full-fledged ministerial students.[9] And yet, recent literature has shown that, as newly arrived women seminarians seeking ordained ministries and pastorates, they stood at the center of the Southern Baptist battles in the late twentieth century.[10] They also predicted the movements and divisions in American Christianity and politics, with a widening gap between the left and the right. Their stories, then, help us better understand the denominational battles and the rise of the larger culture wars, with its polarization of American religion and culture. As soon as the religious right moved beyond denominational concerns and took a broader national stage, it carried with it many of the same challenges to women's freedom and full equality as expressed in the SBC controversy, a development that further politicized our participants and the liberal Christian demographic they represent. In listening to our participants more recently, in 2016, we found that the divides between progressive and conservative evangelicals have only widened, particularly in entering the era of the Trump presidency.

Women's Experiences before the Takeover

Founded as the denomination's first seminary in 1859, Southern is the "Mother Seminary" of Southern Baptists. Women first found some access to the seminary with the founding of the Woman's Missionary Union (WMU) Training School in 1907 as a missionary preparatory school for women. The Training School was separate from Southern and in no way was intended to prepare women for pastoral ministry. Women could sit in on seminary classes, but they could not officially enroll in its divinity program until 1948, although the School of Church Music allowed women to enroll starting in 1944.[11]

During the 1970s and 1980s, Southern offered highly respected academic programs within a theologically moderate framework that generally supported women, although the institution was still adjusting to the increasing presence of women. By the early 1980s, women made up about a third of the approximately 3,500 student body, and, while most women still enrolled in the programs in education and church music, significant numbers began to enroll in the School of Theology, including its MDiv degree program.[12] By the 1984–85 academic year, 217 women made up about 13 percent of students pursing the MDiv.[13] No women served on the faculty of the School of Theology until 1984, when Molly Marshall joined the theology faculty and Pamela Scalise joined the biblical studies faculty. A few women did teach Christian education and music, but, by far, women at Southern received their theological education from men, who, although trying to be allies, did not always understand the challenges faced by their women students. Nonetheless, all of our participants praised the education they received at Southern. Every one of them felt her education reflected a quality comparable to other leading seminaries across the country. Their difficult experiences were barriers to overcome, but they did not prevent these women from making the most of their educational opportunities.

Our participants spoke of loving the Southern Seminary they once knew. They appreciated their education and the friendships they made, many of which have lasted across their lives. Despite their critiques of the sexist behavior of some male professors and fellow students, they nevertheless called the pretakeover seminary "open minded," "forward-looking," "justice-seeking," and "a great basic theological education." Jael described "excellent professors and an incredible group of PhD students as peers and colleagues," concluding, "I think I got an absolutely superb academic preparation." Gertrude found her PhD studies to be "exhilarating." She elaborated: "They were arduous, but I feel like I got a very good grounding. . . . [Southern] helped me hone practices of scholarship; it introduced me to significant scholars whom I would not have known otherwise. . . . It grounded me in a broader stream of scholarship; it helped me make connections and sharpened me by being with persons of nimble acumen, both professors and fellow students. It introduced me to the craft of scholarship for the church as well as the guild." Willie, likewise, said she was intellectually stimulated at the seminary, "just soaking up everything." PR agreed: "You know, I went to a great place. There was so much self-discovery there." Taylor said Southern gave her a good education, good friends and colleagues, and good professors and "opened [her] eyes to a world [she] did not even know existed." Leah claimed that she would put her Southern education alongside anyone else's. Similarly, Sheila commented that her experience at Southern had a "huge impact on [her] formation, including both as a scholar and a clinician in pastoral care and therapy." Over and over again, the participants underscored that the seminary gave them a "good education" and opened up worlds they had not previously known. Even as they were aware of the struggles they faced as women at Southern at that particular historical moment, they treasured the theological education they had claimed. Meredith enthused that her seminary experience was "wonderful for [her] own intellectual and spiritual discovery." The seminary, in its moderate heyday, provided a place for her to leave the fundamentalism of her childhood and see possibilities of liberation for herself.

Disillusionment and Feminist Awakenings

Even while they embraced the educational opportunities at Southern during its final years as a moderate seminary, women experienced overt and covert sexism from some faculty and male students in the 1970s and 1980s. Most of the male faculty affirmed women in ministry, although their own privilege, especially in terms of power in church and society, often obscured the workings of gender for them. While some read feminist writers and worked very hard to develop a gender lens, many were simply benevolent patriarchs, hoping to welcome women without making too many deep structural changes in theological education at Southern.[14]

Thus, on the one hand, Southern was a place where these women were able to create a place for themselves and find their voice. On the other hand, sexism defined the context in which they were exploring their identities as professionals and women in ministry. Deb explained, "They were the best of times, and they were the worst of times, indeed." Leah, too, experienced Southern both as a positive and a frustrating institution in this era. She noted one faculty member she admired for his deep theological knowledge, but, she indicated, he "didn't get the gender issue at all . . . he didn't understand feminism at all."

Leah described how she was often the only woman in her PhD seminars. "It was difficult, you know. I was passed over in conversation. I'd say something, and someone would respond to the man who'd gone before me." RP remembered when a professor asked her to speak in his introductory class to "give a woman's perspective." With as much of a straight face as she could muster, RP curtsied and said, "Professor, God didn't give me any other choice." Jael spoke of how one professor told her no woman would ever teach Hebrew at Southern. "Well," Jael told us, "I did teach Hebrew" at Southern, as did other women after her. Meredith emphasized, "It was a fight. It was always a fight." She told of male students making fun of her when she was pregnant and a professor telling her his class would have been better without her presence. Meredith referred to a lot of men at the seminary as "Neanderthals." "But I kept on going," she commented. "I tried to work around the edges, work underneath, the subterranean role kind of thing, trying to figure out ways women could be involved there." As a result, she indicated that she developed an antenna for picking up gender discrimination. "I can sniff it out like an animal," she remarked. Mabel called her experience "the good, the bad, the ugly!"

Repeatedly, the participants asserted that their experiences at Southern made them more resilient. According to Jael, "We were finding our place, and those of us who were there could not afford to be average; we couldn't afford to be anything other than our very best." She added, "Southern made me tough." The sexism at the seminary "toughened me up," said Patsy. "It required me to meet head on, to become a woman in ministry that isn't put off now by sexism or any other barrier that is put in my way. So was it hard? Yes. Was it worth it? Yes." Mabel added, "Having been at Southern at that point in time, we had to learn to live with paradox and embrace it."

Yet the seminary was open enough for students to feel free to explore feminist possibilities within the institution. Flannery said, "I absolutely agree it was not Camelot, but within it, in that moment, it felt like it. You know, it was because it was this place where we were learning things and we were fighting for something we believed in, and, I mean, I loved seminary. It was the hardest, most painful thing I'd ever done, and, at the same time, I loved it. . . . It was sexist and misogynistic and patriarchal to its core, but, again, for this little fundamentalist girl who came out of Georgia, it was pretty progressive and feminist and all those things." Deb wondered whether Southern, if the fundamentalists had not taken it over, might have become increasingly proactive in addressing sexism and eventually become a Camelot for women.

Some of these women were already feminists when they enrolled at Southern Seminary; the rest became feminists there. All of them identify as feminists now. Jael said, "I was a feminist long before I got to Southern. It was because I was a feminist that I survived at Southern." Florence also came to seminary as a feminist, having had her consciousness raised as a teenager during the height of the women's movement in the 1960s and 1970s. Others became feminists while at Southern. For a number of them, it was the sexism they experienced even at a moderate seminary that first led them to feminism. ECS described herself as coming to seminary "unarmed" and so started learning about feminism to fight for her place at the seminary. She read Betty Friedan's *The Feminine Mystique* (1963) at the end of her first year at the seminary, as the experience of encountering sexism as a woman in a Baptist seminary connected her with the secular feminist movement that had been underway for well over a decade at that point. Meredith explained that

Southern played the role of adversary in her development as a feminist. She recollected, "The social demands of that culture were so uncomfortable that I felt that if I wanted to do anything I had to look at things, I had to break away from the pack because there would be no way the pack could provide me with answers." Instead she turned to the voices of the women's movement and started applying feminist theories to her work in the church. At the same time, others found institutional support for their feminist explorations during the 1970s and 1980s. Deb, for example, said the academic freedom and solid scholarship at the institution introduced her to the works of feminists such as Mary Daly and Letty Russell, creating a "time of awakening" for her.

Perspectives after the Takeover

In 1984, as fundamentalists continued to take control of the SBC, the denomination itself declared women unfit to serve as pastors, and, by the mid-1990s, Southern itself was under the control of fundamentalists, with the appointment of Albert R. Mohler Jr. as president in 1993. In this new era, the faculty excluded women from taking preaching classes and denied them access to courses in pastoral ministry.[15]

Our participants, who witnessed firsthand the fundamentalist ascendancy in the SBC and Southern Seminary, reflected that the experience profoundly shaped their identities and deepened their commitments to feminism. RP held that "being there in all of the tumult solidified for good or ill the life lesson of 'be true to yourself' and that you can't be anyone other than who you are." Leah learned "useful political lessons" from being a PhD student at Southern during that tumultuous time. "It certainly made me, I think, appropriately cautious about institutional life." She continued, "My experiences there are really responsible for the core of my identity as a woman, as a Christian, and as a professional." Leah insisted that the controversy while she was at Southern absolutely played a role in her development as a feminist. "I had a Christa [female Christ] on the wall in my office," she noted proudly. Deb explained that a lot of women at Southern during the controversy were experiencing a moment of feminist consciousness-raising.

Meredith stated that she was proud of her "scars" from the fundamentalist purge of moderates—including feminists—from SBC leadership. Because of the wounds, she said, "I was able to identify those places of discrimination better than I would have I think if I would not have gone through that experience." Sophia underscored that what she learned at Southern has served her well. "It may have been the first major battle I was in, but it wasn't the last . . . I learned to speak, to believe in expressing oneself positively and not defensively, and bearing witness to my experience of truth . . . I learned about gender dynamics and the subtleties of gender dynamics." RP noted with irony, "It was great training for things that they didn't realize they were training me for." Gertrude agreed, affirming, "I am probably more fearless in undertaking hard issues." Flannery said that the time at Southern "sharpened us." Leah related that her experiences at Southern gave her "some courage and a voice and confidence and some political savvy that was really, really useful."

Certainly, these women needed a strong sense of self because most of them continued to face barriers, skepticism, and hostility after Southern, as they entered their ministerial careers and related vocations inside (early on for some) and outside the SBC (eventually for everyone). Jael explained that when she preached during SBC missionary orientation, some of her fellow missionaries-in-training made a show of ignoring her by reading newspapers or engaging in other activities. By the end of the training, the mission board revealed that her appointment and her husband's too were both in jeopardy because of their more liberal leanings. They did achieve their appointment, but Jael said she "kept everything at arm's length, and that's how [they] survived." Others ended up as the only woman on the religion faculty at various, though primarily Baptist, institutions, where they often faced criticism as women teaching theology, biblical studies, or Christian ministry. Others faced battles as pastors in churches and denominations still struggling with the idea of women in leadership. Nonetheless, as Flannery spoke, she spoke for many of these women: "I look at who we became, and everybody is really successful in doing all sorts of things and strong feminists, and, in some weird way, I think that took that horrible moment [of the fundamentalist takeover] and all the pain that came with it and the things that happened to us after seminary, and people still found a way to be strong and to accomplish amazing things."

While the participants unanimously felt appreciation for the Southern they attended before fundamentalists gained control, they had fewer kind words for today's Southern. While the Southern of the 1970s and 1980s at least held out the possibility for their inclusion as equals, the current Southern overtly embraces women's subordination in the home and exclusion from ordained ministry. With this wholesale embrace of explicit patriarchal norms (described by advocates as "complementarianism"), it is not surprising that the women in our study have nothing positive to say about today's fundamentalist-controlled seminary. They called the seminary: "a joke," "a sad, unfortunate disaster," "laughable," "irrelevant," "an embarrassment," "a foreign country that I wouldn't recognize if I went there," and "a dark spot on the earth." Jael said, "I can't imagine a woman going there now." Martha commented, "The institution we knew died and was taken over by the white male supremacist fundamentalist Christians . . . we don't really have an alma mater." Florence remembered Southern with affection, but now she's "written it off." Like a number of other participants, she noted that she simply tosses the alumni magazine into the recycle bin without reading it whenever it comes. Several participants mentioned that they cringe when they tell people where they earned their PhD or they quickly explain that they attended the seminary "BF," meaning "before the fundamentalists" or "before the fall." PR said, "I'm not ashamed that I went there and am actually very grateful I went there. But I mean I have nothing, I have no connection to the place, and, like I said, they wouldn't recognize me, and I wouldn't recognize them." ECS noted, "Golly gee, they'd probably shoot us if we tried to come [back]."

Most discussed Southern with a sense of loss. When we interviewed them in 2016, their sadness and grief was not as palpable as it was in the early 1990s, but it was nevertheless evident. Gertrude said, "I grieve what it became. I grieve the loss of progressive thinking and leadership shining a light on ignorance on Southern Baptists. I really find its huge resources put to the service of repression and patriarchy profoundly disturbing." Sophia stated, "I will grieve the loss of the seminary for the rest of my life." Like others, she feels she can no longer go back to the campus. "This place that was formative for me is now a place I wasn't a part of. It's everything I detest in religion, in academia." Willie added, "I think it's sad, genuinely sad." Deb agreed. "It's very sad to me. So there is some sense of loss that it's not the institution that it was when I was there, and it's not an institution that I can be proud of today to say, you know, that I can say that I received a degree from Southern Baptist Theological Seminary." Sheila stated, "I loved Southern and a part of me always will. . . . Now I weep to see what it has become." Like Flannery, she does not hang her diplomas on her office wall.

Despite these vivid descriptions of disillusionment and sorrow, the women in our study have detached themselves from Southern Baptist life much more so now than they had in their first interviews. Many avoid thinking of Southern, as it exists now, altogether. Martha pointed out that the Southern she knew has "disappeared," stating, "Our institution doesn't exist anymore." She described a period of mourning after the takeover of the seminary but noted that time is now long past. Florence used the analogy of cutting apron strings. Severing the tie to the seminary was at first like untying the apron string but then became more like cutting the strings off and then throwing the apron away. Taylor said, "I feel no attachment whatsoever with the school as it is now. No attachment whatsoever." After leaving Southern and watching the completion of the takeover, the women we interviewed in 1997 had experienced anger for years. Now, however, although they do not mince words about the fundamentalist-controlled SBC, they are also more likely to describe an absence of feelings toward the Southern of today. Emerson explained, "There's this whole piece of me, the anger that I had for so long is just kind of gone because I probably have not thought about Southern seminary in I don't know how many years. I haven't even been back since I graduated . . . since I left I've had no connections whatsoever so I really don't have any feelings per se." Mabel affirmed that "the pain has definitely diminished. It's easier to remember the good." Leah said she feels better with the distance. Several participants likewise acknowledged that their feelings had mellowed in the past few years. Most are simply resigned to letting Southern go. Like Camelot, the place they loved no longer exists.

Feminism and Social Justice

The participants acknowledged that the fundamentalist takeover of the SBC caused them to move deeper into feminist thought and practice than they might have otherwise, and they see this as a good thing. Flannery explained, "Becoming a feminist was all in this context of women being on center in this Baptist battle, and the inerrancy stuff was just a façade because they wouldn't come right out and say, 'Women have progressed too far,' and so it sent me on this trajectory that, maybe had it not been so tumultuous, maybe I wouldn't be so radical and left-wing, but when I saw the alternative. . . ." Florence agreed. "I've certainly gotten more progressive and more liberal . . . and I've tried to act on that as well." Taylor added that being at Southern during that time of controversy "pushed me more to the left, politically, theologically, philosophically. . . . If I had gone to Vanderbilt or Candler I might still be as liberal as I am, but I do think the situation at the time pushed me more toward the left." Patsy said her theology has become more and more liberal over the past years as she has read progressive theologians. "My theology would scare the pants off most Baptists I know," she quipped. Because of their own experiences of discrimination, they are highly attuned to issues of race, class, sexuality, and other forms of difference, and they are deeply and passionately committed to social justice.

To be sure, the feminisms embraced by most of these women are not especially radical by broader secular standards on the whole, although they bring a keen awareness of contemporary understandings of intersectionality to their expressions of feminism. Most are willing to work within existing structures to bring about greater equity; few are ready to do away with gender as a social category; and almost all of them still see value in Christian faith and have hope for the Christian church to become a place of love, inclusion, and justice.

Overall, these women share fairly consistent definitions of feminism around equality and equity for women. Jael said, "To be a feminist is to say that regardless of biology, regardless of society's gender standards, that a person is able to be and become all that they're capable of being, full humanity." Sophia added, "Women must be equal partners in the conversation, whatever the conversation is, whether it's political, or whether it's economic, or whether it's Christian, or whether it's educational. . . . To have a conversation where women are not equal participants and equal also in terms of the power dynamics [is] having a false conversation." Sheila noted that feminism allows her to have "both the ability and responsibility to make choices" for herself: "I am not confined to a box of someone else's definition. Nor can I avoid responsible behavior and action because of my gender."

Mabel said that, for her, feminism is about working toward reaching one's potential regardless of gender and "bringing to light injustices of the world, no matter where those injustices are, not just for women." Several connected their feminism with humanism to express the breadth of their commitment to justice for all people. Some still struggle with the contradictions between cultural expectations of Southern women—to be nice—and their own callings to bring about social change. Patsy explained, "I'm still very conscious, in fact, I laugh at myself around this, I have a great awareness of what it means to be female and Southern, a Southern lady. I think that has encouraged me to develop an approach to conflict and debate that is a little softer and maybe a little better received, not as aggressive. [Yet] I'm very assertive."

Others articulated systematic visions for feminist politics. For Gertrude, being a feminist means she "will do everything [she] can to interrogate and dismantle places and practices of injustice based on gender." Deb commented on the role of feminism in offering "critical analyses of systems and structures" that "promote sexism and misogyny." Martha said that, for her, feminism means action and coalition-building, and she highlighted her involvement in a living-wage campaign centered on women's undervalued and underpaid work at her institution.

For these women, feminism is a call, an affirmation, and a challenge for them to be true to themselves as women and to improve the world for others. For them, feminism is a call deeply intertwined with their call to ministry; both are calls to transform the world in particular ways. They have reimagined calling in light of gender, other forms of difference, and a broader world, and their sense of call reaches far beyond the expectations of those churches that first sent them to seminary to spend a career serving Southern Baptists. Whether they came to seminary as feminists or became feminist while they were there, they embraced feminism's attention to gender and action for social change. Their experience at Southern heightened their awareness of gender oppression and provided them with tools to develop as feminists, well beyond most of their professors' own understandings of social justice. Feminism became a tool of resilience for them, further developing the strong sense of self that led them to seminary in the first place. Feminism gave them a way to explain their experiences at the seminary and an action plan for moving forward. In their careers, feminism has been a guiding philosophy, ensuring their own work would be liberatory and not oppressive.

During the time these women were students at Southern, the seminary emphasized social justice issues such as hunger, peace, and civil rights. These issues stood apart from any feminist analysis offered by professors who were either unaware or uninterested in feminism as a critical lens. So, these women students themselves brought feminist analysis to the seminary's social justice emphasis. Their experiences, both in the classroom and in extracurricular activities, strengthened their commitments to social justice, and, since their time at Southern, these women have centered social justice in their work. Their own experiences of oppression at the seminary and in their careers have sensitized them to systems of power and privilege, and, in their thinking and acting, they prioritize justice on behalf of all marginalized people. Sheila stated that since leaving Southern social justice issues have become central rather than peripheral. She said the most pressing issues for people of faith today are social justice ones, which involve "applying the Gospel values to the poor, the marginalized, the disenfranchised, those hurting." ECS said her understanding of gender, along with her understanding of the Bible and her own faith, gave her "this tremendous sense of justice . . . it's just really about justice."

For Flannery, postcolonial feminist theology "has just blown [her] out of the water . . . to think about the imperial context" of these issues: "It's just moving more in the progressive directions . . . [I'm] even more dedicated to social justice . . . more dedicated to peace and being a pacifist. So just a good ol' lefty." Gertrude agreed that postcolonial feminist theology is important because it challenges "white women's hegemony." Other participants pointed to reproductive justice, death with dignity, antinuclear movements, anti-death penalty movements, religious pluralism, and relationships with Muslims as important contemporary social justice issues. Leah noted that she is "way left of center in terms of theology, you know, all the grounded theology, black theology, womanist theology." Gertrude added that the most pressing issues for people of faith are "how we embody our faiths, our call for justice. And, if it remains simply theoretical, it moves the church into greater irrelevance in the world." Sophia explained that her understanding of social justice has broadened and deepened in the last few years but has remained connected to her seminary training: "I think again, to go back to what I learned at Southern, appreciating what it means to appreciate God's love and God's justice and figuring out how to live that in the world." She said that since the 2014 police killing and riots in Ferguson, Missouri, her understandings of social justice have become more concrete. "How do you practice love and justice in this context? . . . How do you talk about loving your neighbor?"

Most of the participants mentioned sexuality as an example of how their commitment to social justice issues had grown since we first interviewed them in the 1990s. All of these women had become supporters of LGBTQ+ equality. A number of them have come out since seminary themselves. For them, coming out was another form of resilience. Deb pointed to her own coming-out process as a watershed moment. Others highlighted their experiences of gender oppression as an entry to supporting LGBTQ+ folks. Emerson said her experiences as a woman at Southern "set [her] on a course of looking at gender roles in even broader and bigger ways, today even, and thinking about sexuality . . . being much more open [about homosexuality and transgender identities]." ECS expressed surprise when a friend told her it was a radical thing for her friend to use a sermon at a denominational gathering to call people to embrace LGBTQ+ brothers and sisters. "You're kidding me!" was her response. Gertrude noted that her "theology of human sexuality has progressed in a number of ways," and she works intentionally to make her institution a place that is safe for LGBTQ+ people. Jael indicated that she makes sure her LGBTQ+ students feel welcome in the classroom, and she continues to learn about sexuality and to keep up with the changing vocabulary of sexual identity.

For all of these women, social justice served as a key component of their identities. As feminists, they were cognizant of the role of gender in systems of oppression, including the church and higher education, and their experiences have helped them develop intersectional lenses that allow them to examine gender oppression across differences among women. They made connections between gender oppression and all other forms of oppression, and they linked sexism to injustice for all marginalized people. They were committed to putting their ideas into action, and so they worked to make positive changes in the world around them. They were realistic about the enormity of the task, but that did not dissuade them from taking action however possible.

Women Role Models

Most of these women did not have role models when at Southern. While a couple of women taught in the Schools of Christian Education and Church Music by the early 1980s, the School of Theology only added women to its faculty starting in the mid-1980s, with Molly Marshall joining the faculty in theology and Pamela Scalise in Old Testament. While many participants did describe how important the support of individual male faculty members was to them, they lamented the lack of female faculty available to them.

Deb remarked on the irony of her situation at Southern. "Here I am a closeted lesbian writing a literary feminist interpretation of [a story of a biblical woman], and I have three white straight men on my dissertation committee." ECS thought having more women on the faculty would also have been good for the male students. "I think it would have mattered if we'd had a woman faculty member as a regular faculty member." Instead, she took classes as often as she could from a woman faculty member at the nearby Presbyterian seminary. Meredith shared, "I had to figure [teaching] out on my own, which is not a bad thing, but I did not have any women who could walk that way in the lecture hall for me, whose pedagogy I could emulate . . . and, boy, did I spend a lot of time trying to figure that out in the decade after Southern Seminary." Flannery agreed that women in her cohort had to figure out how to be feminist teachers on their own. She explained, "While I felt very supported by my professors, they didn't know the feminist stuff, so we had to find it and read it on our own . . . that attuned me to wanting to be aware of women students, students across all sorts of differences, and to make sure that their experiences and perspectives were on center as much as the dominant narrative. And so I think it had a huge impact because I . . . didn't have women who were my role models because there were so few at

Southern, despite its stated commitment to women. You know, we were a third of the student body but a teeny tiny bit of the faculty. And so that made me pretty sensitive."

The lack of female role models at Southern has made these women attentive to the ways they themselves can serve as mentors for other women, and it has also had an impact on their pedagogical strategies. Patsy noted, "I am a female role model and a mentor to other females who are now coming through seminary because I want them to have what I didn't have when I was going through the process. So the lack of what I needed back then heightened my awareness and made me more concerned to offer that to other females now." Jael commented that she ensures that her students not only read works by women but also learn to read in feminist ways. "I teach my students to read with suspicion, to look at the world and always ask who's advantaged and who's disadvantaged by this perspective." Gertrude said that she purposefully tries to educate both men and women about gender relations. "Gender equity is a core value here," she insisted, "and so we instantiate it every way we can." She went on, "I just think we learn the practices of ministry better when we have female scholars as well as men. I think that we understand some of the 'shadowfied' history and theological construction if we have women as well as men teaching. I think it is critical for students to see both men and women embodying a vocation to which they may aspire." Willie said that early in her career, while teaching at an evangelical Christian college in which she was the only woman on the religion faculty, she "had a one-woman responsibility to let students know there was a female presence" and that her feminism affected the curriculum she chose and the way she presented it. Deb too explained that, largely because of her Southern experience, she purposefully teaches all of her courses from feminist points of view. She chooses textbooks that center women and uses women's issues to explore larger societal issues. Likewise, Emerson makes conscious decisions to make sure women are represented. Speaking of the absence of women role models in her own theological education, Emerson said, "I think it has heightened my awareness to make sure whether I am forming committees or groups or inviting student involvement on something, it has made me very aware and sensitive to include a mixture of men and women and also a mixture of racial and cultural differences. . . . It has really heightened my awareness to be inclusive and to hear all voices and to make sure there is a diversity of representation." Leah's sentiments echoed those of most of the participants: "I felt like I was able to make some important difference, not only for myself as a woman, but for young women at [my institution] . . . I did a lot of things for the sake of my own gender and young women who followed me at [my Baptist college], and I think a lot of that was because of consciousness-raising from my experience at Southern."

Conclusion

These women did not go to seminary to become feminist role models or pioneers, and they certainly did not go to engage in a fight over women's issues; they went to answer their calling to ministry that was born out of their Southern Baptist heritage and local church upbringing. Nonetheless, while they were at Southern, gender became front and center of the Baptist battles and the growing controversy on campus, profoundly affecting their sense of call.

As we discovered through both sets of interviews, across years of struggles, these participants have demonstrated a persistent and deepening commitment to feminism and social justice. While their hope for a Camelot in Southern Baptist life faded like a distant dream, fundamentalist attempts to prevent women's entrance into ministry still proved impossible, as feminist transformations across American society opened new paths of resistance, resilience, and opportunity for women both within and outside Baptist life. Because of the controversy, these women, rather than abandoning their sense of call, reimagined it, coming to see it as a rallying cry to feminism, community, and social justice. Their interviews and stories, then, help us think about Southern Baptist history as a catalyst for women's transformation, albeit in unexpected ways.

Notes

1. In Southern Baptist life, a "call" or "calling" is a deeply and personally felt sense that God is guiding someone to a vocation in ministry. For more on Southern Baptist women's sense of calling, see Susan M. Shaw, *God Speaks to Us, Too: Southern Baptist Women on Church, Home, and Society* (Lexington: Univ. of Kentucky Press, 2008).
2. H. Leon McBeth, "The Role of Women in Southern Baptist History," in *No Longer Ignored: A Collection of Articles on Baptist Women*, ed. Charles W. Desweese and Pamela R. Durso (Atlanta, GA: Baptist History and Heritage Society, 2007), 25. For the statistics on the 1981–82 academic year, see Presidential Annual Report

to the Board of Trustees, 1981–1982, Southern Baptist Theological Seminary, Seminary Archives, Louisville, KY.

3. We use the terms "fundamentalists" and "moderates" to refer to the two factions of the controversy because these were the terms used during the conflict while Tisa and Susan were students at Southern Seminary and the terms used by the women we interviewed.
4. Susan M. Shaw and Tisa Lewis, "'Once There Was a Camelot': Women Doctoral Graduates of the Southern Baptist Theological Seminary, 1982–1992, Talk about the Seminary, the Fundamentalist Takeover, and Their Lives since SBTS," *Review and Expositor* 95 (1998): 397–423.
5. Duke McCall, "Camelot" (commencement address), Dec. 14, 1984, Alumni Memorial Chapel, Southern Baptist Theological Seminary, Audio Visual Collection, https://repository.sbts.edu/handle/10392/4196/.
6. Kennedy herself was referencing the Arthurian legend, which the 1958 novel *The Once and Future King* and the 1960s musical *Camelot* had popularized.
7. All participant names are pseudonyms selected by the participants themselves. While many of the names selected are simply aliases for the sake of this study, a number reflect the wit and irony of participants. For example, Gertrude of Helfta, or Gertrude the Great, was a Benedictine nun and theologian whose mystical visions led her to a life of contemplation and devotion. Jael is a biblical character who drove a tent peg through the head of a sleeping commander of enemy forces. Flannery from Georgia is a reference to the Roman Catholic writer Flannery O'Connor. Some of these pseudonyms have been shortened to a single name for ease of reading.
8. Mark Chaves, *Ordaining Women: Culture and Conflict in Religious Organizations* (Cambridge, MA: Harvard Univ. Press, 1997); Barbara Brown Zikmund, Adair T. Lummis, and Patricia M. Y. Chang, *Clergy Women: An Uphill Calling* (Louisville, KY: Westminster John Knox Press, 1998); *The Non-Ordination of Women and the Politics of Power,* ed. Elizabeth Schussler Fiorenza and Herman Haring (Maryknoll, NY: Orbis Books, 1999); Roxanne Mountford, *The Gendered Pulpit: Preaching in American Protestant Spaces* (Carbondale: Southern Illinois Univ. Press, 2003); Nicole Hoggard Creegan and Christine Pohl, *Living on the Boundaries: Evangelical Women, Feminism and the Theological Academy* (Downers Grove, IL: InterVarsity Press, 2005).
9. Gregory A. Wills, *Southern Baptist Theological Seminary 1859–2009* (New York, NY: Oxford Univ. Press, 2009). While at times critical of conservatives as well as moderates, Wills did not include the voices of the women that we highlight here and view as significant to the story.
10. Eileen Campbell-Reed, *Anatomy of a Schism: How Clergywomen's Narratives Reinterpret the Fracturing of the Southern Baptist Convention* (Knoxville: Univ. of Tennessee Press, 2016); Elizabeth Flowers, *Into the Pulpit: Southern Baptist*

Women and Power since World War II (Chapel Hill: Univ. of North Carolina Press, 2012); Susan M. Shaw, *God Speaks to Us, Too.*

11. The first woman entered the BD program (which would become the MDiv) in 1949. The seminary only allowed women entrance into the BD program upon completion of the Master's of Religious Education at the Training School.
12. These numbers include students enrolled in Boyce Bible School, a division of the seminary that offered theological education to people who did not have a college degree. In the seminary's graduate programs, enrollment in 1984–85 was 1,896 men and 628 women. For a record of these numbers, see Presidential Annual Report to the Board of Trustees, 1984–1985.
13. Presidential Annual Report to the Board of Trustees, 1984–1985.
14. The story of Southern Seminary is primarily a story of whiteness. The faculty and the student body have always been overwhelmingly white, as are the participants in our interviews.
15. According to the seminary's catalog, "Christian Preaching (30000), Preaching Practicum (30020), and Pastoral Ministry (40301) are reserved for, but not required of men." See p. 70, *2019–2020 Academic Catalog*, Catalogs and Forms, Admissions, Southern Baptist Theological Seminary, http://www.sbts.edu/admissions/catalogs-and-forms/.

Nine

FROM MOLLY MARSHALL TO SARAH PALIN

Southern Baptist Gender Battles and the Politics of Complementarianism

Karen K. Seat

From the 1960s to the 1980s, some Southern Baptists saw possibilities for a feminist awakening in their denomination with the rise of prominent women leaders such as Rev. Dr. Molly Marshall, appointed in 1984 as the first woman on the faculty of theology at the denomination's flagship Southern Baptist Theological Seminary. These hopes were short-lived, as Marshall was forced out of her position by 1994, and the denomination explicitly turned away from the work of evangelical feminists in 2000 as it codified women's exclusion from the pastorate and wives' submission to husbands in its revised confessional document, the Baptist Faith and Message. But the Southern Baptist Convention (SBC) did not simply revert back to a pre-feminist status quo imagined by some anti-feminists in the "conservative resurgence." By the turn of the twenty-first century, the influence of feminism had inexorably changed American culture—including the normalization of women's fuller participation in public life—and thereby shaped American evangelical religion, including the SBC, in ways never imagined or intended by earlier generations of feminists or anti-feminists.

By the 2000s, it was clear that conservative leaders in the SBC, in conversation with other conservative Protestants who had gone through similar battles to purge feminism from their denominations, were championing a new gender map altogether in light of changing times. This drew national attention during the 2008 US presidential election, when these opponents of evangelical feminism celebrated Alaska Governor Sarah Palin's rise as the vice presidential candidate on the Republican ticket. In less than three decades, ascendant gender ideologies in the SBC had moved away from the feminist possibilities represented by Molly Marshall—now a symbol of a gender path not taken—to a very different vision of gender as represented by denominational leaders' embrace of politically conservative women such as Palin.

The conservatives who took control of the SBC after 1979 have often been described as "fundamentalists," but they were not old-time fundamentalists who eschewed the messy world of coalition building and compromise required to engage in democratic politics in the United States. Since 1979, leaders of the SBC have worked in partnership with a wide range of conservatives to shape local and national party politics and have been instrumental in conservative evangelicals' unbroken embrace of the Republican Party since the 1980 election of Ronald Reagan. As they simultaneously purged women leaders from their denomination in the name of biblical fidelity and maneuvered to become a vital force in the unwieldy world of American politics, Southern Baptist leaders joined forces with other conservative Protestants to develop a new theology of gender they dubbed "complementarianism." Conservative Southern Baptists' embrace of complementarianism's softer patriarchy—accepting the realities of universal suffrage and women's wage labor while demanding a loving gender hierarchy in the "private sphere"—enabled SBC leaders to derail feminist stirrings within their denomination while preserving their relevance in American culture.

The SBC's dual commitment to complementarianism and Republican politics was put to the test on a grand scale with Governor Sarah Palin's dramatic entrance into national politics as the vice presidential candidate on the 2008 Republican ticket. The public statements of support for Palin by Southern Baptist leaders brought into sharp focus complementarians' departure from the kinds of patriarchy advocated by fundamentalists historically. The popularity that Palin (and other notable Republican women) have had among conservative evangelicals illuminates just how unique complementarian theology has become in the history of Protestants' grappling with gender. The stories of Southern Baptist leaders' energetic engagement with the figures of Molly Marshall and Sarah Palin illustrate the evolution of gender discourses during the growth of a new conservatism in the SBC from 1979 through the first decade of the twenty-first century.

Southern Baptist Gender Battles

Southern Baptists have roots in old-time patriarchy, as can be seen in the 1923 book *Feminism: Woman and Her Work*, published by Southern Baptist pastors, scholars, and convention leaders three years after women gained national suffrage in the United States and five years after the SBC voted to allow female messengers to its annual meeting. Published as a screed against equal rights for women in civic and religious life, the volume reprinted William Patrick Harvey's 1892 assertion that supporters of universal suffrage were products of groups considered to be the antithesis of established Southern culture: "They abound chiefly among Mormons, Spiritualists, Universalists, Unitarians, Free Lovers, Anarchists, and Infidels."[1] The volume portrayed women's political participation as alien to the Southern Baptist way, as its contributors' approach to the Bible supported a seamlessly patriarchal view of the world. While subsequent generations of Southern Baptists eased into an acceptance of women's suffrage, the patriarchal theology advocated by their forebears was taken for granted by many in the denomination. Barred from the pulpit, Southern Baptist women poured their energy and talents into the denomination through extensive grassroots fundraising and missionary work, especially through the Woman's Missionary Union.

However, as new waves of feminism in the late twentieth century shook American evangelicalism to its core, Southern Baptists underwent a radical reappraisal of the denomination's approach to gender. Out of the shakedown, most Southern Baptists gravitated to two new theologies of gender that emerged in the late twentieth century, replacing previous forms of patriarchal theology; these new approaches came to be labeled "egalitarianism" and "complementarianism." By the twenty-first century, very few self-proclaimed "patriarchalists" remained in SBC leadership. The old-school patriarchs of the SBC who opposed women's suffrage in the 1920s surely would have been startled by the enthusiastic embrace of women's participation in public life later demonstrated by their denominational descendants, egalitarians and complementarians alike.

Egalitarians sought a comprehensive reinterpretation of biblical texts to support women's full participation in religious life and society at large, while complementarians—a term created in the 1980s by advocates of this approach—insisted that both egalitarians and old-school patriarchalists had gotten it wrong. Complementarians, while aligning themselves with the fundamentalist tradition of biblical literalism and patriarchy, were willing to open the door to women's participation in economic and civic pursuits, as long as women remained submissive in church and home.[2] This distinctive move has been described by Wayne Grudem and others as "two-point" complementarianism.[3] While their forebears had promoted women's submission in three areas, or "three points"—church, home, and society—complementarians argued that the Bible only required women's submission in two areas, or "two points"—the church and the home. This dramatically opened the door to the possibility that even conservative evangelicals committed to "biblical inerrancy" could accept women's leadership in the vast world outside of church and home life. The rise of complementarianism was a significant evolution in SBC history, one that had broad ramifications within the SBC and in American culture.

In the 1980s and 1990s, the divergence of "egalitarian" and "complementarian" approaches to gender was central to the Southern Baptist schism, as the fierce battles between Southern Baptist "moderates" and "fundamentalists" regularly focused on the proper ways to approach gender and gender roles in light of scripture. Moderates often embraced the egalitarian understanding of biblical teachings regarding women, including an acceptance of women's ordination, while fundamentalists opposed this passionately, claiming that such "biblical feminism" was leading the denomination far afield from traditional Baptist fidelity to the Bible. As fundamentalists gained ascendency by the 1990s, the new conservative leadership in the SBC purged egalitarian moderates from their posts. The forced resignation of Molly Marshall from the faculty of the Southern Baptist Theological Seminary in 1995 is an iconic moment of the expansion of complementarians in the denomination.

The Rise of Complementarianism in the SBC

During the women's movement of the 1960s and 1970s, women involved in numerous Christian denominations actively worked to bring feminist principles of gender equality in all realms of life into their denominational institutions, and Southern Baptist women were no different. Like others in this period, feminist-inspired Southern Baptists began to vocalize their concerns about the treatment of women within the denomination.[4] Initially, some women were able to pave new paths in Southern Baptist life because of the decentralized nature of Baptist polity and the critical Baptist theological embrace of "the priesthood of the believer." Also described as "soul competency," Baptists have long claimed that the individual has direct access to God and thus direct authority to discern God's call to ministry. Local Southern Baptist churches traditionally have had the authority to ordain whomever they choose, and in 1964, Addie Davis became the first woman to be ordained by a Southern Baptist church.[5] Deluged with a storm of letters from around the country opposing her ordination, she remained firm in her conviction that "a dream born of God within one's heart should be heeded."[6] In the following two decades, despite widespread opposition, some five hundred women would be ordained by local Southern Baptist churches.[7] The majority of women who received ordination by 1986 graduated from either Southern Seminary or Southeastern Baptist Theological Seminary, the two seminaries in the denomination that were most welcoming at the time to faculty and students interested in developing new paths of leadership for women in the denomination.[8]

Alarmed by the growing Southern Baptist engagement with broader intellectual and cultural movements such as feminism, SBC conservatives organized to reclaim the denomination, and they were especially keen to put a stop to the influence of feminist biblical scholarship undergirding women's ordination. Paige Patterson, a leading architect of the conservative resurgence in the SBC, stated that conservatives in the mid-twentieth century felt as if the "the denominational raft was swept along by the white water currents that propelled American Baptists, British Baptists, United Methodists, and a host of other denominations to a mooring far removed from the havens of their founders."[9] Conservatives were convinced that new ways of interpreting the Bible were a foreign and dangerous infiltration into the heart of Southern Baptist commitment to biblical authority. Referencing the German origins of modern biblical scholarship in his description of mid-twentieth-century SBC seminary faculty, Patterson quipped that, "someone had visited Deutschland and returned with a 'Tubingen gourd' and poisoned the life-giving gospel stew that the [SBC] was supposed to be warming," leading to a growing number of Southern Baptist "professors and leaders who had imbibed deeply at the wells of historical-critical scholarship."[10] Conservatives focused on taking control of the denomination's two "liberal" seminaries, and, as Elizabeth Flowers states, in "1987 Southeastern fell swiftly to the conservatives" while "Southern followed much later, in 1995, after experiencing nearly a decade of tensions."[11]

Convinced that moderate Southern Baptists had brought foreign influences into the convention, Southern Baptist conservatives found alliances of their own outside the SBC with like-minded Protestants who were entrenched in similar battles within their own denominations. Ultimately, the unity Southern Baptists had once enjoyed was fully shattered by the end of the twentieth century, as moderates left the denomination and conservatives who had gained ascendency reached out beyond the regional roots of the convention to join a nationwide conservative/fundamentalist movement.

The creation of the transdenominational International Council on Biblical Inerrancy (ICBI) in the late 1970s played a major role in bolstering the conservative agenda within the SBC. Conservative Southern Baptists found allies outside the denomination such as Jay Grimstead, who helped initiate the ICBI with the vision of creating a "theological 'army' of scholars" who would go "into battle as a united team" to challenge those they viewed as non-inerrantists.[12] Decades later, Norman Geisler, a major leader of the ICBI, wrote that "foremost" among the vast influence of the ICBI was "that it helped reverse decades of the drift from inerrancy in one of the largest Protestant denominations in the United States—the Southern Baptist Convention."[13] More than three hundred Protestant church leaders, including Southern Baptists such as Paige Patterson and his wife Dorothy, attended the inaugural ICBI conference in 1978, which mapped out a decade-long program for breathing new life into the fundamentalist concept of "inerrancy" as a core commitment in modern evangelical thinking.

The renewed focus on inerrancy led to rising concerns regarding how to approach biblical statements regarding women's submission and silence. In a world where law and custom was turning toward gender equality, how were biblical inerrantists to live by biblical passages such as 1 Timothy 2:11–14, which states, "A woman should learn in quietness and full submission. I do not permit a woman to teach or to have authority over a man; she must be silent. For Adam was formed first, then Eve. And Adam was not the one deceived; it was the woman who was deceived and became a sinner"?[14]

To respond to these questions anew, another transdenominational organization was formed, just as the ICBI was concluding its work.[15] In 1987, conservative Southern Baptists joined with other evangelicals, including Wayne Grudem and John Piper, to form the Council on Biblical Manhood and Womanhood (CBMW). Dorothy Patterson was involved in founding the CBMW and was a major figure, along with her husband Paige, in disseminating complementarianism in the SBC and beyond.[16] The goal of the CBMW, as outlined in its 1988 manifesto titled the "Danvers Statement," was to reverse the work of "feminist egalitarianism with accompanying distortions or neglect of the glad harmony portrayed in Scripture between the loving, humble leadership of redeemed husbands and the intelligent, willing support of that leadership by redeemed wives."[17] Founders of the CBMW agreed to use the term "complementarian" to describe their particular theology, eager to abandon the "baggage"[18] of the term "patriarchy" and appeal to modern sensibilities (although later complementarians, such as Russell Moore, would suggest that complementarians should consider reclaiming the term "patriarchy" as a positive word).[19] Complementarians undertook a close study of the Bible to determine just how much patriarchy was required by scripture and felt free to shed any forms of patriarchy that they did not see endorsed by their reading of the Bible. Asserting that the Bible did indeed require male headship in marriage and church offices, a key component to their platform was that there was nothing oppressive or unjust whatsoever in women's submission to male headship in the home or church, because "God's word" would not require anything that was not good.

In 1991, Grudem and Piper first published the foundational text of the complementarian movement, *Recovering Biblical Manhood and Womanhood: A Response to Evangelical Feminism* (1991, 2006), with chapter contributions from Paige and Dorothy Patterson. In their 1991 preface, Grudem and Piper stated that they preferred "the term *complementarian*, since it suggests both equality and beneficial differences between men and women."[20] For complementarians, "equality" meant "of equal value"; thus, as Piper and Grudem stressed, "We hope that thousands of Christian women who read this book . . . will feel *fully equal* to men in status before God, and in importance to the family and the church. We pray that, at the same time, this vision of equality and complementarity will enable Christian women to give wholehearted affirmation to Biblically balanced male leadership in the home and church."[21]

One of the major criticisms complementarians faced from their egalitarian counterparts was that they were advocating a gender hierarchy by drawing from sections in the Bible that had been used in the recent past to support racism and slavery. This was a point that was especially sensitive to Southern Baptists, as their denomination had been formed in the 1840s explicitly due to its support of race-based slavery. In response, complementarians argued that it was right for Christian inerrantists to preserve male headship in modern times even while moving away from older American Protestant theologies supporting race-based hierarchies, because "male and female personhood, with some corresponding role distinctions, is rooted in God's act of creation before the sinful distortions of the status quo were established. . . . The existence of slavery is not rooted in any creation ordinance, but the existence of marriage is."[22] Since 1 Timothy 2:13 refers to Adam's creation before Eve as a justification for women's silence, complementarians argue, the admonition that women should not "teach or have authority over a man" was not a culturally or historically conditioned command, as egalitarians would claim, but a reference to God's intent for the order of creation (since Adam was formed first, then Eve). Thus the term "order of creation" is a favorite of complementarians and can be found frequently throughout their writings.

The twin goals of the ICBI and the CBMW were ultimately reflected in the Southern Baptist Convention's revised confessional document, the Baptist Faith and Message, which was adopted during Paige Patterson's presidency of the Southern Baptist Convention from 1998 to 2000, after much fanfare and national news coverage.[23] As Patterson wrote in his history of the SBC schism and conservative resurgence, the two significant achievements of the revision were the elaborated text on biblical inerrancy and the new text reflecting complementarian theology.[24] He carefully commissioned what he described as a "blue ribbon" committee to finalize revisions to the text, including complementarians such as his wife Dorothy Patterson and Richard Land, then the president of the SBC's Ethics and Religious Liberty Commission and a major influence in engaging the SBC with conservative politics nationally. The new text in the Baptist Faith and Message, as Flowers has pointed out, "borrowed liberally, often word for word, from the [CBMW] 'Danvers Statement.'"[25] Complementarian theology permeates the 2000 Baptist Faith and Message, including statements that "while both men and women are gifted for service in the church, the office of pastor is limited to men as qualified by Scripture," and that, while "the husband and wife are of equal worth before God, since both are created in God's image," nevertheless "a wife is to submit herself graciously to the servant leadership of her husband even as the church willingly submits to the headship of Christ."[26] According to the 2000 Baptist Faith and Message, Genesis 1:27 means that "the gift of gender is thus part of the goodness of God's creation"—suggesting that the complementarian focus on distinct male and female genders is the key point of this biblical passage ("in the image of God he created them; male and female he created them"), rather than other possible interpretations, such as biblical feminist interpretations of gender equality. The 2000 Baptist Faith and Message codified complementarianism as the prevailing gender ideology for the SBC as the denomination entered the twenty-first century.

Molly Marshall

During the years of fracture in the Southern Baptist Convention, Molly Marshall became one of the most prominent symbols of the brief rise of egalitarian theology and practice in the SBC before the complementarian takeover. Thus, she has been the recipient of an outpouring of appreciation from Baptist egalitarians, as well as the recipient of a tirade of scorn and outrage from complementarians. Centrifugal currents within the SBC from the 1960s through the 1990s made possible Marshall's ordination and tenure as the first woman professor of theology at a Southern Baptist seminary even as fundamentalists launched a campaign that would ultimately force her resignation.

Marshall was a dedicated Southern Baptist who earned her MDiv at Southern Baptist Theological Seminary in 1976 and went on to complete her PhD there in 1983, the same year she was ordained by a local Southern Baptist church and became a pastor of a Southern Baptist congregation. She joined the faculty of Southern Seminary in 1984, as the first female faculty member of the School of Theology, and had a brief but illustrious tenure there, becoming the associate dean of the School of Theology in 1988 and receiving Southern Seminary's Louvenia and Findley Edge Award for Teaching Excellence in 1993. She was pressured to resign from Southern Seminary in 1994. Much has been written about Marshall's life and influence as a Baptist theologian,[27] and the 1996 film *Battle for the Minds* covers in detail her forced departure from Southern Seminary.[28] However, little has been written regarding how her story, as imagined by conservative Southern Baptists, came to function in complementarian discourse as a symbolic morality tale about the dangers of feminism and the importance of the complementarian triumph.

To be clear, the ongoing vitriol aimed at Marshall is a sign that antifeminists have not been able to claim full victory in Baptist life. After leaving Southern, she joined the faculty of Central Baptist Theological Seminary (affiliated with American Baptist Churches USA),[29] and she continued her distinguished career, serving as the president of Central Seminary from 2004 to 2020.[30] To date, she has published seven books and numerous articles and chapters. In 2004, she was honored with the William H. Whitsitt Baptist Heritage Society Courage Award during the annual meeting of the Cooperative Baptist Fellowship, an organization of moderates who left the SBC.[31] In 2014, the National Association of Baptist Professors of Religion (NABPR) published a Festschrift in honor of Marshall, comprised of contributions with titles such as "Molly T. Marshall: Theological Midwife, 'Alive in the Heat of the Holy Spirit'" (Mark S. Medley, Festschrift editor) and "Molly Truman Marshall: Living Icon for Beholding the Spirit's Renewal of the Church" (Eileen Campbell-Reed).[32] In her contribution to the Festschrift,

Eileen Campbell-Reed captured Marshall's significance for egalitarians in contemporary Baptist debates about gender: "At stake in the years of Molly Marshall's adult life was a deep and profound struggle over the meaning of human being, an attempt to reimagine and reclaim the full humanity of women, and a longing for encounter with the living God. In her preaching and teaching, writing and organizing, leading and serving, Molly Marshall had a sense of these struggles, and she articulated them at every opportunity and engaged directly in what became for many an all-out battle."[33]

During her career within the Southern Baptist Convention, Marshall's signature achievement was making the case that feminist theology was not a foreign imposition into Baptist life but was something that grew organically out of traditional Baptist ways of thinking and living. She emphasized that women following their call to become ordained pastors was rooted in the Baptist tradition itself, stating, "Baptists have historically celebrated freedom of conscience (sometimes called 'soul freedom'). . . . Each person has the freedom, ability, and responsibility to respond to God for herself or himself." Moreover, she wrote, "Baptists historically have encouraged what Walter Shurden calls 'Bible freedom'—the principle that people have a right to interpret the scriptures in different, even opposing, ways."[34] In the year of her ordination, she published an article in which she stated, "The longer I study the Scriptures, the more convinced I become of the bedrock theological support for women being afforded equal access to all positions of vocational ministry."[35] In this and subsequent publications, she highlighted what she called "enduring theological principles" found in scripture, including the principle that male and female being created in the image of God meant that men and women could serve equally as members of the body of Christ. Marshall, like other egalitarians, frequently highlighted examples of Jesus commissioning women to be "proclaiming witnesses" of his resurrection and women functioning as leaders in Pauline churches. Thus, she wrote during the height of Southern Baptist gender battles in 1986, "Rather than allowing a lingering perception of women ministers as interlopers in Baptist life, we must stress that our movement is thoroughly informed by Baptist theological distinctive. It is because we are Baptists that we courageously persevere in the face of mounting opposition."[36] Robert Shippey, a former colleague of Marshall's at Southern, proclaimed, "She has been a pioneer paving the way for others to follow—not just female students aspiring to her stature—but for all of us who have valued Baptist liberty, Christian compassion, and integrity."[37]

Marshall's influence made her a prime target of the leaders of the conservative resurgence. In *Battle for the Minds*, filmed in 1995 during Marshall's last days at Southern Seminary, R. Gene Puckett, then editor of the *Biblical Recorder* and a founding director of the Associated Baptist Press,[38] put it this way: "Molly is very brilliant, very well educated, very personable, very influential when she speaks. So there is a certain kind of magnetism and dynamic quality in Molly Marshall's life. Therefore, she constitutes a very real threat and an issue not to be ignored any time you deal with this issue [women's ordination]. I think she was made to be uncomfortable on the faculty of Southern because she was a threat to some of the men, probably starting with the president of the seminary [R. Albert Mohler]."[39]

While the ordination of Addie Davis had provoked an unorganized storm of outrage in 1964, when Marshall joined the faculty of the School of Theology at Southern in 1984, while also serving as the ordained pastor of a Southern Baptist church, fundamentalists were sufficiently organized to successfully pass a resolution rejecting women's ordination at the annual convention later that year. Titled "On Ordination and the Role of Women in Ministry," the resolution denounced the egalitarian position and declared that normative Southern Baptist practice was to accept that the Bible "excludes women from pastoral leadership . . . to preserve a submission God requires because the man was first in creation and the woman was first in the Edenic fall."[40] When I interviewed Marshall in 2009, she said, "Gender became the means by which fundamentalists tried to argue that liberal seminaries did not take the Bible seriously. . . . It was Exhibit A. . . . I was elected to the faculty in the spring of 1984 at Southern . . . the resolution on women was [passed in] June of 1984, and at that point the fundamentalists were already asking, 'Why do you have a woman on your faculty who is serving as a pastor?' In a very simplistic approach to biblical hermeneutics, if you affirm women in the pastoral role—the ordination of women—therefore you are not an inerrantist and you do not believe [the Bible]."

Southern Seminary hung on to its egalitarian stance for almost another decade after the 1984 SBC resolution. In 1993, Southern Seminary President Roy Honeycutt, a longtime supporter of Marshall, was forced to retire by the newly fundamentalist-controlled board of trustees.[41] The trustees replaced Honeycutt with R. Albert Mohler, a recent and fervent convert to the Southern Baptist fundamentalist platform.[42] Mohler announced that Southern Seminary leadership would now expect "that all those who are added to this faculty will uphold that the pastorate is a male office." He then began to build a case to file charges against Marshall in order to dismiss her from her tenured position on the faculty. She was informed in 1994 that she would have to resign or else the president would formally bring charges against her.

At that point, Marshall concluded that it would serve no purpose to face a "kangaroo court" at what she believed would essentially be a "heresy trial." She submitted her resignation in 1994 and left the seminary in 1995.[43]

Since then, complementarians, now fully in control of the SBC and its seminaries, highlight Molly Marshall's story as an example of an "enemy from within" who was attempting to destroy Southern Baptist commitment to biblical orthodoxy. The "Molly Marshall" created by this discourse continues to serve as a symbol of the threat posed by a liberal, feminist culture detracting from biblical truth and as an example of a victorious battle in the conservative fight against feminism. In this narrative, Marshall was a pariah, a conduit of liberalism into the heart of Southern Baptist life; thus the triumph of the conservative leadership was not just about purging Marshall but about the salvation of the denomination itself. For example, a 2009 article by a Southern Baptist preacher, Tobby Smith (who named his son Piper after John Piper, the co-editor of *Biblical Manhood and Womanhood*[44]), identifies Marshall as one of the chief "villains" conservative leaders encountered at the end of the twentieth century, stating, "The terms heroes and villains could be considered unloving, unkind, and down right [*sic*] mean spirited, but this writer seems to think that it is appropriate when one begins to consider what convinced bible believing people like Paul Pressler, Paige Patterson, and R. Albert Mohler were up against during the years of controversy; specifically they were up against certain foes who embraced modernity to its most extreme point. In short, the conservatives faced the likes of liberalism in the countenance of . . . Molly Marshall-Green."[45] A 2007 CBMW article identified the infiltration of gender equality into Southern Seminary literally with the physical presence of Marshall on campus, stating that the "Southern Baptist Theological Seminary's egalitarian shift began as early as 1973 with the arrival of a new student by the name of Molly Marshall."[46] A 2013 film produced by Southern Seminary, titled *Recovering a Vision: The Presidency of R. Albert Mohler Jr.*, highlights Molly Marshall and Diana Garland—along with ominous background music and black-and-white photos of each of them, similar to the unflattering depictions of opponents in political campaign ads—as the film's two examples of faculty who departed from the seminary as a result of Mohler's "prophetic leadership."[47] In his pro-conservative history of Southern Seminary published in 2009,[48] Southern professor Gregory Wills implies that Marshall had no real convictions or integrity at all, suggesting she tried to cover up her controversial views when under investigation by the administration and that she "chose to resign and take a monetary settlement rather than fight the charges" against her.[49]

Russell Moore—a longtime supporter of complementarianism who joined the faculty of Southern Seminary's School of Theology in 2001 and then went on to become the dean of the School of Theology before becoming the president of the SBC's Ethics and Religious Liberty Commission—wrote soon after his arrival at Southern that "the reason Norton 237 is occupied by Russell Moore rather than Molly Marshall" was that ordinary Southern Baptist churches had "revolted" against the "bankruptcy of evangelical ecclesiology" represented by egalitarian moderates such as Marshall.[50] In 2005, Moore went on to more fully articulate his view of the threat posed by Marshall:

> The gender issue is not an isolated issue. Instead, it is connected organically to the way one views God, Scripture, salvation, eschatology, indeed the meaning of life itself. This means that evangelical complementarians must go beyond simply explaining what women can and cannot do in the church. We must place the gender issue within the framework of a theology of Christian patriarchy, a theology rooted in the glorious mystery of the Fatherhood of God and his purposes in Christ.
>
> Evangelical feminism is a real and present danger to the church. And its power is not just in misinterpreting a few Mosaic and Pauline texts. Instead it has the power to uproot the entire mosaic of Christian truth. Molly Marshall is just another sad example that feminist theology isn't just about who has 'Reverend' listed on the office door. It is about more than who wins 'evangelicalism.' Instead, it is about the evangel itself.[51]

Because of the complementarian belief that correct views and practices regarding gender roles are central to an authentic Christianity based on biblical inerrancy, Southern Baptist seminaries have now been thoroughly revamped to promote complementarian theology. Their websites clearly state that courses designed for those preparing for the pastorate are for men only. SBC seminaries affirm the Danvers Statement of the CBMW, with links to that statement on their websites. While in the 1990s students at Southern Seminary were holding vigils to protest the eradication of egalitarianism from the institution, in 2008, when an ABC news reporter visited Southern's campus and asked a female student if she ever felt it was unfair that the pastorate track was open only to men, she cheerfully responded, "Of course . . . because I'm a sinner!"[52] Mohler commended the student for speaking "so faithfully."[53] Numerous Southern Baptists, including many women, have been convinced that, in the words of Russell Moore, "Patriarchy is good for women, good for children, and good for families."[54] Yet, as the presidential campaign of 2008 would make clear, while new Southern Baptist leaders had indeed shown themselves to be lovers of patriarchy, theirs was not the patriarchy of their forefathers.

Sarah Palin

After years of making headlines for their battles against feminism, it came as a surprise to the outside world when conservative evangelicals, including Southern Baptist leaders, supported Sarah Palin as the vice presidential candidate on the Republican ticket in 2008. David P. Gushee, who earned his MDiv at Southern Seminary in 1987, before fundamentalists gained control there, represented this general sense of astonishment, especially among Baptist egalitarians who had left the SBC after the conservative takeover. In a 2008 *USA Today* article titled "The Palin Predicament," Gushee posed a number of questions to complementarians, including:

> Are you prepared to renounce publicly any further claim that God's plan is for men rather than women to exercise leadership in society, the workplace and public life? Do you acknowledge having become full-fledged egalitarians in this sphere at least? If you agree that God can call a woman to serve as President, does this have any implications for your views on women's leadership in church life? Do you believe that women carry primary responsibility for the care of children in the home? If so, does this affect your support for Palin? If not, are you willing to change your position and instead argue for flexibility in the distribution of childcare responsibilities according to the needs of the family?[55]

The fact that Palin, especially as a mother with young children, was pursuing high political office certainly seemed to put her outside of complementarian understandings of biblical womanhood.

To be sure, complementarians knew this day would come, committed as they were to conservative US politics. Back in the summer of 2007—right after Hillary Clinton had announced her intention to run for president and a year before Sarah Palin became the GOP vice presidential candidate—Russell Moore, when guest hosting the *Albert Mohler Radio Program*, invited discussion regarding whether or not evangelicals should support a woman for US president. All but one of those who called into the program stated that, while they would not support Clinton, they would support a woman for president, if someone like Margaret Thatcher, for example, were a candidate. Moore concluded the program by conceding that the Bible did not explicitly prohibit women from holding high political office. Yet he predicted that complementarians would struggle with the implications of evangelicals supporting a woman for president. On this 2007 radio program, Moore stated, "I do think that the more that we see women serving in these kinds of roles—president of the United States—the more that we are going to have difficulty teaching young girls that there is something unique about the role of godly womanhood, about being a wife and a mother and a helpmate and about having this unique role as a Titus 2 woman. It means we're going to have to do a whole lot more explaining. We shouldn't think that being president is the best thing for women, even if scripture doesn't prohibit it."[56]

Immediately after John McCain selected Palin as his running mate in 2008, complementarians did indeed begin the work of doing "a whole lot more explaining," as Moore had predicted. Prominent Southern Baptists such as Albert Mohler and Richard Land, in concert with the Council on Biblical Manhood and Womanhood,[57] quickly went to work sending out public messaging that there was no "Palin Predicament" for complementarians. As Mohler and Land were extremely influential figures in the nation's largest Protestant denomination, they were cognizant that what they said about Palin could influence the outcome of the Republican bid for the White House. Their response was that they had never said that women were to be subordinate to men in the public sphere but only in the home and the church. Nevertheless, complementarians struggled to provide a cogent response to the issues raised by McCain's choice of a woman. Ultimately, this struggle reflected the challenge of coherency for complementarian theology itself, especially when taken to such an extreme conclusion as promoting women's spiritual submission and women's political leadership at the same time.

Mohler, in a September 2008 article titled "Palin Can Serve Family and Country" published on the *Newsweek/Washington Post* blog *On Faith*, wrote that Southern Baptists' "confession of faith [the Baptist Faith and Message] does not speak to the appropriateness of women serving in political office. It does speak to the priority of motherhood and responsibilities in the home, but it does not specify any public role that is closed to women. The reason for this is simple—the New Testament does not speak to this question in any direct sense. The distinction is perfectly clear. Where the New Testament speaks, we are bound. Where it does not speak, believers are not bound."[58] Eager to explain that the SBC did not teach that women were inferior to men, Richard Land wrote in a piece for the *Baptist Press* that "Southern Baptists and similarly inclined Evangelicals have no problem with a woman serving in a leadership role in public policy or business. There is no inconsistency or hypocrisy involved in taking such a position, and there is no belief in any inferiority of women whatsoever."[59]

At the same time, complementarians also maintained that one reason it was acceptable to support Palin was because roles in the "secular" public sphere (even the public roles of vice president and president of the United States) were not as important as the leadership positions reserved for men in the church and home. Mohler wrote that any suggestion that complementarians were being inconsistent for supporting Palin while denying ordination for women was flawed, because it assumed that there was "no distinction between the church and the world." Barrett Duke, then director of the Research Institute and vice president for Research and Public Policy at the SBC's Ethics and Religious Liberty Commission, circulated a paper clarifying that women were barred from *spiritual* headship but not from secular leadership, stating that "God's design for male headship in the home and the church does not require the exclusion of women from leadership in public life, where spiritual headship is not involved."[60] David Kotter, representing the position of the Council on Biblical Manhood and Womanhood regarding Palin, echoed this position when he wrote, "Complementarians only seem to be inconsistent if one overlooks the priority of the church and misses the distinction between the church and civil government. . . . Government has been instituted since the Fall, whereas manhood and womanhood, marriage and family, and the fellowship of all true believers are part of the design of creation."[61]

Complementarians nevertheless did continue to reveal ambivalence about Palin in the early days of her vice presidential candidacy. They were at pains to make clear that their support of Palin should not be taken as tacit support for the idea that men and women were the same or that women in general should forego the home as their primary sphere, and they expressed worries about the prospect of Palin juggling both family and high political office. Mohler wrote that, while he was "elated about [Palin's] pro-life commitments and political philosophy," if he were her pastor he "would be concerned about how she could balance these responsibilities [of political office] and what this would mean for her family and her roles as wife and mother." He also stated that he would be less than happy if this caused "Christian young women to believe that being vice president of the United States is more important than being a wife and mother." Yet, he opined, the risk of this outcome was low, because "God has placed in the hearts of most women a deep desire for the fulfillment of marriage and the raising of children as a life priority," and thus, he concluded, "feminists are bewildered and frustrated by the fact that the vast majority of women find their greatest joy and fulfillment in the roles of wife and mother."[62] Kotter concluded his CBMW series on Palin by stating that voters should not worry that they might "be complicit in tempting [Palin] to work outside the home, since this decision apparently has already been made." Kotter stressed, "Let me be clear: I am not arguing that [Palin's] was a wise choice, only that it . . . would not necessarily be wrong to vote for Governor Palin." He was at pains to point out that "Christian voters are only presented with the question of who is likely to rule the country in a way that is just and most consistent with the Word of God," not whether or not they should vote for a woman—implying that Palin was the candidate most likely to "rule" in this way, because of her position on abortion and other issues important to conservative evangelicals.[63] Ultimately, complementarians' commitments to key conservative political goals trumped any concerns about gender propriety. Southern Baptist theologian Denny Burk, for example, wrote that he agreed with John Piper's point when comparing the 2008 Obama/Biden ticket with the McCain/Palin ticket that "defending abortion is far worse sin for a man than serving as Vice President is for a woman."[64]

Complementarians' explanations for supporting Palin in the fall of 2008 did leave them open to the challenge that they were soft-pedaling their commitment to biblical authority to accommodate modern culture, a critique that complementarians had long leveled against egalitarians. Outside the SBC, advocates of biblical patriarchy were among the most vocal critics of complementarians' support for a woman pursuing political office and charged that complementarians were promoting an inconsistent theology and worldview by supporting Palin. These patriarchalists asserted that male headship over *all* areas of life was inscribed in God's order for creation. As patriarchalist William Einwechter wrote in a September 2008 article titled "Sarah Palin and the Complementarian Compromise," male headship "is an essential order that knows no exceptions." Einwechter continued:

> Do Kotter and his fellow complementarians realize what they have done to their own argument for male headship in the church? The New Testament does not explicitly forbid women from the office of elder either. . . . But, in spite of this, complementarians still maintain that women are forbidden to service as elders; and they do so on the basis of the general role relationship of men and women established at creation. . . . They do not seem to understand it, but, by their enthusiastic support of a wife and mother of five children (one being an infant) for vice president, they are jeopardizing their own ability to defend complementarianism in the home and in the church. How so? They have denied, at least in part, the biblical doctrine of the created order of male headship, and the biblical doctrine of the unique, non-transferable roles of men and women in God's plan. . . . They are laying the ax to the root of their own doctrine of male headship in the church."[65]

Doug Phillips, then president of the (later scandal-ridden) patriarchalist organization Vision Forum Ministries,[66] similarly charged that complementarians had created new theological arguments in support of Palin, ones that contradicted their previous claims, and that "their legitimization of a mother of young children to serve as President of the United States undermines, if not altogether destroys, their view of complementarianism in the family because of the absurdity of the claim that a woman can lead a nation as chief executive and still properly prioritize her non-optional, biblically required duty to serve as a helpmeet to her husband." Phillips captured the significance of the moment when he stated that "many of the same conservative leaders who have previously distinguished themselves by opposing the very type of egalitarian feminist model of family and leadership embodied in the candidacy of Sarah Palin are now talking like full-fledged egalitarians. . . . There appears to be a historic shift in the cultural and political agenda of social conservatives and Christians."[67]

Palin did not become vice president, of course, but her candidacy was indeed a watershed moment for complementarian discourse. By 2009, as Palin continued her celebrity status among rank-and-file evangelicals, leading complementarians appeared to have moved past any hesitation or ambivalence they once may have had about women pursuing the US presidency. In July 2009, when Moore again hosted the *Albert Mohler Radio Program*, he stated that he had been "*very* enthusiastic about Palin," especially how she had modeled her pro-life commitment by giving birth to a child with Down syndrome. Moore professed his dismay over Palin's sudden resignation from her position as governor of Alaska, especially because he was concerned this would hurt her chances for a 2012 run for the White House. Richard Land came on the show to offer words of comfort, stating that he believed Palin's resignation was actually a "shrewd move" that would help her position herself to run for the presidency in 2012. Land emphasized that she needed to promote her book and campaign throughout the lower forty-eight states to overcome her enemies, which he identified primarily as feminists. Land stated that the reason Palin had enemies all over the country was because "she poses an existential threat to liberal feminism in the United States." Land went on to explain: "She threatens to redefine what it means to be a modern woman. She is a conservative. She is a mother. She has five children, the last one being a Down syndrome child. She is a hunter, a crack shot . . . and a governor, and has a husband. And she's good-looking. All of those are existential threats to radical leftist feminism."[68] Evangelical complementarians had chafed at the outside world's caricatures of them as bigoted chauvinists, and some even seemed to enjoy the example that Palin portrayed to the world, that a conservative Christian woman could "have it all"—motherhood to five children, being a "crack shot," *and* the US presidency.

Palin's celebrity status signaled that, in the twenty-first century, it was entirely up for grabs what a modern woman could be in conservative evangelical subcultures. When Moore asked Land if he thought evangelicals would support Palin for president in 2012, Land replied, "I know some places where evangelical women have brought their daughters to see Palin to show them that they can be evangelicals, they can be mothers, and can be professional women, too."[69] Palin had a broad appeal to evangelical women, many of whom eagerly embraced the notion that they could have positions of equality and leadership in the public sphere, if not in the home and the church. Southern Baptist leaders thereby remained in sync with their constituencies, through the evolution of their gender theology and rhetoric.

Epilogue

Sarah Palin's entrance onto the national stage was a turning point for complementarians, as they fine-tuned their message and enjoyed a chance to demonstrate to the world their less patriarchal side. During congresswoman Michele Bachmann's presidential campaign during the Republican primaries in 2011 through 2012, there was hardly a ripple among conservative evangelicals regarding her gender, and in the summer of 2011 she had a turn as a favorite presidential candidate among white evangelicals.[70] According to one news source, when inquiring with Richard Land in 2011 as to whether or not conservative Christians believed that a President Michele Bachmann "would have to obey her husband when it comes to public policy," Land made clear that this was a "silly question."[71] Sarah Palin's vice presidential candidacy of 2008 had clarified complementarians' position that women were restricted from leadership only in the case of *spiritual* headship. In spite of a command that women submit to men at church and in their homes, political leadership was not off-limits. This idea was picked up by Bachmann herself in 2011 when she was asked on a Christian radio show to explain her views on wifely submission. Bachmann stated, "I respond to [my husband] as a wife. But when it comes to being a leader, whether I'm running a business or being a member of Congress . . . This is not a spiritual position, it is a position of authority in our government; it is very different from that of a wife to her husband."[72] Bachmann even explained her foray into politics as an outcome of her husband's spiritual sway, as *she* went to law school in submission to her *husband's* message from God.[73]

This is an interesting reversal of sorts. Throughout history, a major configuration of patriarchal Christian theology has posited that males and females have spiritual equality in Christ, but in all earthly realms men are to rule over women; and in early American evangelical patriarchy, women's civic influence was to come only from their moral and spiritual influence on their husbands' public lives. Now, in the modern patriarchy of the complementarians' world, a woman can be president of the United States, as long as she accepts the spiritual headship of her husband in the home.

Notes

1. W. P. Harvey, "Shall Women Preach?" in *Feminism: Woman and Her Work*, ed. J. W. Porter (Louisville, KY: Baptist Book Concern, 1923; reprint, Bloomfield, NM: The Historic Baptist, 1994), 188.
2. "Fundamentalist" is a contested term; here I use it to signify an inerrantist reading of the Bible as the basis for rejecting feminism and other modern phenomena.
3. This distinction was made by Wayne Grudem and was picked up and expanded by his PhD student Maynard C. Mostrom Jr. in his dissertation under Grudem's supervision. The terms *two-point* and *three-point* have been used by patriarchalists as well. See Maynard C. Mostrom Jr., "A Historical Survey of the Complementarian Theology of Gender in American Protestant Fundamentalism from 1870 to 2005" (DMin diss., Phoenix Seminary, 2006), 43–45 and n74; and William Einwechter, "The Palin Predicament Resolved," Vision Forum Ministries, Sept. 23, 2008, accessed Sept. 25, 2019 at https://web.archive.org/web/20080928072521/http://www.visionforumministries.org/issues/ballot_box/the_palin_predicament_resolved.aspx.
4. While conservative Southern Baptists sought to undermine evangelical feminism by charging that "secular" feminism, rather than the Bible, had influenced Christians, an outpouring of Christian feminist scholarship in the late twentieth century, disseminated through popular outlets such as *Daughters of Sarah*, convinced many that feminist goals of human equality were in harmony with Christian faith.
5. David T. Morgan, *Southern Baptist Sisters: In Search of Status, 1845–2000* (Macon, GA: Mercer Univ. Press, 2003), 172.
6. Quoted in Keith E. Durso and Pamela R. Durso, "'Cherish the Dream God Has Given You': The Story of Addie Davis," in *Courage and Hope: The Stories of Ten Baptist Women Ministers*, eds. Pamela R. Durso and Keith E. Durso (Macon, GA: Mercer Univ. Press, 2005), 30.

7. Nancy Tatom Ammerman, *Baptist Battles: Social Change and Religious Conflict in the Southern Baptist Convention* (New Brunswick, NJ: Rutgers Univ. Press, 1990), 89.
8. Elizabeth H. Flowers, *Into the Pulpit: Southern Baptist Women and Power since World War II* (Chapel Hill: Univ. of North Carolina Press, 2012), 119.
9. Paige Patterson, *Anatomy of a Reformation: The Southern Baptist Convention, 1978–2004* (Fort Worth, TX: Seminary Hill Press, n.d.), 4.
10. Patterson, *Anatomy of a Reformation*, 1, 3.
11. Flowers, *Into the Pulpit*, 120.
12. Jay Grimstead, "How the International Council on Biblical Inerrancy Began," accessed Mar. 5, 2019, http://www.reformation.net/articles-by-dr-j-grimstead/how-the-international-council-on-biblical-inerrancy-began.
13. Norman L. Geisler and William C. Roach, *Defending Inerrancy: Affirming the Accuracy of Scripture for a New Generation* (Grand Rapids, MI : Baker Books, 2011), 34.
14. The 1984 New International Version (NIV) translation here was used widely by Southern Baptists until the 2000s. Controversy over "gender neutral" language in new NIV editions led the SBC to pass a resolution in 2011 stating that the denomination could not "commend the 2011 NIV to Southern Baptists or the larger Christian community," and many Southern Baptists and other conservative evangelicals now use the English Standard Version (ESV) instead. See "On the Gender-Neutral 2011 New International Version" (resolution, Southern Baptist Convention, Phoenix, AZ, June 14–15, 2011), http://www.sbc.net/resolutions/1218/on-the-genderneutral-2011-new-international-version.
15. The ICBI was organized to operate for ten years, from 1977-1987, during which it held three summits and produced books promoting biblical inerrancy. See Geisler and Roach, *Defending Inerrancy*, 23.
16. "Our History," Council on Biblical Manhood and Womanhood, accessed Aug. 22, 2018, https://cbmw.org/about/history.
17. Danvers Statement, Council on Biblical Manhood and Womanhood, accessed Aug. 22, 2018, https://cbmw.org/about/danvers-statement.
18. In my personal interview with James Borland, a founder of CBMW, he explained that a new term was sought because the term "patriarchy" had "way too much baggage." James Borland, interview by author, June 18, 2012.
19. Moore wrote, "If complementarians are to reclaim the debate [against feminism], we must not fear making a claim that is disturbingly counter-cultural and yet strikingly biblical, a claim that the less-than-evangelical feminists understand increasingly: Christianity is undergirded by a vision of patriarchy," in *JETS* 49, no. 3 (Sept. 2006): 573.
20. John Piper and Wayne Grudem, "Preface (1991)," in *Recovering Biblical Manhood and Womanhood: A Response to Evangelical Feminism*, eds. John Piper and

Wayne Grudem (Wheaton, IL: Crossway Books, 1991, 2006), xv. Emphasis in the original.

21. Piper and Grudem, "Preface (1991)," xv . Emphasis in the original.
22. Piper and Grudem, "An Overview of Central Concerns: Questions and Answers," in *Recovering Biblical Manhood and Womanhood*, 65.
23. For example, the 1998 resolution to amend the Baptist Faith and Message with a section on "The Family" made the front page of the *New York Times.* See Gustav Niebuhr, "Southern Baptists Declare Wife Should 'Submit' to Her Husband: Denomination Moves to Emphasize Family Life," *New York Times*, June 10, 1998, A1.
24. Paige Patterson, *Anatomy of a Reformation*, 13–15.
25. Flowers, *Into the Pulpit*, 145.
26. "Comparison of 1925, 1963 and 2000 Baptist Faith and Message," SBC.net, accessed Aug. 4, 2018, http://www.sbc.net/bfm2000/bfmcomparison.asp.
27. See, for example, Pamela R. Durso, "Molly Marshall: A Woman of Faith and Courage," reprinted in *The Exiled Generations: Legacies of the Southern Baptist Convention Holy War*, ed. Carl L. Kell (Knoxville: Univ. of Tennessee Press, 2014), Appendix 1; Eileen R. Campbell-Reed, "Molly Truman Marshall: Midwife of Grace, Sign of Hope," *Folio* 11, no. 3 (Winter 1994); Susan M. Shaw, *God Speaks to Us, Too: Southern Baptist Women on Church, Home, and Society* (Lexington: Univ. of Kentucky Press, 2008), 169–71; Elizabeth H. Flowers, *Into the Pulpit: Southern Baptist Women and Power since World War II* (Chapel Hill: Univ. of North Carolina Press, 2012), 95–99, 152–54; and *Perspectives in Religious Studies* 41, no. 2 (Summer 2014), a Festschrift in honor of Molly Marshall published by the National Association of Baptist Professors of Religion (NABPR). Marshall wrote a biographical chapter, "God Does Indeed Call to Ministry Whom God Will, Gender Notwithstanding," in *Courage and Hope: The Stories of Ten Baptist Women Ministers*, eds. Pamela R. Durso and Keith E. Durso (Macon, GA: Mercer Univ. Press, 2005), 120–31.
28. *Battle for the Minds*, produced and directed by Steven Lipscomb, aired June 10, 1997, on PBS, http://www.pbs.org/pov/battlefortheminds.
29. Marshall began her work at Central Seminary immediately after leaving Southern Baptist Theological Seminary in December 1994. Central Seminary is not affiliated with the Southern Baptist Convention. According to Central's website, it is "connected in various ways with ABC-USA, CBF, ChurchNet, NBC, DOC, UCC, AME, UM, PCUSA, and the various regional areas associated with these groups." Accessed Aug. 4, 2018, http://www.cbts.edu/about-us/affiliation.
30. Jeff Brumley, "Marshall to Retire from Central Seminary in 2020," *Baptist News Global*, May 20, 2019, https://baptistnews.com/article/marshall-to-retire-from-central-seminary-in-2020/#.XY1HdkZKiUk.
31. Doug Weaver, "Molly Marshall to Receive Whitsitt Society's Courage Award," EthicsDaily, June 21, 2004, https://ethicsdaily.com/molly-marshall-to-receive-whitsitt-societys-courage-award-cms-4343.

32. *Perspectives in Religious Studies* 41, no. 2 (Summer 2014).
33. Eileen Campbell-Reed, "Molly Truman Marshall: Living Icon for Beholding the Spirit's Renewal of the Church," *Perspectives in Religious Studies* 41, no. 2 (Summer 2014): 122.
34. Marshall, "Weaving New Cloth: Overcoming Sexism in Ordination Policies," in *Equal at the Creation: Sexism, Society and Christian Thought*, eds. Joseph Martos and Pierre Hegy (Toronto: Univ. of Toronto Press, 1998), 174–75.
35. Marshall, "Women in Ministry: A Biblical Theology," *Folio: A Newsletter for Southern Baptist Women in Ministry* 1, no. 2 (Fall 1983): 1. See also Molly Marshall-Green, "Women in Ministry," in *Formation for Christian Ministry*, eds. Anne Davis and Wade Rowatt Jr. (Louisville, KY: Review and Expositor, 1981), 125–37.
36. Marshall, "Toward Encompassing Theological Vision for Women in Light of Baptist Tradition," *Folio: A Newsletter for Southern Baptist Women in Ministry* 4, no. 2 (Autumn 1986): 1.
37. Quoted in Pamela R. Durso, "Molly Marshall: A Woman of Faith and Courage," *The Whitsitt Journal* (Spring 2004): 1.
38. Bob Allen, "Longtime Editor R.G. Puckett Dies," *Baptist New Global*, May 13, 2013, https://baptistnews.com/article/longtime-editor-r-g-puckett-dies/#.W3cY8ehKi70.
39. *Battle for the Minds*, 57:25–58:10.
40. "Resolution on Ordination and the Role of Women in Ministry" (resolution, Southern Baptist Convention, Kansas City, MO, June 12–14, 1984), http://www.sbc.net/resolutions/1088.
41. Durso, "Molly Marshall: A Woman of Faith and Courage," 6.
42. Gregory A. Wills, *Southern Baptist Theological Seminary, 1859–2009* (New York, NY: Oxford Univ. Press, 2009), 512.
43. Quotes taken from *Battle for the Minds*.
44. Tobby Smith, "Who Is Tobby Smith Anyway?" *Raised3rdDay* (blog), accessed July 12, 2019, https://raised3rdday.wordpress.com/who-is-tobby-smith-anyway.
45. Tobby Smith, "From Modernity to Mohler: How Things Changed from Liberalism to Conservatism at the Southern Baptist Theological Seminary," accessed Dec. 18, 2009, http://www.ncmbc.org/Articles/Pastor%20Tobby/From%20Modernity%20to%20Mohler.htm. During the early part of her career, Molly Marshall used the hyphenated name Marshall-Green. In recent years, she has gone by Molly Marshall or Molly Truman Marshall.
46. Jason Duesing and Tomas White, "Neanderthals Chasing Bigfoot? The State of the Gender Debate in the Southern Baptist Convention," *Journal for Biblical Manhood and Womanhood* 12, no. 2 (Fall 2007): 8.
47. *Recovering a Vision: The Presidency of R. Albert Mohler Jr.* (Southern Productions, Oct. 17, 2013), accessed June 11, 2015, http://www.sbts.edu/resources/uncategorized/recovering-a-vision-the-presidency-of-r-albert-mohler-jr. Depending on the publication, the departures of Marshall and Garland have been characterized variously as voluntary resignations, forced resignations, or, in the case of Garland,

being outright fired from the seminary. A 2015 article about Baylor University renaming its School of Social Work after Diana Garland, for example, states that before "joining the Baylor faculty in 1997, Garland was fired as dean of the Carver School of Social Work at Southern Baptist Theological Seminary after publicly criticizing the seminary's president in 1995." See "Baylor Renames School of Social Work for Dean Diana Garland," *Baptist News Global*, Apr. 27, 2015, https://baptistnews.com/ministry/people/item/30028-baylor-renames-school-of-social-work-for-dean-diana-garland#sthash.SDA10OSo.dpuf. The 2013 Southern Seminary film simply states that she resigned, noting that "many" considered it a "forced resignation."

48. In his review of this book, Dwight A. Moody drolly points out that, according to Wills's 546-page tome, "for fully three quarters of the [150-year] history now being celebrated, or exactly 137 years, Southern Seminary is contaminated by that cluster of ideological diseases known as Arminianism, modernism and liberalism. That leaves only thirty-seven years of theological righteousness. . . . In other words, this entire historical narrative . . . is oriented toward one purpose: to explain why 'the conservative takeover' had to happen" ("*Southern Baptist Theological Seminary 1859–2009*: A Review Article," *Review and Expositor* 106 [Spring 2009]: 260–61). The Southern Seminary film, *Recovering a Vision: The Presidency of R. Albert* Mohler Jr. (Southern Productions, Oct. 17, 2013), reflects the thesis of Wills's book and features excerpts from an interview with Wills. Accessed June 11, 2015, http://www.sbts.edu/resources/uncategorized/recovering-a-vision-the-presidency-of-r-albert-mohler-jr.
49. Wills, *Southern Baptist Theological Seminary, 1859–2009* (New York, NY: Oxford Univ. Press, 2009), 505, 520.
50. Russell Moore, "What's Next for Evangelical Theology?" *Moore to the Point* (blog), Nov. 26, 2003, http://www.russellmoore.com/2003/11/26/whats-next-for-evangelical-theology.
51. Russell Moore, "Evangelical Feminism Lurches Leftward: Is Molly Marshall an 'Evangelical' Feminist?" *Moore to the Point* (blog), Aug. 4, 2005, http://www.russellmoore.com/2005/08/04/evangelical-feminism-lurches-leftward-is-molly-marshall-an-evangelical-feminist.
52. R. Albert Mohler Jr., "Media Advisory—ABC World News Comes to Southern Seminary," AlbertMohler.com, Sept. 29, 2008, http://www.albertmohler.com/2008/09/29/media-advisory-abc-world-news-comes-to-southern-seminary.
53. Mohler, "Media Advisory."
54. Jeff Robinson, "Many Evangelicals Unwittingly Live as Feminists, Moore Says," *Baptist Press*, Nov. 28, 2005, http://www.bpnews.net/bpnews.asp?ID=22161.
55. David P. Gushee, "The Palin Predicament," *USA Today*, Sept. 15, 2008, 12A.
56. "Hillary Clinton and the Gender Wars," *Albert Mohler Radio Program*, Mar. 16, 2007, http://www.albertmohler.com/2007/03/16/hillary-clinton-and-the-gender-wars.
57. See David Kotter, "Does Sarah Palin Present a Dilemma for Complementar-

ians?" Parts 1–4, Council on Biblical Manhood and Womanhood, Sept. 3, 5, 8, 10, 2008, accessed Nov. 30, 2009, http://www.cbmw.org/Blog/Posts/Does-Sarah-Palin-present-a-Dilemma-for-Complementarians-Part-1, https://cbmw.org/uncategorized/does-sarah-palin-present-a-dilemma-for-complementarians-part-2, https://cbmw.org/uncategorized/does-sarah-palin-present-a-dilemma-for-complementarians-part-3, https://cbmw.org/uncategorized/does-sarah-palin-present-a-dilemma-for-complementarians-part-4.

58. R. Albert Mohler Jr., "Palin Can Serve Family and Country," *Newsweek/Washington Post, On Faith* (blog), Sept. 5, 2008, accessed Dec. 28, 2009, http://newsweek.washingtonpost.com/onfaith/panelists/r_albert_mohler_jr/2008/09/a_tale_of_two_offices.html.
59. Richard Land, "Baptists, the Bible and Women: There Is No 'Palin Predicament' for Southern Baptists or Evangelicals," *Baptist Press*, Sept. 19, 2008, http://www.bpnews.net/28959.
60. Quoted in Nathan A. Finn, "Gender and the Vice Presidency," *Baptist Press*, Sept. 5, 2008, http://www.bpnews.net/28848; Barrett Duke, interview by author, July 11, 2011.
61. Kotter, "Does Sarah Palin Present a Dilemma for Complementarians?" Part 1, Council on Biblical Manhood and Womanhood, Sept. 3, 2008.
62. Mohler, "Palin Can Serve Family and Country."
63. Kotter, "Does Sarah Palin Present a Dilemma for Complementarians?" Part 4, Council on Biblical Manhood and Womanhood, Sept. 10, 2008.
64. John Piper, "Why a Woman Shouldn't Run for Vice President, but Wise People May Still Vote for Her," DesiringGod.org, Nov. 2, 2008, https://www.desiringgod.org/articles/why-a-woman-shouldnt-run-for-vice-president-but-wise-people-may-still-vote-for-her; Quoted in Denny Burk, "A Female President?" *The Journal for Biblical Manhood and Womanhood* (Fall 2011): 7.
65. William Einwechter, "Sarah Palin and the Complementarian Compromise," Vision Forum Ministries, Sept. 8, 2008, accessed Nov. 16, 2009, http://www.visionforumministries.org/issues/ballot_box/sarah_palin_and_the_complement.aspx.
66. In the fall of 2013, Doug Phillips resigned after a sex scandal, and Vision Forum Ministries closed operations. See Sarah Pulliam Baily, "Doug Phillips Extramarital Affair Forces Resignation from Vision Forum Ministries," *Huffington Post*, last updated Nov. 13, 2013, http://www.huffingtonpost.com/2013/11/07/doug-phillips-affair_n_4235191.html.
67. Doug Phillips, "*USA Today* Editorial Challenges Semi-complementarians for Compromise; CBMW Answers; VFM Responds," Vision Forum Ministries, Sept. 25, 2008, accessed Nov. 16, 2009, http://www.visionforum.com/hottopics/blogs/dwp/2008/09/#n9.
68. "Sarah Palin: Where Has She Gone?" *Albert Mohler Radio Program*, July 6, 2009, http://www.albertmohler.com/2009/07/06/sarah-palin-where-has-she-gone.
69. "Sarah Palin: Where Has She Gone?" *Albert Mohler Radio Program*.

70. Beth Reinhard, “Michele Bachmann Wins the Ames Straw Poll,” *The Atlantic*, Aug. 13, 2011, https://www.theatlantic.com/politics/archive/2011/08/michele-bachmann-wins-the-ames-straw-poll/243564.
71. Bob Smietana, “Should Wives Submit? Debate Resurges,” *The Tennessean*, Aug. 29, 2011.
72. Michele Bachmann, interview on the *Steve Deace Radio Show*, Dec. 19, 2011, accessed Jan. 2, 2012, http://stevedeace.com/news/national-politics/deace-show-podcast-12–19–11.
73. “Bachmann: ‘God Called Me to Run for Congress,’” YouTube video, accessed Oct. 1, 2011, http://www.youtube.com/watch?v=lorUBomKvYo&feature=related. See also Libby Copeland, “Hail to the Housewife: Can Michele Bachmann Be the Leader of the Free World and Still Obey Her Husband like a Good Evangelical?” *Slate*, June 30, 2011, accessed De. 8, 2019 at https://slate.com/human-interest/2011/06/michele-bachmann-and-evangelicals-can-a-woman-really-be-accepted-as-a-leader.html.

Ten

"MY HUSBAND WEARS THE COWBOY BOOTS IN OUR FAMILY"

The Preacherly Paradox of Beth Moore

Courtney Pace

In a 2007 segment of Beth Moore's *Believing God* DVD series, an audience member described her transformation, immediately demonstrating "the Beth Moore effect." Early in the multiweek study, the young woman wore a nature-toned, plaid flannel shirt without makeup and with simple, unstyled hair. Several weeks later, she was a striking contrast to her former self in a pink flannel shirt, sporting carefully coiffed curls and brightly made-up. She praised Moore's studies for helping her grow spiritually, engaging more deeply in faith practices and understanding, which in this case was conflated with adopting Southern gender norms.[1] As seen with this woman, the Beth Moore effect resembles an evangelical beauty regimen, in which a spiritual makeover often includes changes in physical appearance, with matching accessories in the latest fashions. In any marketplace, though, fashions change, making the seemingly seamless beauty regimen more complicated than initially meets the eye and sometimes, as more recent events around Beth Moore and the #MeToo movement have shown, rather unpredictable.[2]

From about 1994 to 2016, Moore succeeded dazzlingly as the consummate Southern Baptist woman evangelist, marketing her ministry almost solely to women. Born Wanda Elizabeth Green in 1957 on an army base in Green Bay, Wisconsin, she grew up in Arkadelphia, Arkansas, where her family operated a movie theater. As a teenager in a Southern Baptist church, she first discerned her call to ministry in music, missions, and biblical literacy.[3] She earned a degree in political science from Southwest Texas State University, where she met Keith Moore. Shortly after marrying in 1978, Keith started a plumbing company, and Moore stayed at home to raise daughters Amanda (b. 1983) and Melissa (b. 1986).[4]

As a stay-at-home wife and mother, Moore was active within First Baptist Church of Houston, Texas, where she started a women's Bible study from her own desire to study the Bible for spiritual growth. To say the Bible study "took off" would be an understatement. By the early 1990s, Moore's Tuesday night interdenominational Bible studies at the Baptist megachurch drew thousands of women; online streaming later added thousands more. In 1994, Moore founded Living Proof Ministries (LPM). Lee Sizemore of LifeWay, the Southern Baptist Convention's (SBC) publishing house, took notice and partnered with Moore. Moore's ministry soon topped LifeWay's sales, with Moore publishing nearly four dozen books, mostly Bible studies with accompanying workbooks and DVDs.[5] She sold out arenas and concert venues as she traveled nationally for Living Proof Live conferences. LPM became a family business, eventually employing both of her daughters, and expanded to radio, *Living Proof with Beth Moore,* and regular television appearances through *Wednesdays with Beth*, a segment on James Robison's *LIFE TODAY*.[6] Most importantly to the SBC, LPM fed the literature and programming of the growing conservative women's ministry movement, encouraging women to pursue unordained, often volunteer, "ministries," teaching and evangelizing women and children. A 2010 feature on Beth Moore in *Christianity Today* placed Moore alongside male luminaries of the twentieth and twenty-first centuries: "In the evangelical spectrum . . . if Billy Graham functions as an evangelist, Rick Warren as a pastor, and John Piper as a teacher, then Moore serves as an exhorter." The article quoted Joe Stowell, former president of Moody Bible Institute, who praised Moore's work in this capacity: "An exhorter is calling you enthusiastically to grow with Jesus."[7]

The use of the historical term *exhorter* to describe Beth Moore, rather than *preacher*, *pastor*, or *evangelist*, is revealing, harkening back to the Great Awakenings of the eighteenth and nineteenth centuries, when some women mounted church pulpits and camp-meeting platforms to deliver testimonies and messages, witness to the Spirit, and pray. Often accompanied by passionate weeping, their proclamations stirred onlookers' emotions, as their exhorting—not preaching—called these onlookers toward Christ. Since these emotions were acceptable outlets for eighteenth- and nineteenth-century women, female revivalists still functioned within realms of respectability, though sometimes courting controversy.[8] As Southern Baptists grew more denominationally minded, early twentieth-century SBC women led their congregations and the convention itself through an expanding missionary movement. Seen as missional authorities, mission teachers, or missionaries—rather than ministers, evangelists, or preachers, even when mounting the pulpit—women created agency for themselves via respectability politics using alternative titles for their ministry. Briefly, from the 1960s through the 1980s, some SBC women pursued official positions of ordained ministry and earned master of divinity degrees at SBC seminaries as part of their ordination journey. The late-twentieth century conservative takeover of the SBC closed those doors, after which Southern Baptist women returned to previous means to ministry.

Throughout most of her career, until 2019, Moore did not claim the term *preacher* for herself. Like other Southern Baptists since the conservative takeover, Moore embraced complementarianism.[9] By the 1990s, *complementarianism* had become the favored term among conservative evangelicals for a patriarchal theology that celebrates different roles and responsibilities for men and women in familial and ecclesial life, wherein men hold positions of leadership and authority and women play supporting, submissive roles, primarily as wives and mothers. Moore's success was paradoxical, as her teaching and performance reinforced women's submission within complementarianism, even as she functioned like a preacher for an ever-growing audience. She achieved this under the name *women's ministry*, a term which emerged as early as the 1970s to account for growing programs focused on women's ministry to women.[10] The caveat, "to women," proved crucial as an entry point for Moore's ministry, but as her celebrity status grew, the boundaries between female and male ministry blurred, with Moore's ministry explicitly reinforcing Southern Baptist gender and power norms while simultaneously, and implicitly, challenging those norms.

Moore's story continued to change and unfold, though, while I was writing this chapter, and from 2016 onwards, her implicit challenge to current SBC gender norms became explicit. This change was primarily in reaction to the election of Donald Trump and the advent of the #MeToo movement, especially as these developments implicated SBC pastors and leaders. Openly defying a majority of evangelical leaders, Moore denounced Trump and later endorsed the #MeToo movement, joining forces with many women in sharing both her own story of childhood sexual abuse and later harassment by evangelical officials. This chapter, then, considers her ministry from the early 1990s until 2016, with the final section looking at Moore in the era of

Trump, from 2016 to 2019, asking whether Moore's preacherly paradox is sustainable in a complementarian Southern Baptist context.

Womanhood

For most of her tenure, at least until 2016, Moore's teachings on gender relations promoted complementarian patriarchy in marriage and family. According to Moore, the roles of wife and mother epitomized womanhood. Moreover, while Moore sometimes rhetorically promoted interracial cooperation, claiming in 2016 that her works reached "women of all ages, races, and denominations," her work perpetuated and maintained white, middle- and upper-class, heteronormative Southern gender norms as Christian orthopraxis.[11] Though herself a woman behind a pulpit, at conferences and in DVD appearances, her language reinforced patriarchal ideals through encouraging women's explicit affirmation of male authority as necessary for Christian faith, starting with women's roles in marriage and family.

Moore affirmed complementarianism by consistently stating that she operated under the headship of her husband. When discussing marriage roles, she emphasized submissive respect for her husband and faith that God ordained the marital hierarchy. In one of her first books, *Breaking Free,* which she published in 1999 and revised nearly a decade later, she credited Keith for his responsibility over their finances and security, downplaying her role as the family's primary breadwinner.[12] To honor Keith's request for a regular schedule, she often acknowledged that she limited her travel to every other Friday night: "We walk the dogs together and eat out together all the time and lie on the floor with pillows and watch TV. My man demanded attention and he got it, and my man demanded a normal home life and he got it."[13] At a 2009 Focus on the Family conference, she shared Keith's response to someone's question about how he maintains spiritual headship over her: "I don't have to keep up with her. She's not the one that gives me the office. God has given me the office."[14] Keith's statement likewise attempted to explain possible contradictions: although he read his wife's books for his own spiritual formation, and she chose the text for her family's daily Bible meditations, he nevertheless remained the head. Writing in 2005, Moore herself stated: "With God's help I was able to do every single bit of this [daily devotionals] without undermining my husband's authority. He certainly wasn't *against* the plan. He thoroughly approved. He just didn't always participate. . . . I didn't require it of my husband because I am not his boss."[15]

Moore's teachings on marriage and her representation of her personal life closely mirrored the 2000 SBC Baptist Faith and Message (BFM) section on marriage and family, a key complementarian text: "[The husband] has the God-given responsibility to provide for, to protect, and to lead his family. A wife is to submit herself graciously to the servant leadership of her husband even as the church willingly submits to the headship of Christ. She, being in the image of God as is her husband and thus equal to him, has the God-given responsibility to respect her husband and to serve as his helper in managing the household and nurturing the next generation." Moore consistently portrayed her personal life as that of a submissive wife, happily married to Keith (now for over forty years), and a proud mother and grandmother. Though she functioned as the minister in her family, her rhetoric clearly placed her within Southern Baptist complementarianism.

Despite her audience being women, only two of her dozens of Bible studies reference women in the title: *A Woman's Heart: God's Dwelling Place* (1995) and *Esther: It's Tough Being a Woman* (2008). And some might argue that her studies reinforced a number of gender stereotypes about women. Her praise of Esther, for instance, celebrated clever use of beauty and feminine wiles: "Esther's full intent was to dress for success."[16] She later elaborated: "You and I know that the providence of a sovereign God was the overarching reason for her success, but few of us would deny that He used her approach: mannerly, feminine, sweet, smart, and shrewd."[17] In another example from *So Long, Insecurity* (2010), she "started flipping through scripture" to find examples of biblical characters with insecurity and quipped that Eve was "our first runner up," stating, "I feel sure all our female troubles [with insecurity] began with her."[18] She then blamed Sarah's insecurity for Hagar's oppression and granted Leah and Rachel the "Most Insecure Women in the Word Award."[19] Perhaps not surprisingly, Mary, the mother of Jesus, received more positive attention, with her love for her baby and submission to God.[20] But for most of her teaching ministry to women, male biblical figures dominated, with some of her most popular Bible studies being on the patriarchs, Daniel, David, and John.

Gender Performance

One of the most effective aspects of Moore's complementarian ministry was, and has certainly continued to be, her performance of white Southern gender norms of femininity. First, Moore has been recognized as attractive by the standards of affluent Southern white culture, which has produced its fair share of Miss Americas. Her carefully styled blond hair and twinkling mascaraed eyes are part of her trademark. She has stayed consistently thin and fashionable, typically dressed in a "rustic chic" or "country club casual" style, never repeating an outfit on camera. High heels have been standard, except when introducing a video series on location, in which case she might wear sandals or boots to match her setting. Not surprisingly, her DVDs credit a makeup artist and hair stylist. Second, her wholesome good looks have enhanced her energetic and youthful personality. A key to the success of her gender performance has been her funny, relatable personality, exuding charismatic charm. In addition, Moore's sets have been designed to appeal to women in her target demographic. The stage might be elaborately decorated like Tuscan Italy, a well-appointed living room, the desert, or an idyllic garden, to match her topic.

Moore's conspicuously feminine appearance has matched her rhetorical style as a charming, engaging, and often humorously self-deprecating "girl-next-door" personality. For example, she has compared Christianity to the school carpool, CliffsNotes, the lights above her bathroom mirror, her hair-dryer, and types of shoes. In *Get Out of That Pit* (2009), Moore even quoted text printed on her Starbucks cup as a theological insight.[21] At another point, in *So Long, Insecurity*, she exalted Starbucks, somewhat tongue-in-cheek, for confirming she had chosen the right doctor: "But once I arrived [at the doctor's office] and saw the Starbucks on the first floor of the high-rise, I rested in God's perfect will."[22] All of this she delivered in classic Texas twang.

Moore has described her husband using hypermasculine terms: driving or standing next to a pickup truck, traveling and returning from a hunting trip, fixing things around their home, or offering advice the way only a wise cowboy can. She also compared her love of her husband to her love of Christ, echoing Southern Baptist complementarians' focus on the parallel between the relationship of a wife and husband and the church and Christ. In *Breaking Free,* she exclaimed: "One of the reasons I wanted children was to bear offspring who were the image of my husband. I wanted little Keiths and Keithettes! I didn't want them to look like me. I've always thought Keith was far more beautiful than I. You see, the same is true of our spiritual offspring. Once we fall in love with Christ, we are so taken with His beauty, we want children who look just like Him."[23]

Complementing her husband's masculinity, Moore has prioritized an overtly feminine appearance for herself, discussing her own appearance in nearly every study, workbook, and DVD. In *Esther,* she listed the products she uses daily: "face wash, refining lotion, moisturizer, makeup primer, foundation, highlighter, bronzer, blush, frosty beige eye shadow, frosty brown eye shadow, eyeliner, mascara, lip-stain, lipstick, and lip gloss."[24] Her former career as an aerobics instructor surprises few.

Yet even as Moore seems to reinforce a culture that prioritizes physical appearance, she also has critiqued this culture, even naming body image as one of the primary crises facing Christian women today. In *Living Beyond Yourself*, she claimed: "We are the first media driven culture. This one is getting to us. . . . If we don't get this thing where we have a spiritual perspective toward it, it is literally going to eat us alive."[25] Insisting women envision the problem spiritually, she attacked women who falsely spiritualize disordered body image: "We want to be so spiritual, and we rename our obsessions." And she likewise challenged the abuse of spiritual practices, noting that a "fast for prayer" could mask anorexia.[26] In *Breaking Free*, she listed five primary sins: pride, idolatry, unbelief, prayerlessness, and legalism.[27] The latter, she stated, happen when "regulations replace relationship," "microscopes replace mirrors," and "performance replaces passion."[28] Throughout her ministry, Moore frequently discussed overcoming her perfectionism, particularly about appearance.

The obvious contradiction of her gender performance with her call for women to rise above appearance insecurity has reflected Moore's own apparent struggle with these tensions, with Moore addressing her own past struggle between acquiescence to gender norms and desiring liberation from them. She humorously describes *So Long, Insecurity* as "the closest [she will] ever come to an autobiography," jesting about her own appearance insecurity as well as relationship insecurity.[29] In *Breaking Free*, she acknowledged her high school conflation of appearance and self-worth: "To feel I looked OK, everything had to be right. No humidity, good hair, lots of makeup, no clumps in the mascara. I worked so hard at trying to look good. Too hard. I believed that nothing about me was naturally beautiful. How thankful I am for the freedom God has increasingly given me in Christ. I'm in the throes of middle age—a friend says, 'Time is a great healer but a lousy beautician.' Yet I am happier and more satisfied than I've ever been. The secret? I'm learning to see myself as beautiful to Christ."[30]

Yet even while attempting to move beyond rigid beauty standards, Moore criticized women who "hide themselves" in "masculine" appearances. In *So Long, Insecurity*, she wrote: "Countless women are so insecure about their womanhood that they act like men . . . women who hide themselves behind a masculine exterior so no one can get to their vulnerable female interior."[31]

Later in the text, she suggested that women defying typical affluent Southern patriarchal norms must be in psychological denial of their femininity as a self-defense mechanism since "all insecurity is a cover-up for unbelief."[32] Thus, she normalized her particular understanding of femininity as prescriptive for what all Christian women *should* want, claiming that a Christian woman who does not perform gender similarly must be in unbelief.

Throughout her public ministry, Moore's gender performance has, for the most part, implied that a woman's worth is directly linked to her attractiveness according to specific standards. She has consistently communicated that women's spiritual maturity is inextricably linked to Southern gender norms, a norm that has traditionally included women's explicit exclusion from the upper hierarchies of church leadership. Moreover, if the success of her ministry has given Moore power within the SBC, at least temporarily, her female followers lack that authority in their local contexts.

Church Leadership

After codifying complementarian marriage in 1998, the SBC further revised the Baptist Faith and Message in 2000 to include the statement that "the office of pastor is limited to men as qualified by Scripture." Moore affirmed this patriarchal hierarchy, insisting on the necessity for pastors and preachers to be male. And she has persisted in her insistence. Like most complementarians, at least until recently, Moore attributed male authority not to inequality but to a need for order, a burden men are called to bear. Just like "a monster cannot have two heads, the buck has to stop with somebody," she quipped. She also insisted that she was not "nervous" to submit, and even playfully quoted Tony Evans's definition of submission: "learning to duck so God can hit your husband."[33] Imagining women with household authority, she said: "We would not want it. We would want them to have it. . . . God holds your husband responsible for the welfare of your home and your marriage."[34]

At Focus on the Family 2009, during which Moore was the only female speaker, she opened with a disclaimer: "I would never dream of lording authority over you. . . . I am serving you by serving your wives." Looking to conference coordinator Gary Smalley, Moore said, "I need your cover for this," seeking his spiritual cover over her, since he was the male in charge and she was operating within the authority he had given her.[35] During a Living Proof Live event around the same time, Moore acknowledged men in her audience while simultaneously limiting her ministry to women: "The gentlemen who had such courage to come into this place tonight, into this estrogen fest if you will ever find one in your entire life, we are so blessed to have you. I do not desire to have any kind of authority over you."[36] These statements demonstrated Moore's embrace of women's submissive role in complementarian deference to male headship in church and home.

At the same time, and again until recently, Moore largely avoided questions regarding the biblical roles of women in ministry, with a few exceptions. In *Breaking Free,* she emphasized that Isaiah's wife was known as a "prophetess," humorously adding: "I like Isaiah already, don't you?"[37] Discussing her morning Bible reading, Moore wrote: "I practice what I'm 'preaching' here almost every day."[38] Her quotation marks around "preaching" suggested intentional playfulness, or hesitation, with the word. "Scripture's strong leaning toward male gender references never has bothered me," she declared, "I'm perfectly at home with the generalization including females as well as males."[39]

Complicating the picture, Moore sometimes blended egalitarian and complementarian approaches to scripture. In *Beloved Disciple* (2002), for instance, she taught her audience to "see ourselves as beloved disciples," suggesting that just as God called John, described in the New Testament as the "beloved disciple," God calls believers today, both male and female.[40] Likewise, in *So Long, Insecurity*, she assumed Paul's address to "brothers" included women: "The thought never occurred to me that Jesus didn't call girls to follow Him alongside the boys. . . . We might be commissioned to do different things, but Jesus ministers next to men and women alike. . . . [Called] is used in reference to the way every Christian, regardless of gender, first comes to Christ (Romans 8:30)."[41] While Moore interpreted Ephesians 5:21–33 (typically used by complementarians to justify male headship over women) as a literal assignment of gender roles, when teaching 1 Timothy 2 (which says women should learn in silence), she emphasized the importance of mentors, ignoring the call for women's silence.[42] Interestingly, when speaking about Christians' inheritance of the Old Testament priesthood, she emphasized that all now serve as "believer-priests," and she failed to distinguish between men and women: "Just as Aaron was a type, or picture, of Christ, our Great High priest, the sons who were permitted to serve with Aaron are types, or pictures, of New Testament believer-priests—you and me!" Moving to 1 Peter 2:9, she underscored that "we" are "also priests after the order of Melchizedek."[43]

Additionally, as for her personal life, she regularly described her marital relationship as one of "mutual respect," and in her teaching, spoke directly to men on how to be good husbands, bumping up against her own message of complementarian submission.[44] With some exegetical shrewdness, she did, once, note differing translations of the same Hebrew word as "valor" for men in Judges 6 and as "noble" for women in Proverbs 31: "Why must it be translated differently in Proverbs 31 just because she was a woman? Is it because it doesn't take as much courage to be a woman as it takes to be a man?"[45] Rather than fully critiquing patriarchy, however, Moore frequently repeated that, because God ordained the hierarchy, it must be trusted.[46]

Preacher

While, until 2019, Moore claimed to teach, not preach, referencing Living Proof Ministries as a "teaching ministry," her ministry nevertheless mirrored what evangelical men do when preaching. In her DVDs, for instance, she stood behind what she called a "Bible stand"—which certainly would be called a "pulpit" if she were a man—and exposited the biblical text for those gathered to hear her, which contradicted historical notions of exhorting as being something different from expositing, at least in its more personal and extemporaneous content. She not only explained her understanding of the text but also its contemporary relevance. Moore's speaking engagements consistently followed this setup. Her primary audience has been women, and she has marketed herself accordingly. Yet, from the start, men have attended her speaking engagements, and she has acknowledged male readership in her books.[47]

How Moore managed to have a flourishing ministry in a complementarian SBC culture reveals the subversion of absolute patriarchy possible for women who know how to navigate cultural gender norms. Without being overly controversial—as she did have her critics—or explicitly bucking the SBC's gender hierarchy, Moore found a way to preach. Her dynamic and engaging performance emulated preaching in its traditional sense, clearly challenging her audience to make specific mental and behavioral shifts toward accepting her preacherly presence. She stood behind a pulpit with her Bible like a preacher, she waved her arms like a preacher, and she spoke with passionate homiletic technique like a preacher, even drawing from the call-and-response tradition: "Somebody in this room wants to say 'Hallelujah!' Can I get an Amen?"[48] For a brief season in the early 2000s, Moore traded her pulpit for a wicker plant stand or a barstool and table, perhaps softening her image amidst the newly released 2000 BFM or as part of a trend among conservative preachers nationwide at that time to appear more accessible to their congregations, but most of her video supplements were filmed at her church where she taught from the actual church pulpit.

Early on, some Southern Baptists recognized Moore's ministry as preaching. A minority called Moore "one of the most dangerous persons in the SBC . . . because she is a woman who exercises proclamation gifts."[49] Josh Buice, pastor of Pray's Mill Baptist Church in Douglasville, Georgia, argued strongly against Moore based on his assessment of her as an "ecumenical Charismatic," a woman in ministry, and an allegorical rather than literal interpreter of the biblical text, as well as her claims to have heard directly from God rather than exclusively through the biblical text.[50] A Facebook group called "Beth Moore—Exposed," created in 2012, critiqued women in ministry in general and Moore in particular as "a wolf in sheep's clothing who is misleading her followers down a dangerous dead-end path" because she was a "False Teacher, False Prophet, Counterfeit Christian, and Dangerous Bible-Twister who is preaching a different gospel and a different Jesus than what is taught in the Bible."[51]

Despite such criticism, however, the denominational leadership celebrated Moore as a vital leader for women in the church, even as they advocated the patriarchal vision of complementarianism. Those at LifeWay, for instance, referenced her work as "teaching" because of her gender, though if she were a Southern Baptist man, she most certainly would have been ordained and her "teaching" recognized as "preaching." Essentially, Moore found room to preach by another name.

But why did the SBC promote what it so vilified? Several possibilities emerge. First, for most of her ministry, she preached what they wanted her to say, calling women to embrace, not buck, the gender hierarchy as a matter of spiritual necessity. Second, she appeared as they wanted her, and indeed all women, to look. Her exuberant femininity maintained a certain respectability and acceptability within conservative evangelicalism so that, when behind a pulpit, she reinforced the Southern white culture so familiar to most members of the SBC. Her gender performance nullified most accusations of preaching, creating space for her independence and leadership. Keith may have worn the boots, but through her successful performance of femininity, Beth effectively wore the pants. Though she performed submissive femininity, she was a famous, well-compensated public religious leader. Few other Southern Baptist women managed this paradox as successfully.

Over time, however, Moore's performance began to undermine the very binary she claimed to support. As women flocked to women's ministry programs at SBC seminaries, becoming the next Beth Moore presented an appealing possibility. Although Moore did not challenge the SBC status quo in the content of her teaching or her display of femininity, she nevertheless embodied an alternative identity for Southern Baptist women as a confident public figure, who was Spirit-filled, respectful of men and women, and, most significantly, visible behind the pulpit. Thus, as a preacherly paradox, her ministry challenged new generations of Southern Baptist women to follow what they perceived as God's call in new, untraditional ways. While Moore was not the only woman whose leadership presented a paradoxical dilemma for Southern Baptist women, she was certainly the most visible. And for most of her ministerial career, it seemed that paradox would hold, until Donald Trump and the #MeToo movement emerged.

Epilogue

In October 2016, as Donald Trump was in the final weeks of campaigning for the upcoming presidential election, a leaked recording of his 2005 conversation with former *Access Hollywood* host Billy Bush exposed Trump bragging about his nonconsensual sexual encounters with women. This tape functioned as a turning point for Moore's public persona. Moore had long shared her story as a sexual violence survivor; but until October 2016, her audience had been women, and her purpose for sharing focused on women's recovery. With the Trump incident, however, she turned to social media as a platform to critique men's abuse of power and rally other Southern Baptists, men and women, to her side.

Moore's first tweet in response to Trump read: "Wake up, Sleepers, to what women have dealt with all along in environments of gross entitlement & power. Are we sickened? Yes. Surprised? NO. Try to absorb how acceptable the disesteem and objectifying of women has been when some Christian leaders don't think it's that big a deal."[52] In the same thread, Moore drew attention to herself: "I'm one among many women sexually abused, misused, stared down, heckled, talked naughty to. Like we liked it. We didn't. We're tired of it."[53] Other than a few notable exceptions—such as the anti-Trump stance of the president of the SBC's Ethics and Religious Liberty Commission, Russell Moore (no relation to Beth Moore)—many leading Southern Baptists did not condemn Trump for his history of sexual impropriety. Prominent evangelicals within the SBC and beyond continued their loyalty to his campaign, including Robert Jeffress, pastor of First Baptist Dallas, and other evangelical leaders such as Jerry Falwell Jr. of Liberty University and Billy Graham's son Franklin Graham of Samaritan's Purse. Despite the "family values" rhetoric of the SBC and Beth Moore's efforts to expose the dissonance between those values and Trump's campaign, since his election, the SBC and other conservative evangelical groups have continued to defend and even idolize Trump as divinely chosen to restore conservative Christian values to America.

Suddenly Moore found herself at the center of a brewing controversy. But rather than silencing her, it emboldened her to reject what she viewed as evangelicals' alliance with the GOP under Trump. For Moore, the alliance prioritized politics over accountability. In November 2017, she tweeted: "This idea that God puts up with secret sins from His servants for the greater good is a total crock."[54] Thus, while exhibiting a somewhat compliant complementarian attitude previous to 2016, when it came to matters of sexual harassment and abuse, Moore demonstrated and called women as well as men to independent thinking, even if it meant a loss of approval: "Risk being the only one in your familiar circle who changes your mind if that's what it takes. To never change your mind is to never change. ROCK THE BOAT. And if it needs sinking, let Jesus sink it. . . . I'm so tired of aphorisms from people with their heads in the sand I could throw up. Let's get our heads out, eyes open & serve in this mess."[55]

As Moore would have it, "responsibility for the gospel" resided with the church, not the state.[56] Critiquing the ongoing evangelical-GOP alliance, Moore tweeted: "The consistent casting off of restraint of any leader who wields considerable power—1st & foremost in the house of God—ought to terrify us."[57] And then, "There are issues & times when we must land on 1 side or the other. This tweet is about going past party lines in allegiance to Jesus alone."[58] Addressing a Public Religion Research Institute poll finding—"White evangelical protestants are now more tolerant of immoral behavior by elected officials than the average American"—Moore replied, "This is what happens when we sell our souls to buy our wins. The huge irony is that we do it in Jesus' name. I don't think He's taking credit for this."[59] Officially disavowing herself of affiliations, she tweeted: "If you want me to answer to it, don't call me evangelical/ conservative/ liberal/ Baptist/ Pentecostal/ Republican/ Democrat. It's Jesus follower."[60]

In October 2017, when numerous Hollywood women accused movie mogul Harvey Weinstein of sexual assault and harassment, the #MeToo hashtag, originated by Tarana Burke ten years prior, took off, with more than nineteen million respondents using the hashtag within the next year to claim victimization. Moore immediately returned to Twitter to address the sexual abuse of girls and women at the hands of powerful men: "A well-meaning mentor told me at 25 that people couldn't handle hearing about sexual abuse, and it would sink my ministry. It didn't. #MeToo."[61] As #MeToo accusations spread, and more men were implicated, male leaders of the SBC and conservative evangelicalism largely stayed silent. Moore responded to their seeming indifference by escalating her rhetoric: "One reason why we can't seem to repent and get on with the business of God is because we are having serious trouble calling things what they are. . . . Sexual assault is not an issue. It's a crime. CRIME. Crime."[62] And if that were not enough, she hit hard: "It's been a harrowing trip to Oz for many evangelicals this year, the curtain pulled back on the wizards of cause. We found a Bible all right, seemingly used instead of applied, leveraged instead of obeyed, cut and pasted piecemeal into a pledge of allegiance to serve the served."[63]

Moore was clearly testing the overwhelming good graces she had once enjoyed, and graces that had often looked over her preacherly presence in the denomination. On March 16, 2017, in a hint of things to come, she even doctored a photo to present herself dressed as a man, with noted credentials, and tweeted: "I'm sometimes asked if I speak to men's groups. No. But the Brother Reverend Doctor Seth Moore is, on rare occasion, available."[64]

At this point, though, her critique was primarily aimed at the acquiescence of male SBC leadership to sexual violence against women in exchange for political power grabs. In spring 2018, #MeToo then moved to Southern Baptist circles, with thousands of evangelical women calling for the firing of Paige Patterson, president of Southwestern Baptist Theological Seminary, after sermons surfaced in which Patterson flagrantly objectified women's and young girls' bodies and urged abused wives to prayerfully stay with their husbands rather than seek safety for themselves and their children. As the protest spread, other evangelical leaders were indicted, including Willow Creek's founding pastor Bill Hybels and the young Southern Baptist minister from Memphis Andy Savage, whom many had viewed as the heir to conservative Southern Baptist legend and former SBC president Adrian Rogers.

On May 3, 2018, Moore posted "A Letter to My Brothers" on her blog. As a candid memoir of her experience as a woman leader in evangelicalism, it served as a searing condemnation of its patriarchal leadership.[65] In recounting her SBC rearing, walking the aisle to accept both her salvation and calling, and her interdenominational ministry, Moore made clear that her call had been "to teach and to serve women." While adding that "being a woman called to leadership within and simultaneously beyond those walls was complicated to say the least," Moore emphasized that she had "worked within the system." Then, she disclosed the harsh reality of sexism within that system:

> As a woman leader in the conservative Evangelical world, I learned early to show constant pronounced deference—not just proper respect which I was glad to show—to male leaders, and when placed in situations to serve alongside them, to do so apologetically. I issued disclaimers ad nauseam. I wore flats instead of heels when I knew I'd be serving alongside a man of shorter stature so I wouldn't be taller than he. I've ridden elevators in hotels packed with fellow leaders who were serving at the same event and not been spoken to, and, even more awkwardly, in the same vehicles where I was never acknowledged. I've been in team meetings where I was either ignored or made fun of, the latter of which I was expected to understand was all in good fun. I am a laugher. I can take jokes and make jokes. I know good fun when I'm having it and I also know when I'm being dismissed and ridiculed. I was the elephant in the room with a skirt on. I've been talked down to by male seminary students and held my tongue when I wanted to say, "Brother, I was getting up before dawn to pray and pore over the Scriptures when you were still in your pull ups."

Anticipating critique that such treatment stemmed from her lack of education rather than sexism, she responded that those were the same: "Where was a woman in my generation and denomination to get seminary training to actually teach the Scriptures?" Admittedly, Moore did begin theological education at Southwestern Baptist Theological Seminary in 1988, commuting from Houston to Fort Worth. However, she writes, "[after] a short time . . . of reading the environment and coming to the realization of what my opportunities would and would not be, I took a different route." She educated herself through reading and tutors: "My road was messy but it was the only reasonable avenue open to me."

Moore described critiques from "a segment of hyper-fundamentalists based on snippets taken out of context and tied together," men who simultaneously would not read her work because they "refused to study what a woman had taught" while urging pastors "to disallow their women to do [Moore's] 'heretical' studies." Moore "accepted these kinds of challenges for all of these years" because she recognized the reality of evangelicalism and deemed such "difficulties" as "norms for servants of Christ." She continued: "I accepted the peculiarities accompanying female leadership in a conservative Christian world because I chose to believe that, whether or not some of the actions and attitudes seemed godly to me, they were rooted in deep convictions based on [biblical] passages." It was Trump's rise, championed by the SBC, that awakened her to "misogyny, objectification and astonishing disesteem of women" and a "demoralizing realization." According to Moore, "scripture was not the reason for the colossal disregard and disrespect of women among many of these men. It was only the excuse. Sin was the reason." She could no longer give her SBC "Brothers" the benefit of the doubt: "This is where I cry foul and not for my own sake . . . [but] for sake of my gender, for the sake of our sisters in Christ and for the sake of other female leaders who will be faced with similar challenges. I do so for the sake of my brothers because Christlikeness is at stake and many of you are in positions to foster Christlikeness in your sons and in the men under your influence. The dignity with which Christ treated women in the Gospels is fiercely beautiful and it was not conditional upon their understanding their place."

Moore's letter named the hypocrisy of Bible-loving churches who were "quick to teach submission" and "often slow to point out that women were also among the first followers of Christ (Luke 8), that the first recorded word out of His resurrected mouth was 'woman' (John 20:15), and that same woman was the first evangelist." And she called for repentance: "I'm asking that you would simply have no tolerance for misogyny and dismissiveness toward women in your spheres of influence." If the church wished to imitate Christ, according to Moore, it must imitate "His attitude and actions toward women." She then apologized for her past "acquiescence and silence," which made her "complicit in perpetuating an atmosphere in which a damaging relational dynamic has flourished." Later that year, in a rare interview with a reporter about her public ministry, she declared, tellingly: "The old way is over. The stakes are too high."[66]

In terms of gender, the "old way" might be seen as a strict adherence to complementarianism, which once again precluded preaching. Thus, much to some complementarians' dismay, in May 2019 Moore tweeted to the popular evangelical women's author Vicki Courtney, who had commented on Twitter that "Yours truly is PREACHING 3 services at a SB [Southern Baptist] church on Mother's Day," that she, Moore, was "doing Mother's Day too," adding the tongue in cheek comment: "Let's please, Vicki, don't tell anyone this."[67] When the popular Southern Baptist theologian and author Owen Strachan reminded Moore on social media that "women do not preach on Sunday to the church" and that complementarians "will not capitulate" on this issue, Moore dismissed him: "I am going to say this with as much respect & as much self restraint as I can possibly muster. I would be terrified to be a woman you'd approve of."[68]

By 2020, the Beth Moore effect was not as predictable as once before. If

Moore had not explicitly rejected patriarchy, she certainly condemned the reality of its practice—and not only its tolerance of sexual violence but also its marginalization of women in Southern Baptist churches. In other words, she finally moved off script and, in so doing, exposed the lengths to which some evangelical leaders had gone to maintain their power. For all intents and purposes, then, the paradox could not hold, and as with many women in Southern Baptist history, Moore found herself preaching to those who denied her access to a pulpit.[69]

Notes

1. Beth Moore, *Believing God* (Nashville, TN: LifeWay Church Resources, 2005), DVD.
2. The #MeToo movement was originated by Tarana Burke in 2007 but gained mainstream popularity in 2017, largely fueled by white female celebrities speaking against sexual harassment in Hollywood.
3. Here, a call to ministry refers to sensing that God has chosen the believer for leadership or ministry service, whether to a titled position or otherwise, and that one's sense of vocation and self-will from then on includes this ministerial purpose. Some discern a call to ministry generally, and others to specific kinds of service.
4. In the 1990s, they adopted a four-year-old son, Michael, who was later returned to his birth mother. See "Beth Moore—Breaking Free!," *JOY! Magazine*, Jan. 2009, https://www.joymag.co.za/article.php?id=12.
5. See Carol Pipes, "LifeWay Celebrates 20 Years with Beth Moore," LifeWay, news release, Feb. 13, 2015, https://blog.lifeway.com/newsroom/2015/02/13/lifeway-celebrates-20-years-with-beth-moore/.
6. In 2011, Beth and Keith Moore began attending Bayou City Fellowship, a church planted by their son-in-law, Curtis Jones, formerly employed by LPM.
7. Sarah Pulliam Bailey, "Why Women Want Moore," *Christianity Today*, Aug. 13, 2010, 25.
8. Catherine Brekus, *Strangers and Pilgrims: Female Preaching in America, 1740–1845* (Chapel Hill: Univ. of North Carolina, 2000).
9. Egalitarianism, in contrast, teaches that God calls men and women to leadership within the church and that domestic responsibilities should be shared equally between spouses.
10. For more about the history of the shift from women's organizing around missions to evangelical women's ministry programs, see Elizabeth Flowers, *Into the Pulpit: Southern Baptist Women and Power since World War II* (Chapel Hill: Univ. of North Carolina Press, 2012); and Susan Shaw, *God Speaks to Us, Too: Southern Baptist Women on Church, Home, and Society* (Lexington: Univ. Press of Kentucky, 2008).

11. "About Beth Moore," Living Proof Ministries, accessed Nov. 14, 2016, http://www.lproof.org/about.
12. Beth Moore, *Breaking Free: Discover the Victory of Total Surrender* (Nashville, TN: Broadman and Holman, 2007), 49.
13. Bailey, "Why Women Want Moore," 23.
14. Beth Moore, *Insights on Marriage: A Video Teaching by Beth Moore* (Houston, TX: Living Proof Ministries, 2010), DVD.
15. Beth Moore, *Feathers from My Nest* (Nashville, TN: Broadman and Holman, 2005), 61.
16. Beth Moore, *Esther: It's Tough Being a Woman* (Nashville, TN: LifeWay Christian Resources, 2008), 109.
17. Moore, *Esther*, 157.
18. Beth Moore, *So Long, Insecurity* (Carol Stream, IL: Tyndale House, 2010), 45.
19. Moore, *So Long, Insecurity*, 51.
20. See, for example, Beth Moore, *Things Pondered: From the Heart of a Lesser Woman* (Nashville: Broadman and Holman, 2004).
21. Beth Moore, *Get Out of That Pit: Straight Talk about God's Deliverance* (Nashville, TN: Thomas Nelson, 2009), 208. In the mid- to late-2000s, Starbucks cups had "The Way I See It" sayings on them, many of which offended conservative evangelical sensibilities.
22. Moore, *So Long, Insecurity*, 176.
23. Moore, *Breaking Free*, 160.
24. Moore, *Esther*, 37.
25. Beth Moore, *Living Beyond Yourself* (Nashville, TN: LifeWay Church Resources, 2004), DVD.
26. Moore, *Living Beyond Yourself.*
27. Moore, *Breaking Free*, 53.
28. Moore, *Breaking Free*, 77.
29. Moore, *So Long, Insecurity*, xi.
30. Moore, *Breaking Free*, 151.
31. Moore, *So Long, Insecurity*, 139.
32. Moore, *So Long, Insecurity*, 160.
33. Moore, *Insights on Marriage.*
34. Moore, *Insights on Marriage.*
35. Moore, *Insights on Marriage.*
36. Bailey, "Why Women Want Moore," 23.
37. Moore, *Breaking Free*, 12.
38. Moore, *Breaking Free*, 208.
39. Moore, *So Long, Insecurity*, 154.
40. Beth Moore, *Beloved Disciple: The Life and Ministry of John* (Nashville, TN: LifeWay Church Resources, 2002, 2008), DVD.
41. Moore, *So Long, Insecurity*, 268–69.

42. Moore, *So Long, Insecurity*, 154.
43. Moore, *A Woman's Heart: God's Dwelling Place* (Nashville, TN: LifeWay Church Resources, 1995), 155.
44. Moore, *Insights on Marriage*.
45. Moore, *So Long, Insecurity*, 152.
46. See, for instance, *A Woman's Heart*, 65.
47. *Breaking Free*, 144, 155. For examples of her teaching men, see her "Wednesdays with Beth" appearances on *LIFE Today*, http://www.lightsource.com/ministry/wednesdays-with-beth/.
48. Moore, *Believing God*; Moore, *A Woman's Heart;* and Beth Moore, *Stepping Up: A Journey through the Psalms of Ascent* (Nashville, TN: LifeWay Church Resources, 2007), DVD.
49. Wm. Dwight McKissic Sr., "Attitudes toward Women in Baptist Life," *New Blog for a Pneuma Time* (blog), Apr. 1, 2010, http://dwightmckissic.wordpress.com/2010/04/01/attitudes-toward-women-in-baptist-life/. McKissic, pastor of Cornerstone Baptist Church in Arlington, Texas, cited this minority opinion to contrast it with his own affirmation of Moore's work and the calling of women in the SBC generally.
50. Josh Buice, "Why Your Pastor Should Say 'No More' to Beth Moore," Delivered by Grace, May 24, 2016, http://www.deliveredbygrace.com/say-no-more-beth-moore/.
51. "Beth Moore—Exposed," Facebook group, accessed Nov. 26, 2016, https://www.facebook.com/Beth-Moore-Exposed-297387470312957/.
52. Beth Moore (@BethMooreLPM), Twitter, Oct. 9, 2016.
53. Moore (@BethMooreLPM), Twitter, Oct. 9, 2016.
54. Moore (@BethMooreLPM), Twitter, Nov. 13, 2017.
55. Moore (@BethMooreLPM), Twitter, Aug. 17, 2017. See also Kristin Kobes Du Mez, "Gender and Authority: Tish Warren, Jen Hatmaker, and the 'Crisis' of the Female Christian Blogosphere in Historical Perspective," *in all things,* Aug. 31, 2017, http://inallthings.org/gender-authority-tish-warren-jen-hatmaker-and-the-crisis-of-the-female-christian-blogosphere-in-historical-perspective/.
56. Beth Moore, "The Scandal of Election 2016," *The LPM Blog*, Oct. 18, 2016, http://blog.lproof.org/2016/10/the-scandal-of-election-2016.html.
57. Moore (@BethMooreLPM), Twitter, July 1, 2017.
58. Moore (@BethMooreLPM), Twitter, July 1, 2017.
59. Moore (@BethMooreLPM), Twitter, Dec. 8, 2017; Public Religion Research Institute (@PPRIpoll), Twitter, Dec. 7, 2017; McKay Coppins, "You Need to Think About It Like a War," *The Atlantic*, Dec. 7, 2017, https://www.theatlantic.com/politics/archive/2017/12/the-vanishing-values-voter/547772/.
60. Moore (@BethMooreLPM), Twitter, July 24, 2017.
61. Moore (@BethMooreLPM), Twitter, Oct. 15, 2017.
62. Moore (@BethMooreLPM), Twitter, Nov. 9, 2017.

63. Moore (@BethMooreLPM), Twitter, Nov. 14, 2017.
64. Moore (@BethMooreLPM), Twitter, Mar. 16, 2017.
65. Beth Moore, "A Letter to My Brothers," *The LPM Blog,* May 3, 2018, https://blog.lproof.org/2018/05/a-letter-to-my-brothers.html.
66. Emma Green, "The Tiny Blond Bible Teacher Taking On the Evangelical Political Machine," *The Atlantic*, Oct. 2018.
67. Moore (@BethMooreLPM), Twitter, Apr. 27, 2019.
68. Owen Strachan (@Ostrachan), Twitter, May 8, 2019; Beth Moore (@BethMooreLPM), Twitter, May 9, 2019.
69. As of the final days of editing this chapter, Moore's name emerged as a potential candidate for 2020 SBC president, sparking debates between Southern Baptists with "hard" versus "soft" views of patriarchy and the gendered hierarchy. See Dave Miller, "A Soft Question for 'Hard Complementarians,'" SBC Voices, June 4, 2019, https://sbcvoices.com/a-soft-question-for-hard-complementarians; and Bob Allen, "Debate over Women in Southern Baptist Pulpits Flares on Social Media," *Baptist News Global*, May 10, 2019, https://baptistnews.com/article/debate-over-women-in-southern-baptist-pulpits-flares-on-social-media/#.XPkJnS-ZNAY.

Contributors

CHELSEA L. CICHOCKI is assistant director for Student Support Services at the University of Connecticut.

ELIZABETH H. FLOWERS is associate professor of the history of Christianity at Baylor University. Prior to this appointment, she served as associate professor of American religious history at Texas Christian University. She is the author of *Into the Pulpit: Southern Baptist Women and Power since World War II.*

KRYN FREEHLING-BURTON is senior instructor in women, gender, and sexuality studies at Oregon State University. She is the playwright for *In the Image of God* and *Baptist Preacher Girl.*

CAROL CRAWFORD HOLCOMB is professor of church history and director of the Center for Baptist Studies at the University of Mary Hardin-Baylor. She is the author of *A Home without Walls: Southern Baptist Women and Social Reform in the Progressive Era.*

TISA LEWIS is past senior director of accreditation and institutional evaluation for the Commission on Accrediting of the Association of Theological Schools. Prior to this appointment, she was professor of human development and Christian education at Montreat College. She coauthored, with Susan Shaw, *Girls Rock! Fifty Years of Women Making Music* and also published *Faith Influences: Gospel Responsibilities in a Changing World.*

JOANNA LILE has taught at Georgetown College, the University of Kentucky, Baptist Seminary of Kentucky, and Transylvania University. Her current research involves Southern Baptist women's education.

MELODY MAXWELL is associate professor of church history at Acadia Divinity College. *The Woman I Am: Southern Baptist Women's Writings, 1906–2006* was her first book, and she coauthored, with T. Laine Scales, *Doing the Word: Southern Baptists' Carver School of Church Social Work and Its Predecessors, 1907–1997.*

O'DESSA MONNIER is a PhD researcher in women's studies at the University of York.

COURTNEY PACE is associate professor of church history at Memphis Theological Seminary. She is the author of *Freedom Faith: The Womanist Vision of Prathia Hall.*

KARI S. ROOD is assistant dean of students for Disability Services and Academic Success at Claremont McKenna College.

T. LAINE SCALES is professor of social work at Baylor University, where she is also recognized as a master teacher. Her books include *All That Fits a Woman: Training Southern Baptist Women for Charity and Missions, 1907–1926*, and, with Melody Maxwell, *Doing the Word: Southern Baptists' Carver School of Church Social Work and Its Predecessors, 1907–1997.*

KAREN K. SEAT is associate professor of US religion at the University of Arizona, where she also serves as head of the Department of Religious Studies and Classics and director of the School of International Languages, Literatures, and Cultures. She is the author of *Providence Has Freed Our Hands: Women's Missions and the American Encounter with Japan.*

SUSAN M. SHAW is professor of women, gender, and sexuality studies at Oregon State University. Her books include *Intersectional Theology: An Introductory Guide*, coauthored with Grace Ji-Sun Kim; *God Speaks to Us, Too: Southern Baptist Women on Church, Home, and Society*; and *Reflective Faith: A Theological Toolbox for Women.*

C. DELANE TEW is professor of history at Samford University. She has published several articles on early twentieth-century Southern Baptist women and missions and served as president of the Baptist History and Heritage Society.

Index